THOU SWELL, THOU WITTY

A Joan Kahn Book

FREDERIC MARVIN

designed by Lydia Link

co-ordinated by Elliott Sirkin

THOU SWELL THOU WITTY

THE LIFE AND LYRICS OF LORENZ HART

edited and with
a memoir by
Dorothy
Hart

HARPER & ROW, PUBLISHERS

NEW YORK, HAGERSTOWN, SAN FRANCISCO, LONDON

FIRST EDITION

Library of Congress Cataloging in Publication Data

Hart, Dorothy.
    Thou swell, thou witty.
    1. Hart, Lorenz Milton, 1895-1943.
    2. Songs—Texts.
I. Title.
ML423.H32H4   784'.092'4   [B]
75-23885
ISBN 0-06-011776-1

SONG LYRICS

ACKNOWLEDGMENTS

My thanks are due to Mel Shauer, Sig Herzig, Gene Zukor, Dick Leonard, Bob Gersten, Bob Lewine, Fred Nolen, Florence Weingart, Max Wilk, Barbara Kennedy and ASCAP.

For their help in tracking down illustrations, I would also like to thank the staffs of The Museum of the City of New York, the Museum of Modern Art, the Lynn Farnol Group and The Performing Arts Research Center of The New York Public Library at Lincoln Center.

I am very grateful to Stanley Musgrove, whose evening-long celebration of the lyrics of Lorenz Hart at the University of Southern California helped to supply so much of the best material in this book. Thanks also to Edith Meiser, George Balanchine, Josh Logan, Vivienne Segal, Irving Berlin, Arthur Schwartz, Marcella Wallace, Gene Kelly, Phil Leavitt, Helen Ford, Richard Rodgers, Nanette Guilford and Frances Manson.

And lastly, very special thanks to Michael Colby, whose enthusiasm and dedication to the theatre are so reminiscent of the young Larry Hart's. And to my son, Lorenz Hart II, who insisted that I could and that I must complete this book, when I faltered so frequently during the two and a half years it took to recollect and re-experience some painful moments.

This is for Teddy

1897-1971

Again, for his research, I would like to thank Michael Colby.

For me, Larry Hart was a constant revelation. His intellect, his enthusiasm, his urbanity and his sentiment all combined to give his lyrics the wit and freshness that helped to change the whole face of the musical theatre.

RICHARD RODGERS

BEGINNINGS

1895-1925

The Hart family, just before the turn of the century. Larry (on the left) was four; Teddy, two.

The heavy gold band worn by Frieda Hart for almost fifty years is inscribed *Max-Frieda November 6, 1886.* She had been Frieda Isenberg, only a year arrived from Hamburg, Germany, and seventeen. Max Hart, who had been Max Hertz in Germany, was nineteen. It was a good marriage despite all the things that went on between that happy day and Max's death in 1928. The apartment on Allen Street, on the Lower East Side, where the newly arrived immigrants lived, was filled with young Max's overpowering vitality and exuberance. And often, wandering in and out at will, were his nine brothers and sisters, and Frieda's eight sisters and her brother. And of course, their respective parents.

Fifty years later Frieda spoke wistfully of those long-ago days, which had been the happiest of her life. She'd only seventeen cents in her purse the day she married, and until they moved uptown there often wasn't much more. But Max was a devoted husband, serving her breakfast in bed every morning—a ritual he continued all his days.

Max was ambitious, with a driving will, and before long he knew all the local politicians. Later, through the force of his personality and willingness to do precinct work for the Tammany Hall politicians, he became friendly with prominent lawyers and judges and even the mayor of New York, Theodore Van Wyck. He named his son Teddy after this good friend.

Max and Frieda were childless for some years, and Frieda often feared that she could never bear a child. Then little Jimmy came along, bringing short-lived joy for the couple who had waited more than five years for that event. But alas, a fire in the tenement in the dead of winter sent Frieda out on the fire escape, clutching the infant, and though she saved herself and the baby, he succumbed to pneumonia several days later.

This tragedy sent the Harts uptown to a brownstone on East 106th Street between Second and Third avenues. Max prospered there. And though the house was still lively with relatives, always a *gemütlich* household, Frieda's difficulty in bearing children depressed her. The doctor was never encouraging, but Lorenz Milton arrived May 2, 1895 (Frieda said she usually got pregnant when the doctor said she couldn't). The Harts became a joyous family again. Max had entered into many business enterprises, owning small railroads and real estate, anything at which he could turn a substantial profit. There are apartment houses in Harlem still around today that bear the names LORENZ and THEODORE over the entrance. Max Hart was a promoter, and it was known in certain circles that if one got into trouble, one called Max Hart. Max always responded regardless of the hour or the misdeed—short of murder. Short of the doings of the regular criminal element. But when *he* found himself in a tight squeeze, his shenanigans sometimes almost led to his going to jail. His deals sometimes skirted the law. Max believed in his investments, risking his own money and that of any relative with a spare thousand or so. No one complained when things were going well. But when they weren't, and the disgruntled took a close look at Max's business methods, it took a friendly lawyer or two to straighten matters out.

When the next Hart baby, Theodore Van Wyck, came along on September 25, 1897, after the same discouraging shake of the head from the doctors, Frieda felt her life was complete, though she would always regret not having a daughter since after Teddy, there were no happy surprises; this time the doctors were right.

The Harts and their children lived at the 106th Street house for six years, and then, as their more affluent acquaintances were doing, they moved farther uptown, to 59 West 119th Street, in Harlem, on the edge of Morningside Heights. It was a street of brownstones with high stoops, where established families, mainly Jewish, lived. There was a Reform synagogue on the street, and farther east were the tenements and apartment houses of the less financially fortunate. There was vitality and hope and the life of the streets that gave New York its color in that era: the sweet-potato man with a hot sweet potato for two cents, and the

Larry age one and a half, dressed as all infant boys from respectable families were dressed in 1896.

hurdy-gurdy with the monkey, and the fortuneteller with his parrot, which, for one cent, pecked out a small square of paper that told your fortune.

Street singers haunted the backyards, singing Yiddish songs or Irving Berlin ballads for a coin tossed by an appreciative listener, and you could always hear someone taking a violin or a piano lesson, which would cost a quarter. The kids played stickball and raced with skates tied to egg crates. On high holidays, the synagogue on the street was noisy with the boys getting sweet wine and sponge cake for free (they never entered it otherwise until their bar mitzvahs). Here at Mt. Zion Larry and Teddy were bar mitzvahed by Rabbi Tintner, who, a few years later, was to help bring the Berlinger boys to thirteen-year-old maturity. Milton Berlinger, who became Milton Berle, and his brothers lived farther east, on 118th Street.

The life of the streets surrounded Teddy and Larry. But they were cushioned by the growing prosperity of Max Hart, who by then had two housemaids, and when the automobile came in, a chauffeur and even a footman. Nothing was too good for the flamboyant head of the household, or his family. It was a happy environment for Teddy and Larry. They were forever proud to be The Boys from Harlem. They were good-natured, active children who found only one embarrassment as they grew up: Papa Max. For though he was warm, loving, enfolding them with wet, fat kisses, Max was also crude, coarse and outrageous.

When the well-known Cantor Rosenblatt, living in the next house, found the summer heat too oppressive indoors, he continued practicing his chants in the backyard that he and the Hart family shared—and when the interminable sounds bothered Max beyond endurance, he poured a bucket of water on the good cantor's head! This was the talk of the neighborhood, of course. A cantor yet—and Rosenblatt, the great one! And how about the time Max was caught outside the door in his nightshirt, when a maid innocently closed the door on him as he retrieved a newspaper. The screams and the oaths and the language aimed at the poor maid until the door was opened! No one could understand how the dignified, quiet, *gnädige Frau* Frieda could tolerate it. But secretly she loved it: Papa was all.

The affluence that was apparent in the life style of 59 West 119th had its critical times. When there were business reverses, Frieda's fortune in jewels made its way stealthily to the pawnbrokers. During one of the financial upheavals, Larry told his mother consolingly, "When we're poor, we can move to the Plaza."

From the age of six, Larry had written verse for every family occasion, reciting with the oratory of the born ham. Max and Frieda's twenty-fifth wedding anniversary was held at Harasted Hall in the Bronx. That was in 1911, a good year for them. Lillian Russell, who was married to Alexander Moore, a former ambassador to Spain, sent a silver service (Moore was involved in some business affairs with Max). The family, and a hundred or so political cronies, were present, and to the tune of "Alexander's Ragtime Band," Larry wrote some verse dedicated to the celebrating couple (see page 23). He passed around the lyrics and then sang them with appropriate sentiment. (It was not one of his most memorable poems; at the age of sixteen, he was perhaps playing down to his audience.)

At school (Columbia Grammar and DeWitt Clinton), Larry belonged to literary societies, was editor of the school papers, and small big man on the school grounds. Larry was popular at school and camp, though he was always by far the smallest boy in the class. (His mother was four feet ten, papa not more than five feet four.) Despite his size, he was a leader in all school activities, except sports. For a time, he entered the running meets at camp (Weingart Institute and Paradox Lake), and was very fast, short legs and all. (Teddy played tennis at camp, and won a few prizes; but as they grew older, with Teddy five feet two and Larry under five feet, they put all their energy into the camp shows.)

Theatre seemed to come natural to both boys, though no one in the family was connected in any way with show business. (Frieda had been stage-struck back in Germany and had approached a theatre manager for an audition, but looking down at her diminutive height, he had told her kindly, "Come back when you grow up." However, Frieda never did "grow up." She remained tiny, and a frustrated actress always.)

Teddy and Larry knew about the theatre from about the age of six, when they were taken to the Irving Place, a German-language theatre on Fourteenth Street. The German stars, among them Christian Rub,

Greta Meyer and Gustave Hamburg, came to the house on 119th Street as guests on numerous occasions. (Frieda never lost her love for her German heritage, and English wasn't spoken in the home until the boys entered school.) Also, Willie Hammerstein, brother of the famous impresario Oscar Hammerstein, and father of Oscar II, was a business partner for a while in some of Max's ventures, and the Harts received tickets regularly to Hammerstein's Victoria Theatre. There wasn't a Broadway show they missed. Cousin Elsie took Larry and Teddy frequently to the Star Theatre, a very good stock company on 107th Street and Lexington Avenue. Uncle Harry took them to Hurtig and Seaman's burlesque, and it was there that Larry got some of his best material for the camp shows he was to write. At home, he wrote and acted in comedy skits. The Hart Brothers, as they were billed, satirized everything they had seen on Broadway. Teddy loved to write, and he often said that if he could spell, he would have been a writer while Larry loved making people laugh, loved to perform, would envy Teddy's comedy talents.

I wonder if reversing the roles of these brothers would have made Larry a happier person.

Larry and Teddy, inseparable companions.

Some snapshots from the family album. Larry (left) age three; Teddy, age five.

Sig Herzig

Sig Herzig, musical-comedy librettist and Hollywood screenwriter, knew Larry at an early age. In the summers of 1908 and 1909, they both attended the Weingart Institute in Highmount, New York—a camp-school that Larry dearly loved.

Weingart Institute was a summer school in the Catskills, a forerunner of the modern camps, and was patronized mostly by the sons of well-to-do German-Jewish families. Lorenz Hart, who immediately became Larry, was there with his brother, Teddy. So were the Bonwit sons, of Bonwit Teller's, a Van Raalte boy, of the underwear firm, and two of the Selznick brothers. Two years later Oscar Hammerstein arrived with Leighton Brill, who afterward became his assistant. Herbert Sondheim, who eventually fathered Steve Sondheim, was also on the roster. Five or six years later Richard Rodgers arrived. But Larry had outgrown Weingart's by then, so the historic meeting between Rodgers and Hart didn't take place at the institute. But even so, Weingart's might well be called a prep school for a Musical Hall of Fame.

The institute was run along strictly disciplinarian lines by Sam Weingart, a martinet from the old country. There were bugle calls for reveille, personal inspection and room inspection, and at least two hours of instruction on weekday mornings. But there was still plenty of time for every form of athletics as well as dramatics, and if it was "culture" you were seeking you joined the Literary Society, which published *The Weingart Review,* the weekly school paper.

I first met Lorenz in 1908 at the institute. He was thirteen, and so short that he looked five years younger— that is, until you talked to him. Then he was ten feet tall. As one of his classmates at the institute remarked: "His brain is so heavy it prevents him from growing in a vertical direction."

Larry immediately became a power in the Literary Society and there was always an article, usually satirical, by him in every issue of the *Review.* In this connection, it is interesting that in Larry's first article he rhymed "Poison Fang" (a secret society) with "hazing gang." Not a world-shattering couplet, to be sure, but it showed that the thirteen-year-old boy was already thinking in terms of rhyme.

At that point, however, Larry was much more interested in acting than in rhyming. Unless further research records something prior, his professional debut took place on Sunday, July 19, 1908, in a farce produced by the Literary Society called *New Brooms.* Larry Hart played Jim Jimalong, the third broom. A month later he appeared as End Man in the institute's minstrel show—the big event of the season. His solo was "Pass It Along to Father," memorable only because it marked Larry's professional debut as a singer. This was the end of Larry's histrionic activities for that summer, although he was always assuming the Shakespearean poses of a frustrated actor. Ironically, his brother Teddy turned out to be the actor in the family.

Although Larry was treasurer of one of the ball teams, he didn't go in for any athletics except running. But his legs were too short to win him medals. You would usually find him with a book under his arm—a heavy book, as to both weight and content. Even at thirteen, he was too sophisticated to be interested in the readings of the Literary Society. They went in for such "classics" as

The Man Without a Country and *Dr. Jekyll and Mr. Hyde.* Yet when an imaginary blonde wrote him a letter in the *Review* asking his advice as to what play to choose for her debut, he advised her to wait for the work he was writing called *Inky Ike, The Ash Barrel Detective.* Even at this date the title has a ring to it.

The summer of 1908 ended in a blaze of glory for Larry. Besides his honors as author and actor, he won a good conduct medal. Let some of those who in later years criticized Larry for occasional bad behavior take note.

In 1909, when Larry came back to Weingart's for his second season, he was, by unanimous consent, jumped over the heads of a dozen eligible older boys, and at fourteen he was made editor in chief of *The Weingart Review.* As editor, his writings were now unsigned, but the Hart touch was unmistakable; the school paper was wittier and more literate. There is only one record of his appearance in a play that season. It was called *A Warm Reception*, and the reviewer facetiously referred to Larry as "our famous tragedian."

Since Larry was a few years older than I was, we weren't close friends. When you're kids you tend to divide into almost exact age groups. In the winter, however, some of us gathered for reunions regardless of age. We would reminisce, exchange news about ourselves, and then shoot crap. I remember going to Larry's home on 119th Street and Lenox Avenue. It was a neat three-story brownstone house with lace curtains at the windows, and the neighborhood was noted as being nice and quiet. This house is still standing and it is still brown. And so is most of the neighborhood.

Larry went to Columbia Grammar and De Witt Clinton for his intermediate education. Then on to Columbia. Clinton and Columbia were also my route, but the two years between us hadn't lessened, and our contacts were still haphazard.

Then suddenly in the middle twenties I began to read about Larry in the columns of the New York papers, where he had become Lorenz again. F.P.A., whose column, "The Conning Tower," was the arbiter of wit at the time, was mentioning Larry's lyrics, as were other columnists. It was a major breakthrough! Outside of a small coterie of Gilbert and Sullivan worshipers, a lyric was never noticed and the lyric writer remained anonymous. And why not? He wrote appropriate and sometimes amusing jingles to accompany the melody.

Then other lyric writers started gaining attention and there was a gush of wonderful words and music as the golden age of the American musical theatre gave birth to a new art form. And Larry was always there to help a fellow craftsman. Modestly, he never took any credit, just as he took no credit for the many books he wrote for his shows. "Lyrics by Lorenz Hart" was enough for him.

One day I met him on Broadway, and he took me by the arm and led me silently to a theatre around the corner. And there on the marquee were those words in lights: "Lyrics by Lorenz Hart." "That's my name," said Larry, pointing upward in naïve wonderment. In that moment he was still the young boy I had first met at Weingart's and emotionally I believe he remained a boy till the day he died, too soon, at the age of forty-eight.

The golden age produced other great talents, and their achievements in many cases equaled Lorenz Hart's. But all of them owe a debt to him as the first to liberate the lyric and make America conscious that the lyric writer is an equal partner of the music writer.

The Weingart Summer School picture, during Larry's last season there. Teddy is up front, second from the left; Larry, looking a little uncomfortable, is the fellow with his arm around a chair in the fourth row. Two summers after Larry's and Teddy's departure, another future theatrical figure would be studying at Weingart: Oscar Hammerstein II.

❧

An Interview With Mr. Lorenz Hart.

"Come in," was the answer to a knock on the door of the private office of the dramatic editor of the Highmount Daily Dope-Sheet. The gentleman who was a reporter for the Pine Hill Daily Screech Owl, opened the door cautiously and tiptoed into the room.

Seeing no one he put on his spectacles to assist his eyesight, and immediately became aware of the presence of the diminutive Mr. Hart, who was promenading the length of the room, gesticulating wildly with all four limbs, at the same time turning his eyes to all points of the compass.

The reporter made profound obeisance to that person, and said, " Have I the honor of addressing Professor Lorenzo Hart ? "

" 'Tis me, indeed, Sir Knight, whom thou hast challenged to —— O! beg pardon, sir, I was just reciting a part from one of my latest plays. Have you ever heard of it ? No ? How uneducated you must be! Why it puts Shakespeare on the blink, and the language in it is simply swell. Its title is ' Lorenzo, the Magnificent,' and I expect it to become famous the wide-world over, wherever the English language is spoke.

" I presume that you wish to interrogate me concerning my past life. Pray, be seated, and put yourself at ease, while I recount to you the story of my career." Finding no time to even insert a syllable edgewise, the reporter sat down, and the speaker continued at the rate of five paragraphs a second.

" To begin with, I was born at a very early age. I was small then, and am still small, because my heavy brain does not permit me to grow in a vertical direction. I began to speak at the age of two weeks. How I managed to exist before that time has puzzled all scientists. My first words were, 'O, paternal ancestor, would'st agitate this infant receptacle.' During my existence, I have kept careful track of my physical growth, as you can see by noticing the hundreds of pictures which adorn the walls of this room. These are my favorite ones," continued Mr. Hart, pointing to a small group in the middle of the room, " they show the extraordinary development of my facial muscles. Sandow is known to have said that if his biceps were of the same strength as the muscle which moves his lower jaw, he could add $500 to his salary every week."

" But what is this ? " asked the reporter pointing to a small frame two inches square

" That ? why that's my diploma from Matteawan Seminary. I received my B S. there. Oh, not Bachelor of Science, but Bachelor of Speech."

" But, Mr. Hart," interrupted the reporter, " we would like to know your opinion on one subject, and this is, ' what do you think of the readings at the Literary Society's closed meetings ? ' "

" My dear sir," said Mr. Hart, as placing one hand sublimely on his chest, while with the other he tore his hair, he assumed that tragic position, which artists have in vain tried to reproduce, " they are unspeakably simple and abominably childish. The very idea of compelling an intellect like mine to listen to such nonsense as ' The Man Without a Country,' or ' Dr. Jekyll and Mr. Hyde.' Why don't they read such things as Goldsmith's ' De-

3

Mel Shauer

After Weingart, Larry and Teddy began camping at Paradox Lake, where they spent many happy summers. His first summer at Paradox, Larry met Mel Shauer, and they became lifelong friends. Later on, in the nineteen-thirties, when Mel was a producer at Paramount Pictures, and Larry was writing for the movies, the two friends were to share bachelor's quarters in Beverly Hills. A lovely, vital gentleman, Mel is now in his seventies. But his memories of Larry and of Paradox Lake Camp couldn't be fresher.

Every year on the same day around five o'clock, all the kids going to Paradox Lake Camp, in the Adirondacks, would gather at the pier. We all met at the 125th Street dock of the Hudson River Line. It really was a beautiful ride. Our families would kiss us goodbye. We'd get on the boat and look around for our roommates. A senior would be paired with a newcomer. I was a veteran camper. My stateroom mate, whom I was to look after, was Lorenz Hart. He was fifteen.

He'd been at Weingart's the last two summers. This was his first summer at Camp Paradox. From the moment we met he never stopped talking. He was overerudite—a little boring!—and we nicknamed him "Shakespeare Hart" immediately.

In choosing our berths, Larry politely insisted that I take the one I preferred, upper or lower. I was equally polite, and insisted that he make the choice. After a ridiculously polite discussion, he said finally, "I'll take the upper. You should have the lower." He climbed nimbly up to his berth and kept me awake all night spouting Shakespeare and discussing in depth very deep subjects. He was brilliant, but it was the wrong hour!

We laughed about it the next day and became lifelong friends. At Fort Ticonderoga, the Paradox campers took a series of buckboard wagons to drive the twenty-six miles to camp.

Both Larry and Teddy were noted for their generosity and friendliness. They didn't care about their personal belongings, gave everything away, left their clothes all over the place. Teddy used to get "porched" because he left his clothing and baseball glove just anywhere. Every morning, at assembly, they'd say, "Whose is this?" and it was always Teddy's or Larry's. We used to invite the other campers to come in and look inside Larry's trunk. It was a sight! Most kids at camp who got a box of candy in the mail wouldn't share it. Larry and Teddy would say, "If you want it, it's yours." They'd share anything with you.

Papa Hart came up to camp unexpectedly one morning bright and early—at five in the morning. A moment before, those beautiful mountains were so quiet. Papa Hart's arrival was like a cyclone hitting us. His voice bellowed, "Where are my boys? Where's my Lorry? Where's my Teddy?" He had to climb a steep hill to get to us and he yelled all the way, awakening the whole camp. He was quite heavy. When he charged into our tent he bawled out Lorry and Teddy for not meeting him. He walloped Teddy. Teddy was always the one who got slapped. I never saw him raise a hand to Larry. Larry's family was a little bit in awe of him. Then Max Hart came over and introduced himself to us and gave us a friendly swat. Through the years I became familiar with his peculiarities.

Immediately after Larry's arrival at camp he got busy with the weekly shows. That was before radio and television. We had to entertain ourselves. We would also go on long hikes, two and three days at a time. We usually looked a bedraggled, motley group. Teddy used to call it "Rabinowitz's May Party." In those days different streets in New York neighborhoods had a block party on different days in May, and they marched in groups to Central Park.

Larry became the big fixture at camp. Wherever he went there was excitement. He was a nonconformist, a laughmaker. He was a bit racy for those days, too. His logic was completely different from anybody else's, a little unbalanced. This logic was based on what he liked and on what he loved. You could almost see the wheels turning in his mind, never letting up.

There was much fun and some few fights up at the camp. Some fist fights. Larry would fight if he had to. He was a hell of a fighter. When he believed in something, he spoke up and was very argumentative. But at the same time he was so nice and friendly to everybody. And yet always a ringleader.

Another Paradox Lake Camper destined for greater things was Herb Fields, the Spanish dancer in this photo. Herb would eventually contribute the librettos for such Rodgers and Hart shows as *A Connecticut Yankee, Dearest Enemy* and *Peggy-Ann*.

The gang at Paradox Lake during Larry's third summer. Larry is the third of the short boys. Mel, second from the left, is the tall, skinny blond.

Larry may not have been a star athlete, but his wit was so in demand that boys would beg him to join their canoe trips as a nonpaddler. Here Larry is making like Chaplin, Mel is wearing the boater and Teddy has the goatee.

Larry very often attended reunions in New York in the winter. We would meet at each other's homes and put on a little show. The Hart house on 119th Street was, compared to the Shauer household, bohemian and kind of shocking in that era (the rest of us came from conventional homes of conventional parents). At all hours of the night the house in Harlem was open to any and all of Larry's and Teddy's friends. No matter where any of us went for an evening, we'd often wind up there at one or two in the morning. Nobody had to let us in. The door was always open and there was always something going on in the living room or kitchen. There was a poet named Robbins, who more often than not would be sitting in the center of the living room, a dim light on his face, while half a dozen young people sat silently listening to him spout poetry, sometimes of an erotic nature. Larry and Teddy might be upstairs asleep and Mama Hart was nowhere to be seen. Occasionally the old man would join us.

We were free to help ourselves to any food in the kitchen and do whatever we wanted. We considered it a hell of a household. Our homes were never like this!

Larry loved it all. He loved people around him. Loved to see them eat and drink. Everybody was welcome at all times. His father would give him a hundred-dollar bill. Larry would gather a group around him and we'd all go out on the town. Nobody else was allowed to pick up a check, not that any of us had any real money to spend. In those days young people got a small allowance which barely covered one date with a girl a week. I grumbled to my father after seeing the way Larry threw money around, but it didn't get me anywhere. So Larry continued to take his crumpled bills from his back pocket, never a wallet, saying, "Here, I've got it! I've got it!" and insist on paying. From time to time one of us would argue feebly, but Larry paid. Actually, most of the parents disapproved of the Hart household. They thought it too loose.

I used to call Frieda Hart "The Cameo." Larry called her "The Cop." She was a quiet little woman who lived in a world of boisterous kids and a raucous husband. She didn't seem to mind, as often happened, when the front parlor was stripped of furniture and made to look like a meeting place. All kinds of young people would assemble there, everybody talking at the same time: politics, literature, poetry, girls. This went on for hours and hours until dawn. Larry's friends reveled in these sessions. Where else could we have this kind of freedom? Certainly not in our orderly homes. Friends meant everything to Larry, and his generosity was unbelievable.

I've been trying to think if there was anybody during our long friendship that Larry disliked. I don't think I ever heard Larry say, "Well, that so-and-so." Many times, through the years, boys from camp who were now men would run into Larry. They always told me afterward how friendly he was.

A hike to Mt. Marcy, Larry carrying the lantern, Teddy wearing the bowler that he would later make famous as Frankie in *Three Men on a Horse*.

Gene Zukor is next to Larry, and Mel is standing behind Gene.

Eugene Zukor

Another fellow camper at Paradox Lake was Mel Shauer's cousin Gene Zukor, the son of Adolph Zukor, and also a future Paramount producer.

My family was summering at a hotel in Highmount, New York. One Saturday night we were invited to a show given by the boys of Camp Paradox nearby. There was a lot of applause for the kid performers until a little dark boy, looking to be about eight or nine, came on stage. Very seriously, he went into Hamlet's soliloquy. His audience hooted and yelled and gave him the Bronx cheer. Without missing a word, the boy—Larry Hart, as it turned out—continued to the very end, to a burst of cat-calls. I've never seen such self-assurance in someone so young, nor such complete indifference to vocal criticism.

The following summer I became a camp boy at Paradox. We all arrived at the camp with individual steamer trunks. It turned out that Larry, and his brother, Teddy, were to share my tent along with Mel Shauer. Larry's trunk was the last one to be unloaded. The driver of the rig that had brought us to camp had to ask someone to help him carry it in to the tent. As we unpacked our camp clothes, it turned out that Larry's trunk was filled entirely with books!

There was a fifteen-volume set of Shakespeare, a thesaurus, and other books with impressive titles. I was holding two sweaters when Larry grabbed one, insisting that I didn't need two. He took some socks from Mel and a shirt from Teddy. We became good friends and during the years I visited his home on 119th Street fairly often.

Like Mel, coming from a similar background, I was fascinated by a family quite different from any other I'd ever seen. It was a period when you unquestioningly obeyed your parents, followed their mode of life, and continued on in the family business. But those times at the Harts' opened our eyes and minds to what was really another world.

1911-13

Max and Frieda—Silver Wedding Anniversary

{ To be sung to the tune of "Alexander's Ragtime Band" }

VERSE

Oh, my hubby, put your hat on.
Better hurry, the taxi's waiting.
We are going, surely going
To the big array—Silver Wedding Day.
Better hurry, better hurry—
Lord, we don't want to come too late, dear.
Come now, somehow, better better hurry along.

1st REFRAIN

So clink your glass, each lad and lass,
For Max and Frieda's wedding day.
Put on a smile, make life worthwhile–
Let each wrinkle shout Hooray!
For life is much too short and time will always fly–
One, two, twenty-five, the years go rolling by.
This is the bestest night of all—let the laughter fall.
Years of joy, Max a boy, at full two scores is well.
And Mrs. Hart still plays her part,
Though her age I dare not tell.
But if you want to make the evening seem like the dear
    old times,
Clink your glass, each lad and lass,
To Max and Frieda's wedding day.
Way, way back, dear, '86, dear,
Things were not just like they are now, dear—
I was young, dear, you were young, dear,
And we didn't plan to help the census man.
Silver streaks, dear, in my hair, dear,
But our hearts, dear, are as young as ever.
Come now, somehow, jolly up and be young.

2nd REFRAIN

In diesen Haus lass Saus und Braus
Könige von allem sein.
Drink a pile, it's worth your while,
Hab die Katz im Morgenschein.
For life is much too short and the years are rolling
    by—
Eins, zwei, fünf-und-zwanzig,
Let the old times fly.
This is the bestest night of all—
Let the laughter fall.
Nur einmal ist es erlaubt,
Dass der Mensch gut leben kann.
Die Zeit fliegt ja und Sorg beraubt
Alle Jugend von dem Mann.
So if you want to make the evening seem like the dear
    old times,
Clink your glass, each lad and lass,
Zu der Silberfestigung.

Once Larry was in high school, he became an active contributor to the school paper, the *Columbia Grammar School News*. He contributed all kinds of pieces to the paper—poems, letters, articles—and usually signed them with his initials, "L. M. H." Eventually, he was to become the *News*'s editor.

The Rock of Refuge

When you're tired, and languid,
And limped and slow
From the drudge of all study, from
School. "Hall of Woe."
When you feel life, a dead weight,
There's one place to go,
And drown all your sorrow, the
"Ten-twenty show."

Oh! "ten-twenty show!"
Oh! temple of Loew!
Where the brave cowboy shoots the wild buffalo,
Where Virtue e'er triumphs; brave
Dick kills his foe,
It's death to the villain, in

The "ten-twenty show."
Oh! dramas ecstatic
In pictures dramatic,
Appeal to the mass and the aristocratic,
Your pulse beats the faster at "thrillers" emphatic.
In no time you'll change to a "filmofanatic."

Your view is, in fact, not confined to a screen,
For vaudeville hold sway, that execrable queen,
Great "Sandow" and "Venus," "Terpsichore," too
Appear between pictures, in gold review.
Then, horror of horrors, the clogdancers prance
And kick on the boards in true variance,
To all forms of beauty and sanity, too,
But are met with applause, be their merits e'er few!

Oh! ten-twenty show!
Oh! temple of Loew!
There's a world of diversity
Where the lesser stars glow.
If you're troubled and bothered
With the discords of life,
Come to this Rock of Refuge
And forget all your strife.

Wall Street

{ *Also written for the* Columbia News }

Between the dark defiles of stone,
Amidst a dreary din,
The surging souls crowd endlessly—
Each doomed to die or win.
Small atoms in this striving sea,
The fate of nations spin.

The dark defiles of stone will hear
Again that dreary din,
But other surging mobs will crowd
And others die or win.
And some will fall down by the way
Who caused the world to spin.

In race and creed they vary all,
In motive, all are kin!
But short the time is theirs to surge
And for the world to spin!
The dark defiles of stone will hear
Another dreary din.

THE COLUMIA NEWS.

L'ENVOI.

[By L. M. H. '13.]

Spring swiftly sweeps the sands of Time
And Summer days are nigh,
When Work is o'er and Play is king
And Jollity can have its fling,
Heigh-ho, for the bright, blue sky!

For ocean strands or mountain glades
We're bound; we're glad we're free!
We leave school with a merry will
But though we're gone, the school's
    there still,
Resting sleepily.

Shall we return?
Some of us will;

The rest will ride along
On rockets through the sphere of space.
Will they fall?
Are they weak, are they strong?
But the school's there still,

Each morning finds
Its lagging, lazy lads
"Creeping like snails, unwillingly"
Even as did their dads.

So, after all, leave we or stay,
The school's there still, we know.
The pranks we played are played again
By the very sons of the self-same men,
Heigh-ho, we are free, let's go?

Falstaff

⊰ Essay Taking Second Prize in English, 1913 ⊱

There are some people who dearly love all that is good in a man. Our late "letter-writing mayor" devoutly dotes on Epictetus. My tastes are different. Perhaps it shows some inborn rascality I have inherited from a bacchanalian progenitor, but, nevertheless, Falstaff is, and always was, my favorite character in literature.

Many are the happy hours I have spent laughing at the fat knight's pranks. Many are the times I have shut both eyes, stretched out my limbs in my armchair, and have longed to shout out, "Shall I not take mine case in mine Inn?" And though the days of happy Jack are no more, as long as books are read, his jolly orgies in the old "Boar's Head" will delight all lovers of pure fun and revelry.

There are really two Falstaffs in Shakespeare—the Sir John of *Henry IV* and he of *The Merry Wives of Windsor*. They differ in many ways. The former is much cleverer, wittier, and bolder than the dupe of Mistress Page. The Falstaff of *The Merry Wives* is an inferior rascal. He is, however, just as fond of sack, of repartee, and the smile of a pretty lass.

Queen Bess commanded Shakespeare to write a comedy, in which the massive knight was to have been smitten by one of Cupid's arrows. But the great poet knew that real love was impossible for Falstaff. Surely, love could never have occupied any room in that fat heart which was already so well stored with an affection for sack, a desire for sleek laziness, and an overwhelming love of good-fellowship. Hence, Shakespeare made Falstaff feign love and be deservedly beaten at his own game. The Falstaff of the pastoral comedy is a lesser counterpart of the one in *Henry IV*. Therefore I revel rather in the jolly companion of Prince Hal, than in the fat buffoon of Mistress Page. After all, Prince Hal is a much better foil for Falstaff's fun than either Pistol or Bardolf. So when I describe the fat knight, it will be Shakespeare's original creation in *Henry IV*.

Falstaff's physical characteristic is his great size. He is a big man and, as Shakespeare says, "a very ton of a man." His fat, highly flushed face is adorned by a red and gray chin beard, but in soldier-fashion. His little ferret eyes, always blinking, as a result of his habit of winking at every pretty lass, seem out of place under so large a forehead. For Falstaff is bald as a billiard ball. The ever-burning flame on his fat upturned nose shows him to be a true son of Bacchus.

He is carelessly but richly dressed. His doublet and hose are expensive but very dirty and worn. A sword is usually hanging at his side. He walks slowly but with a grandiose swagger and never very far, for he dearly loves his armchair at the inn.

In selecting a companion from the underworld, Prince Hal had all London to choose from. Surely, Falstaff must have been an entertaining rascal to have held so long the Prince's affections. Falstaff was a good fellow. This is a quality which makes anybody lovable. No real man can dislike a good fellow, no matter what grave faults he may have. Falstaff is a thief, a braggart, and a lazy, sensual parasite. But he is a good fellow. He loves his joke over his bottle; he loves his companions around his armchair. Finally, he would go through hell itself for Prince Hal. Can such a man be wholly bad? Is not a sense of humor a quality that, after all, shows a warm and affectionate nature?

When Falstaff, Prince Hal, and the others rob a traveling coach, they do it for the mere bravado and excitement. They are not thieves by nature. They know that most of the time the money will be refunded to the victims by agents of the King. Of course, Falstaff is no friend of truth. His bragging, however, is intended to amuse his hearers, not to give them any illusions.

Falstaff is not a coward. For, even on the battlefield, at the very peril of his life, he is ever joking and thoroughly enjoying himself.

His humor is irresistible. I cannot conceive a funnier scene than Falstaff's delineation of Henry IV. He tries to show Hal in what manner his father would address him. The armchair is his throne and the fat knight looks anything but regal, as he slaps Hal on the back and says: "Peace, good pint-pot; peace, good tickle brain; there is a virtuous man whom I have often noted in their company, but I know not his name."

Prince: "What manner of man, an it like your majesty?"

Falstaff: "A goodly, portly man, i'faith, and a corpulent; of a cheerful look, a pleasing eye and a most noble carriage. And now I remember me, his name is Falstaff; if that man should be lewedly given, he deceiveth me."—Act II, Scene 4.

Shakespeare has drawn no comedy part so life-like, so mirth-provoking as Falstaff. Compare the thinness of Aguecheek, the one-sidedness of Malvolio, the bromidic cynicism of Jacques to this blustering, boisterous boy of Bacchus.

Falstaff strikes but one pathetic note—the scene where Mistress Quickly describes his death. Deserted by Hal, poor and broken in health, the old debauchee dies peacefully in his room in the old inn he loved so well. The affection shown by Pistol, Mistress Quickly, and her husband, proves that Falstaff could not have been without his virtues. No totally bad man can instill such affection in his companions.

Therefore, I love Falstaff, not for his wit alone, nor for his good fellowship: but for all his vices and virtues rolled into that "ton of a man"—for everything that makes him—Falstaff, the most real, the most lovable comedy character Shakespeare has created.

Larry's high-school graduation photo. After high school, Larry enrolled in the Columbia University School of General Studies, but, after a year, he transferred to the Journalism School. He never graduated from Columbia, though his drama reviews in the college paper were widely read and discussed.

*The following letters were written during a trip Larry took abroad with his family in 1912.
The first was published under the headline "From Our Special at the German Court." The
second was addressed to a favorite teacher.*

Savoy Hotel, Berlin
Nov. 13, 1912

Dear Messrs. Editors:

On October 12 we arrived at Bremen after a most pleasant journey. Thence we rode to Hamburg, and stayed a month in the Hanseatic seaport; now we are in Berlin.

Though the life at the German capital is fascinating and gay, Teddy and I are homesick. We long for our New York friends, and especially for those at old C.G.S. I never was patriotic till a German band irritated me by playing "Die Wacht Am Rhein." I never used to think of women's dress till the utter lack of "chic" in the appearance of the German woman hurt my eyes.

I trust the *News*, as of old, is enjoying a prosperous year, and if my good wishes will help it any, take them—all of them. Enclosed please find a dollar for my subscription.

With an honest longing to see you, Mr. Campbell, Mr. Wilson, and everybody in C.G.S., in the very near future, I remain,

Very truly yours,
Lorenz Hart, of '14

Berlin, Nov. 13, 1912

Dear Mr. Wilson:

We are now at Berlin. I am sorry to say I have not met a human being since I stepped off the boat.

I have not seen any water, except in my own glass and under bridges. Beer is cheap and excruciatingly popular.

I am learning the words of "Die Wacht Am Rhein." It's even harder than being kept in for Latin. Wishing you good health and few "brummers and harts," I remain,

Your very naughty pupil,
Lorenz Hart, '14

Larry (third from left) with friends, some time during the First World War. By then, he had left Columbia for good. But that was no deterrent to his writing the lyrics of the Columbia Varsity Shows of 1920 and 1921. You only had to have attended Columbia at some point in your life to qualify as an author of a Varsity Show.

There was nothing else Larry could have been but a writer for the theatre. He was always an omnivorous reader and a listener to music (he couldn't stand Victor Herbert's schmaltzy music but he loved Gilbert and Sullivan). He was inspired by P.G. Wodehouse – just as budding composers of the period were trying to pattern themselves after Wodehouse's partner in the Princess Theatre shows, Jerome Kern. The combination of sentiment and acerbity was always there. The poetry was always there.

In 1917, Larry went to Brant Lake Camp as dramatic counselor, where he worked like a demon. He was already writing acts for small-time vaudevillians, of whom the most well known was Georgie Price. Then, in 1920, through the German actor Gustave Hamburg, Larry went to work for United Plays, a play-reading and translating organization affiliated with the Shuberts. It was his first steady job, and Max was pleased that his son was making all of fifty dollars a week. He had never discouraged Larry's theatre ambitions and had continued to hand out large bills to Larry so he could take out girls. Only, in his own blunt words, Max wanted Larry to "get something for it." Larry and Teddy were glad to get a girl, since the female sex wasn't exactly breaking down their doors. Unfortunately, Max's fanny-pinching and his pitch for their dates made the boys reluctant to bring the girls to their home. Who needed competition from a parent? But it never occurred to either one to tell off the old man! He was a formidable figure.

Larry and Teddy—and no doubt Frieda—had always known that Max Hart had a weakness for the ladies. But when Uncle Elkan, who worked for brother-in-law Max, told Larry that the old man was about to elope with his beautiful new secretary, young Larry took matters into his own hands. He confronted the mismatched couple in the office at 280 Broadway and insisted that the girl be fired immediately and that Max return to the bosom of his family. Anyone who had ever seen Larry in a fury, as he still was when he described this incident to me so many years later, could understand how the bald, pudgy, fifty-year-old lover could be chastened enough by his son's confrontation to return home forthwith.

By the time Larry was working for United Plays, Milton "Doc" Bender had inveigled himself into the family fold, playing the piano for Frieda, keeping Larry laughing with very bad puns, and trying to wangle his way out of a lucrative theatrical dental practice and into the show-business world he loved. Bender, Larry told us, used to hold auditions in his office while extracting teeth—a slight exaggeration perhaps. But Doc left his flourishing dental practice to become an artists' representative or "agent," and proved to have an eye and ear for talent. He eventually revived the careers of or discovered some well-known show personalities, and his enthusiasm for the clients who signed on the dotted line with him was contagious. They were the greatest, the prettiest, the best, the most talented. The superlatives were warranted most of the time. Among others under his managerial wing would be Balanchine, Vivienne Segal and Wynn Murray. He would have been very successful indeed had it not been for the arrogance and even vituperativeness his new-found importance brought to the surface. From an amiable, humorous and rather likable sort, he became intensely disliked. A true lover of music, a respecter of talent, he ignored or derided those who could do him no good in the profession. With the exception of his clients, who were genuinely fond of him for his unflagging zeal in looking after their interests, no one on Broadway had any use for him. He fought the good fight with managers for salary and billing, and was removed bodily at other times for being obnoxious and domineering in his demands. He would have endured much longer, would have survived as an important discoverer of new talent, if he had controlled his more unpleasant traits. As a bachelor who could stay up all night as a roving companion, he attached himself to Larry, ever in pursuit of laughter. Through Larry he gained entrée to people and places denied him as an unpopular agent.

The five years with United Plays, from 1920 to 1925, were extremely productive ones for Larry, who used his expertise in the German language to translate and adapt German and Viennese operettas. During these years he wrote an adaptation of Jean Gilbert's *The Lady in Ermine*, changing the European locale to an American Revolutionary background, and with his friend Mel Shauer he wrote an entire score, which was turned over to the Shuberts for consideration. But they weren't ready to take a chance with an unknown salaried writer. And since any project written by a writer employed by United Plays was owned by the Shuberts, there was no problem in turning over *The Lady in Ermine* to the already established talents of Sigmund Romberg. He returned it to the Viennese setting, wrote a new score in keeping with the period and had a big hit for himself and the Messrs. Shubert. Larry received no credit, but he used much of the material he had researched for the operetta in the first Rodgers and Hart "book" musical, *Dearest Enemy*.

Larry also did some work on the translation of Molnár's *Liliom* while with United Plays, though the final version of the translation was credited to Benjamin Glazer. *Liliom*, a smash success for the Theatre Guild, launched Joseph Schildkraut on his starring career, and Schildkraut himself told me—and Teddy, Arthur Schwartz and several other knowledgeable Broadwayites have confirmed—that Larry did some work on *Liliom*. And who knew better than Schildkraut? But Larry didn't mind too much. So confident was he and so sparked with ideas, he had no doubt at all that his day would come.

By now, Larry had a full-time collaborator for the songs he was writing. In 1919 Richard Rodgers, at sixteen, was looking for a lyricist. Larry was then twenty-three, and considered himself a veteran. Phil Leavitt, a friend of Dick's brother, Morty Rodgers, was induced to introduce the two boys. (Phil was a Columbia man, who had contributed to some of the varsity shows.) That Richard Rodgers and Lorenz Hart recognized each other's enormous talents only a few moments after they met is theatre history. That Larry did not brush off Dick because of his extreme youth; that Dick ignored the eccentric appearance of the tiny figure who greeted him at the door on their first meeting, in formal trousers and a bathrobe, unshaven and unkempt, proved their instant rapport. Despite their contrasting temperaments, a real affection and regard endured throughout their association.

With more friends. Teddy is in the second row, wearing the double-breasted blazer.

Dear Bob;—
this is
me — although you
may doubt it.
I think
if you ran the
group of faculty
photographs across
the double page — it
would look pretty
good.
Across a single page
they would be too small to
look well — Fervent passion.
· Larry

Larry used the above photo as his faculty picture in the 1918 Brant Lake Camp year-book.   Left, the covering letter he sent to Bob Gertzenzang, Brant Lake's owner.

1918

Dear Old School Days

{ *Larry wrote this for the camp paper, when he was drama counselor at Brant Lake* }

When the sky-hooks are connected,
And the tent-keys lock the tents,
Leery lessons we've neglected
Are assigned by learned gents.

When we study hist'ry's pages,
We think Charlemagne a quince.
What are all these princely sages
When you've seen the Brent Lek prince?

As we pore o'er Fenny Cooper
We think Fenimore was drunker
Than old Nero, when this trooper
Went and named his hero Unca.

And geography is rotten.
I suppose I'll can that book,
For its author has forgotten
Where's the Isle of Abel Crook.

Mathematics, too, is futile.
I'll throw it in the shade,
For what statistician brutal
Knows the runs that Leslie made?

After school has made us weary,
Though this camping season's done,
Next July, all bright and cheery,
Yea bo! comes another one.

The Brant Lake all-faculty photograph. Larry is down front, legs crossed Indian style.

Phil Leavitt

Currently living in Scottsdale, Arizona, Phil Leavitt, who introduced Larry to Dick, didn't pursue a career in show business. He was very successful in the wholesale paint business, but, for every Rodgers and Hart opening, he received complimentary tickets.

Looking back (a long way), it seems impossible to recall when I met Lorry Hart. I know that I was in my teens. Herbert Fields introduced me. It was in Lorry's home. At the same time I met Lorry's mother—a sweet lady.

Lorry was short—he came up to my shoulder and I was no giant (about five feet, seven inches in height). He had tiny feet, and tiny hands which he would rub together. That seemed to be a way of heating his mind—of expressing satisfaction with what he was thinking. It was very much like the old Indian way of starting a fire by rubbing sticks together.

I recall that Lorry was doing some translating of plays from the German stage—the Reinhardt Theatre. It was hoped that he would pick a winner and in that way be launched. I believe he was doing this for Sig Rumen at the time.

But Lorry was much more interested in listening to his Victrola playing the popular tunes of the classic Wodehouse-Bolton-Kern hits which were playing at the Princess Theatre in New York. Those shows were the first musicals done without chorus girls and in which the leading characters provided the background for the continuity of the story; the songs were intimately tied to the plot. Lorry felt that this type of production was leading into a new era of theatre. Most of all he was entranced by the lyrics and the music. Each completely fulfilled the other. Lorry would gleefully rub his hands together and beam when he heard something that satisfied him. He knew when he heard a rhyme that appeared to answer what he felt should be heard—and understood. He also knew that he would be able to express himself with poetry, if he should ever find someone he could link up with to write the music.

At the time I was interested in amateur shows—first in high school and then as a member of a group that played football, basketball and baseball. It was known as the Akron Club. I think at that time all the members of our team had allowances of about twenty-five cents a week—much too little to provide for uniforms and the necessary equipment. In that era we had to take care of our own recreational needs. We had no instructors who would organize us. We could not afford the cost, nor did our parents feel that we needed a paid leader. In order to raise money we decided to put on amateur shows. Naturally we took into the shows all the young girls who had either talent or the ability to sell tickets. Mort Rodgers, Dick Rodgers's brother, was a member of the club. He told us his kid brother wrote music, and thought that perhaps

we could use some of his tunes. His father, Mort and Ralph Engelsman would write the lyrics. So we tried out that scheme. The book was a conglomerate by everyone in the cast. The first performance was at the Majestic Hotel. Believe it or not, it was a financial success—earning enough money for our needs. Dick's songs were tuneful, but the lyrics were weak. However, we decided to try again the following year.

When it came time to find a man who might collaborate with Dick, I suggested a fellow I knew who I felt might work out—Lorry Hart. No one else in the club knew Lorry, so I volunteered to take Dick up to Lorry's home and introduce him. So I phoned and made the date.

Dick and I went up to Lorry's, where he greeted us heartily at the door. As I said before, Lorry was a tiny man. But he had an enormous head, which would have been fitting on a six-footer; and it was most attractive. There was a big cigar stuck in his mouth (which looked a bit incongruous) but his welcome was hearty. We walked to the back room, where the Victrola was blasting out "Babes in the Wood." That was quickly turned off and the preliminaries were over quickly. Lorry went into raptures about Bolton, Wodehouse and Kern, then he turned to Dick, asking him to play one or two of his songs. It was love at first hearing. I might as well have not been in the room. The pair of them went into a discussion of music, lyrics, shows, etc.—and by mutual agreement decided to collaborate. It was as easy as that.

Their first work together was the Akron shows. Lorry collaborated on the book, while writing all the lyrics, while Dick Rodgers did the music. We had rehearsals wherever we could get the space. The shows turned out well and money was made. While the book was being rehearsed, Dick would be improvising at the piano. Lorry seemed to have ears that never missed anything and when he would hear a strain that pleased him, he would rush over to the piano, ask that what he had just heard be repeated and make a guide sheet on a piece of paper. He would take it home and come in at the next rehearsal with the completed song. Fantastic!

They had written a song called "Venus," which Lorry thought would be salable. I knew Dorothy Fields quite well (she was the daughter of Lew Fields). So, I asked her if she could get her father to listen to the song. She managed to arrange a date. One afternoon we traveled over to the Fields house in Far Rockaway so the number could be played. Lew Fields did not particularly like "Venus," but he was interested in the collaboration and suggested that Lorry and Dick play some of the other songs. There was one, "Any Old Place With You," that he liked so much that he incorporated it into his Broadway show *A Lonely Romeo*. It was the first Rodgers and Hart song accepted for professional performance. And it was a hit!

In the meantime Lorry was working, and in his spare time acting in Columbia University shows. There, too, he displayed his talents. He initiated a satire on *Scheherazade*, which was being played by the Imperial Russian Ballet group at the Manhattan Opera House. It was a ballet which had been criticized in the newspapers for being lewd. Lorry spoofed it, even down to the point of having men dressed as policemen coming down the aisle blowing whistles and stopping the show. It was so good that the Shuberts copied it the following year for their annual revue. It was the first time any musical show used a ballet.

Later in 1919, when Dick matriculated at Columbia University, the decision was made to write a varsity show. It was submitted by Lorry, Dick and myself, but one Milton Kroopf had a more original idea, so the committee asked Lorry and me to adapt Kroopf's thought. The play that resulted was called *Fly with Me,* and it was quite successful. The following year Dick and Lorry wrote another musical, *You'll Never Know,* that was put on by the varsity show group.

Lew Fields in *A Lonely Romeo,* the show for which he bought "Any Old Place With You." The song was a very early effort. But it's still among the most typically fresh and joyful of the early Rodgers and Hart collaborations. Fields was a successful comedian, half of Weber and Fields. He was also a producer, and presented several of the Rodgers and Hart shows.

1919

Any Old Place With You

{ *Originally sung by Alan Hale and Eve Lynn* }

1st VERSE

There is a railroad around Lover's Lane
And the conductor is you.
My heart goes faster than any old train,
Right on schedule, too.
All is ready for our honeymoon.
I've a route in view.
Our express leaves morning, night and noon.
Travel with me, please do.

1st REFRAIN

We'll melt in Syria,
Freeze in Siberia,
Negligee in Timbuktu.
In dreamy Portugal
I'm goin' to court you, gal.
Ancient Rome we'll paint anew.
Life would be cheerier,
On Lake Superior.
How would Pekin do?
I'm goin' to corner ya
In California.
Any old place with you.

2nd VERSE

We'll madly fly over
Hill and down dale
In little Cupid's express.
I'm at the throttle
And I'll never fail
If you whisper "Yes."
Come with me and let me
Be your guide.
One plus one is one.
Then our headlights
Never can collide,
Till life's long road is done.

2nd REFRAIN

From old Virginia,
Or Abyssinia,
We'll go straight to Halifax.
I've got a mania
For Pennsylvania,
Even ride in London hacks.
I'll call each dude a pest
You like in Budapest.
Oh, for far Peru!
I'll go to hell for ya,
Or Philadelphia,
Any old place with you.

1920

Fly with Me

Presented by the Columbia University Players for a limited run, March 24–27, 1920, at the Astor Grand Ballroom

Music by Richard Rodgers
Book by Milton Kroopf and Philip Leavitt
Directed by Ralph Bunker
Choreographed by Herbert Fields

A College on Broadway

VERSE

On high Olympus, mighty Jove all-powerful
Once asked Minerva, "Where's your holy shrine on earth?"
Apollo, Mars and Mercury cried, "Dad,
With Minnie dear, the same old shrine we've had."

REFRAIN

Bulldogs run around New Haven,
Harvard paints old Cambridge red,
Even poor old Philadelphia really has a college, it is said,
And Williamstown belongs to Williams,
Princeton's tiger stands at bay,
But old New York won't let the world forget
That there's a college on Broadway.

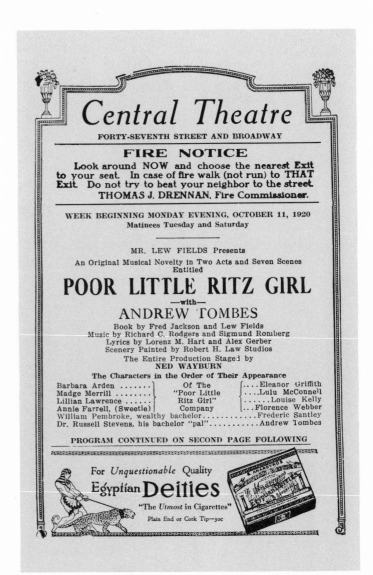

Poor Little Ritz Girl, written after *Fly with Me*, was to have been Larry's first big Broadway break. However, during the Boston tryouts, Lew Fields got cold feet and replaced most of the Rodgers and Hart songs with a score by the more established team of Alex Gerber and (again!) Sigmund Romberg.

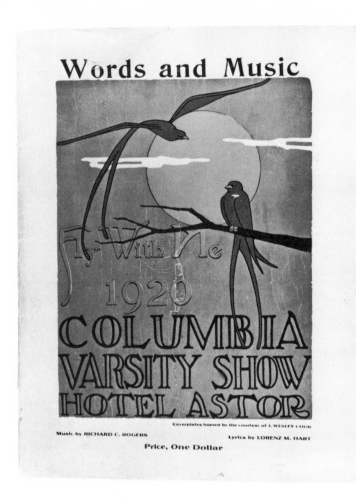

Don't Love Me Like Othello

1st VERSE

Mrs. H.: My romantic fancy isn't hard to please—
That is why my heart belongs to you.
You may not be handsome, like a Grecian frieze—
If you're but affectionate, you'll do.
I don't want a Don Juan with kiss-and-kill-'em
　　eyes—
History is warning me where the danger lies.

1st REFRAIN

Don't love me like Othello—
I'm much too young to die.
An Arrow collar fellow
Can never make me sigh.
Don't love me like King Bluebeard—
His technique was risqué.
And never try to be a cave man—
Don't rave, man,
Behave, man.
But you can treat me like a slave, man,
If you will love and obey.

2nd VERSE

Lowell: Girlies never clamor to make love to me—
That is why you wear my little ring.
You may not emerge like Venus from the sea—
All you have to know is how to cling.
I don't want a Trilby with a larynx in her eyes—
History is warning me where the danger lies.

2nd REFRAIN

Don't love me like Salome—
I'd hate to lose my head.
A Lorelei to comb me
On seaweed must be fed.
Don't love me like Lucretia—
She mixed her drinks, they say.
And never be a bob-haired new girl—
A true girl
Will do, girl.
If I'm to give my name to you, girl,
You'll have to love and obey.

1921

You'll Never Know

Presented by the Columbia University Players for a limited run, April 20–23, 1921, at the Astor Grand Ballroom

Music by Richard Rodgers
Book by Herman Axelrod and Henry W. Hanemann
Directed by Herman Axelrod, Henry W. Hanemann, and Oscar
　Hammerstein II
Choreographed by Herbert Fields

Chorus Girl Blues

1st VERSE

Ma would implore us,
"Don't you be a chorus girl;
Stage life is sinful."
Pa said, "You said a chinful, Pearl!"
I read the "Police Gazette,"
Knew that's the life for this pet.
Now that I'm second from the end,
I'm a different woman, you bet.

1st REFRAIN

I'm tired of ev'ryone
Who says this life's all fun and revel,
That all we do each night
Is frolic and invite the devil.
To travel round they think is great,
So much to see from state to state—
My state is almost half dead
From sleeping three in a bed.
We get so hungry we tear
Food off the arm of a chair,
I've Johnnies by the score,
With flowers at the door they're waiting.
The flowers don't look big—
A steak is more invigorating.
When I've rehearsed all night like mad,
I've no ambition to be bad—
I've got those tight shoes,
Watch your cues,
Darn youse, Chorus Girl Blues!

2nd VERSE

Magazines bore us
That write of the chorus girl.
Say it's a bright life
When they speak of our night-life whirl.
They tell of our limousines,
While we're just subway sardines.
When you inhale the Bronx express,
Mary Garden, you tell what it means.

2nd REFRAIN

They say our souls we risk
Each night to dine on Bisque Tortoni,
While Lulu, Flo and Gert
Know only one dessert, baloney.

We don't get bird's nest soup, fan-tan—
We drink our Campbell's à la can.
Instead of crab meat gratin
We grab for beans in the pan.
Imported cheese we don't miss—
Bite our own holes in the Swiss.
They say we've bottled fizz—
I ask you, how much is that bull worth?
We get our diamond rings,
Our pearls and precious things from Woolworth.
And when my two-by-four I lamp,
I haven't room enough to vamp—
I've got those tight shoes,
Watch your cues,
Darn youse, Chorus Girl Blues!

Donald Kerr and Elise Bonwit in *Poor Little Ritz Girl*

Arthur Schwartz

Arthur Schwartz is, of course, the composer of such cherished melodies as "Dancing in the Dark," "By Myself," "Before I Kiss the World Goodbye," and "That's Entertainment." But how many people recognize him as one of Larry Hart's earliest collaborators? In the early twenties, when Larry was still working for United Plays and writing amateur shows with Dick, Larry continued to return to Brant Lake for the summers, writing and directing camp plays. It was here that he and Arthur met.

One summer during my college days, I was counselor at a boys' camp called Camp Kiwah in Pennsylvania. Another counselor there, called Milton Bender (who was really Dr. Bender, a stage-struck dentist), knew a lot of the Rodgers and Hart songs before they were ever successful. He played those songs for me on the piano when he learned that though I was studying law, I was interested in the theatre and music.

I thought: My God what great lyrics!

When I continued to rave, Bender said, "If you want to meet Larry Hart, don't come back to this camp next summer. Go to Brant Lake Camp, because that's where Larry goes for vacations. He's not a counselor, but there's a little place near the camp for adults who want to holiday there."

I got myself a job at Brant Lake just for the chance to meet Larry. It turned out to be a much better camp. I got more money, better food—and I got to work with Larry Hart, who put on the camp shows every other Saturday. The show I remember best had a song we wrote about a dreamy boy, not the athletic type, who as Larry's title suggested, loved to lie awake in bed. It was the first melody I had written that I felt was any good at all, and I had been trying desperately to write good songs all the time I was going to law school.

This song, titled at camp, "I Love To Lie Awake in Bed," was later, with a new lyric by Howard Dietz, to become a hit years later as "I Guess I'll Have to Change My Plan" in *The Little Show*.

At camp the idea was to give all the kids an opportunity to perform. There was a chorus of the youngest kids we called midgets, the others were called juniors or seniors according to their age group. The midgets were the opening group chorus. There were eight or ten of them in bathing trunks with towels over their shoulders, singing about what they were going to do when they went for a swim. That song was called, appropriately enough, "Down by the Lake." Then there was a waltz melody about the last night at camp, called "Last Night." These were all children's things, of course.

From the start Larry seemed to have an interesting knack for staging things. He knew instinctively the right moments for a song number. He was not only a brilliant lyricist; he was a brilliant theatre man.

In the cabin where I bunked was a fifteen-year-old boy named Marshall Rosanne. His uncle was Elliot Shapiro of Shapiro and Bernstein, a famous music-publishing firm. Uncle Elliot was coming to camp on a weekend visit. I hurried over to Larry's cabin in high excitement.

"Wouldn't you like an audition with a real live music publisher? He's coming to Brant Lake this Sunday. Let's rehearse a few of the songs."

Larry was equally excited. He and Dick had got nowhere with their songs, though they had done two Columbia University varsity shows. In fact, one of the songs we were about to audition was "Don't Love Me Like Othello," from *Fly with Me*.

Now, Elliot Shapiro was not the man with the cigar that you expected to come out of Tin Pan Alley. (I'd seen them look like that in the movies.) He was dignified and grim-faced, and had never heard of Larry Hart or the very new and very young team of Rodgers and Hart. We went to the recreation room (it also doubled as gymnasium), where there was a piano. Mr. Shapiro's face went from grim to grimmer as Larry sang and I played four or five songs.

He shook his head. "It's too collegiate. You fellows" —I think he thought that I was Rodgers—"will never get anywhere unless you change your style. These songs are great for amateur shows. I've got to tell you the truth, fellas. Change your style or give up."

Larry was crushed, of course. He didn't tell Elliot Shapiro that the previous week Billy Rose had been up to camp to see Larry, talking to Larry about lyrics and giving him one hundred dollars a day! No credit and no royalty. Billy and Larry would take a rowboat out on the lake, with some lunch, and at the end of the day Larry had

At Brant Lake, in the early twenties, Larry, second from left, rehearsing a show. Sitting at the piano is Mickey Thomashevsky, of the famous Thomashevsky family of the Yiddish theatre. Mickey wrote the music for most of Larry's Brant Lake shows.

helped write three of Billy Rose's biggest popular hits! You'd be surprised at their names because they don't sound at all like the Larry Hart lyrics we know. But a hundred dollars a day was a lot of money then for a guy who couldn't sell his own songs.

Larry and I remained friends. While visiting at his house in Harlem one evening, a friend, Eddie Ugast, rushed in.

"Do you fellows want to pick up some quick money?"

What else was there to say but "Yes"?

Eddie continued hurriedly. "There's a vaudeville act called Amy and Besser. They're playing in Harlem this week. They need a comedy song. Quick."

Larry and I stayed up most of the night. The act consisted of a straight man and a Jewish comic. The song's title was "I Know My Girl by Her Perfume." The lyrics I have forgotten—something like "I know my girl by her perfume, Estelle has the breath of a Rose. . . ." That was the straight man's line. The Jewish comedian had girls with peculiar smells: Becky smells from herring, some other girls smell from garlic and so on. We were to get seventy-five dollars for the song. We kept working on the song and Eddie Ugast kept telephoning Amy and Besser every hour or so, saying, "They'll have it any minute. They're coming right over."

They wanted it in their act the next day. It must have been three or four in the morning when we had a verse and straight chorus and a comedy chorus. We hurried over to the theatre, close by, and after one reading they said, "We'll take it!"

Ugast acted as agent. He tried to up the price to one hundred dollars, but he settled for the original seventy-five. Twenty-five for him, twenty-five dollars each for Larry and me.

That was the first money I had ever got for a song. But isn't it terrible—or maybe it isn't—that I can't remember that lyric?

After Larry and Dick Rodgers got their own show, I told Larry I still wanted to go into the theatre, even though I was now a lawyer. We obtained Dick's O.K., then Larry got me the job of rehearsal pianist. I went through five weeks of rehearsals and three weeks on the road and learned how a musical comedy is put together.

It was Larry who guided me. He was my adviser—the only one I had. He told me to see him every couple of months and let him hear my latest stuff. At a certain point he said, "I think you're ready, if you've saved enough money to gamble awhile in the theatre—because you can't do both."

Howard Dietz denigrated Larry at one point when Dietz and I were working together. He said, "Larry Hart can rhyme anything—and does." What he meant was pretty obvious: he overrhymed. I don't think so. The construction of a Rodgers and Hart song was usually either a melody first, or a title and melody first; not a lyric

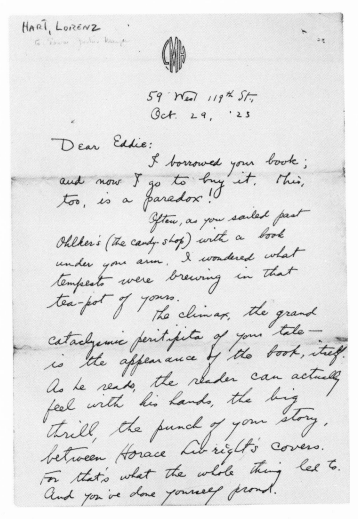

Larry wrote this letter to his friend, the playwright and author Edwin Justus Mayer, in 1923.

first. I mention this because the patterns and schemes of construction of a melody can dictate rhyme. In fact, they do.

I don't find it a fault, because he rhymed most intelligently. There may be some cases of exaggerated rhyming for the purpose of the sound itself, but I don't think so. I think Larry created a style that was personal and was personal to the music as well as the lyrics.

I remember walking down Broadway once with Larry. He was a very short, very nervous man, who constantly rubbed his hands together, smoked cigars, and looked darkly in an upper position with his eyes. This was what Larry said to me: "They said all I could do was triple-rhyme. Now just take a look at this lyric. 'I took one look at you, that's all I meant to do, and then my heart stood still.' I could have said, 'I took one look at you, I threw a book at you,' but I didn't."

That was his way of saying that he did not need to triple-rhyme—to overrhyme. He was right with that melody, not to do that because he had a choice of accents. The melody was undoubtedly written before the words. The title was written first.

As a study of youthful, introspective philosophy, it makes "This Side of Paradise" look like the other side of Barren Island.

The critic in "the Times" is crazy. He cavils because of your good and evil paradox — and your phrase about "too moral to care for morals." Anatol France committed the same fault in "The Revolt of the Angels," so you are castigated in the stocks along with some damn good criminals.

The little reminiscence of Charley touched me, of course! I shall not show your book to the fat bastard — you were

3

unkind to him — and he would certainly crush my copy between the semitically paradoxical hams.

I have no style as a critic. But I know what I know. Your book will _live_. And I am everlastingly grateful to you for having written it.

Lorenz M. Hart.

In Atlantic City. Billy Rose is standing against the backdrop. Eddie Ugast, who sold one of the first Hart-Schwartz songs to a vaudeville act, is sitting in front of Rose, with the hat in his lap.

By 1924, Larry and Dick still hadn't sold a musical score to Broadway, so they tried their hand at writing a straight play. Together with Herb Fields (who had been choreographing many of their amateur shows), they wrote a melodrama called *The Melody Man*. None of them wanted to claim authorship, so they hit on the nom de plume Herbert Richard Lorenz. (In this picture, they're more like Richard Lorenz Herbert.)

I Love To Lie Awake in Bed

I love to lie awake in bed
Right after taps and put the flaps above my head.
I rest my head upon my pillow—
Oh, what a light the moonbeams shed.
I feel so happy I could cry,
And tears are born within the corner of my eye.
To be at home with Ma was never like this.
I could go on forever like this.
I like to lie awake awhile
And go to sleep with a smile.

The Melody Man borrowed a plot from that popular turn-of-the-century tearjerker *The Music Master*. Left to right are Fredric March (who had just changed his name from Frederick Bickel), Betsy Weston and Lew Fields (playing the Melody Man himself, of course!).

BROADWAY and HOLLYWOOD 1925-1935

Edith Meiser

Edith Meiser's career as an actress was just starting when she bowed out of writing the lyrics for the first Garrick Gaieties, *thus giving Larry his first important professional break. She went on, of course, to a long and distinguished acting career, both in musicals and in straight plays.*

I was rather instrumental, very happily, in getting *The Garrick Gaieties* on. All the young performers who were playing small parts for the Theatre Guild got together and said Why don't we do a small revue? The Theatre Guild was in a darling small theatre called the Garrick Theatre. They were building a new theatre. All during the time that they were raising money for the Guild Theatre, which is now the ANTA Theatre, they had big plays going concurrently, like *The Guardsman*, in which I played a small part and understudied Lynn Fontanne.

We did takeoffs, not only of the Guild plays, but of the other plays on Broadway. All this material was written by top comedy writers. They still had revues in those days. We wanted to put on a revue like the *Grand Street Follies*, which satirized topical happenings of the day.

All we'd have to do was find someone to write the music and lyrics. Romney Brent and I were appointed a committee to go out to talk to people who could or would do the score. As a matter of fact, I was supposed to write the lyrics because I had all sorts of ideas that I had already worked on, such as "Gilding the Guild." There was a very nice man, Ben Kaye, a frequent backer of the Guild shows, who said to me one night, "Why don't you see this young man Dick Rodgers, who is the son of a well-known doctor? His father has said that if he doesn't get anywhere soon in show business he's got to get into a more serious and stable business. See if he wouldn't like to write the music for the revue."

We were already in rehearsal. We were going like mad on the sketches. There were no rules or regulations in those days about how long you could rehearse. So Ben Kaye phoned Dick and arranged an appointment for Romney and me to see him. I went uptown across to West End Avenue—which was very elegant in those days—to Dr. Rodgers's apartment. Dick was living with his parents. There was an enormous grand piano in the living room. Dick said, "Well, I'll play you some of the things I wrote for a Columbia University show."

So he did, and I wasn't impressed. Then he played some other things that he had done for amateur shows. Then he played "Manhattan" and I flipped! I told him I would write the lyrics.

Larry and Dick had written something like twenty-five amateur shows when the Theatre Guild came through and gave them their big break with *The Garrick Gaieties*. A few of the many talented young performers who helped make the Gaieties the sensation of New York in the summer of 1925: Sterling Holloway (far right); Philip Loeb (the one with the glasses); and Lee Strasberg (the very intense fellow with the pompadour, bottom left).

I went back to the theatre and said to some of the youngsters who were rehearsing, "I have found the boy!"

Dick came down to rehearsal and played "Manhattan" for them. They all flipped as I had. Then Dick said, "I generally work with a guy named Larry Hart. Would you let him try a few of the ideas that we worked out?" And a few days later Dick brought in the lyrics. Well, I did have the sense to know when I was outclassed. Those lyrics were so absolutely sensational! I remember Larry Hart coming into the theatre. This little bit, almost a dwarf of a man. I always thought he was the American Toulouse-Lautrec. He was that kind of personality. But an enchanting man. He had what is now called charisma. He had such appeal. He was already balding. He had this enormous head and a very heavy beard that had to be shaved twice a day. And of course that big cigar that always stuck out of his mouth. And he was always rubbing his hands together. This was his great gesture when he was pleased. And we adored him. Dick we were terribly fond of, but Larry was adored. He was a pet. He was very, very special. That's not to downgrade Dick at all. We were terribly fond of Dick. In a funny way, you wanted to protect Larry, this funny little ugly man who was so dear. So that was the first *Garrick Gaieties*. The way Herb Fields got in—both boys wanted Herb to have something to do with the show. So Herb wrote a couple of sketches.

There was no one to tell us how to do dance numbers. So Herb, never having been a dancer but having seen so many of his father's shows and having been at the rehearsals, taught us the dance steps. You didn't have to be an awfully good dancer: One, two, three, kick—that kind of thing. For the second *Garrick Gaieties*, Herb did big production numbers.

The early twenties brought the first wave of people from colleges entering the theatre. We were almost all from colleges. Fields, Rodgers and Hart were from Columbia. I was from Vassar. Suddenly colleges were giving courses where the theatre was a serious educational process. The show started as a Sunday Special. Then the Guild decided to put it in for a run and it played the full season.

Larry was so awfully good to us all. We always played in the summer. In those days it was terribly, terribly hot, with no air conditioning. There was one delightful thing that Larry did. He would hire a chauffeured limousine and would take us driving all through those hot nights. We always sang our lungs out. Wherever we went we sang. We'd take a dawn dip in the ocean somewhere out on Long Island, and having cooled off, we'd go back to the city freshened for the night's show. We all thought we were terribly sophisticated, but really we were very naïve. We were innocents.

In later years I would run into Larry in the pool at the Beverly Hills Hotel. Larry lived always for just today. Yesterday didn't exist—tomorrow might never happen. This was a guy who was a Laugh, clown, laugh person. Always fun, always the light, sparkling conversation. But you knew the heart was bleeding under it, always was.

In the later shows Herb and Dick had to lock him in the bathroom and warn, "Don't come out until you've written a lyric."

You know, there were always very attractive chorus girls that Larry was constantly telling jokes to during rehearsals. And he always seemed to be enjoying that more than getting down to work. I've known many lyric writers, and I've done a few myself. You sit there with a rhyming dictionary; with a Roget's *Thesaurus*. But Larry —never. It was purely out of his head. He had one of the most beautiful, full vocabularies I've ever heard.

1925

The Garrick Gaieties

Opened May 17, 1925, at the Garrick Theatre
Reopened June 8, 1925, for a run of 211 performances

Music by Richard Rodgers
Sketches by Benjamin M. Kaye, Arthur Sullivan, Morrie Ryskind, Louis Sorin, Sam Jaffe, Howard J. Green and Edith Meiser
Directed by Philip Loeb
Choreographed by Herbert Fields
Settings and costumes by Carolyn Hancock

Gilding the Guild

⊰ *Originally sung by Betty Starbuck* ⊱

VERSE

We bring drama to your great metropolis.
We are the little-theatre group.
Each of us has built a small Acropolis
To hold our little-theatre troupe.
We'd be very glad to meet you,
And greet you,
And seat you,
And treat you just great.
For all commercial art is hollow,
So follow Apollo
And swallow our bait.
Help to serve the art of your cosmopolis.
If you'll be one of us,
Each son of us,
Will welcome you at the gate.

TRIO-PATTER

The Neighborhood Playhouse may shine
Below the Macy-Gimbel line.
It was built to make a ride
For people on Fifth Avenue.
To Yeats and Synge and Shaw and such
We add an Oriental touch.
We bring out the aesthetic soul
You didn't know you have in you!

We like to serve a mild dish
Of folklore quaintly childish
Or something Oscar Wilde-ish
In a pantomime or dance.
Grand Street folk, we never see 'em—
They think the place is a museum.
And we know just what we do
Because we always take a chance!

DIALOGUE

"The Garrick Gaieties"
Is coming down the street!
Here's where
We meet our meat!

REFRAIN

Gilding the Guild,
Gilding the Guild,
We possess a fine artistic touch.
Money doesn't count.
Not much!
Shuberts may say
Art doesn't pay,
But we've built this
Cozy little shack
Tho' we lack
Shubert's jack!
In our cute little building
We're gilding the Guild!

TRIO-PATTER

The Provincetown Playhouse still owns
The art of Robert Edmond Jones.
From the classic drama
We're a notable secessionist.
We've even made the censors feel
The verity of Gene O'Neill.
The meaning doesn't matter
If the manner is Expressionist!
Our one great contribution
To art is revolution!
Our mood is very "Roosh-in"—
You can tell it at a glance.
Our bare stage may look funny,
But it saves us lots of money,
And we know just what to do
Because we always take a chance!

For your attention, many thanks.
We've brought along subscription blanks
For the actor's theatre,
That the audience may glory in
The dear old "Servant in the House,"
The pride of Mister Ranken Towse,
And plays by Henrik Ibsen
In a manner quite Victorian!
We spurn the bedroom dramas
With heroes in pajamas
For things that pleased our mamas
Such as Candida's romance.
We wear the sock and buskin
To the taste of old John Ruskin.
And we know just what to do
Because we never take a chance.

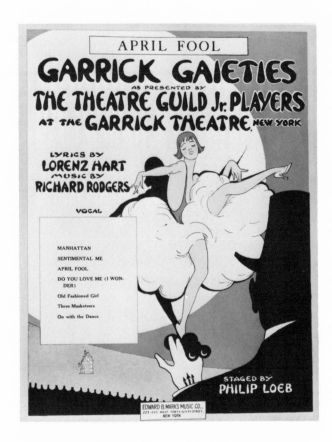

Manhattan

{ *Originally sung by Sterling Holloway and
June Cochrane* }

VERSE

Summer journeys
To Niag'ra
And to other places
Aggravate all our cares.
We'll save our fares.
I've a cozy little flat
In what is known as old Manhattan.
We'll settle down
Right here in town.

1st REFRAIN

We'll have Manhattan,
The Bronx and Staten
Island too.
It's lovely going through
The zoo.
It's very fancy
On old Delancey
Street, you know.
The subway charms us so
When balmy breezes blow
To and fro.
And tell me what street
Compares with Mott Street
In July?
Sweet pushcarts gently gliding by.
The great big city's a wondrous toy
Just made for a girl and boy.
We'll turn Manhattan
Into an isle of joy.

2nd REFRAIN

We'll go to Greenwich,
Where modern men itch
To be free;
And Bowling Green you'll see
With me.
We'll bathe at Brighton
The fish you'll frighten
When you're in.
Your bathing suit so thin
Will make the shellfish grin
Fin to fin.
I'd like to take a
Sail on Jamaica
Bay with you.
And fair Canarsie's lake
We'll view.
The city's bustle cannot destroy
The dreams of a girl and boy.
We'll turn Manhattan
Into an isle of joy.

3rd REFRAIN

We'll go to Yonkers
Where true love conquers
In the wilds.
And starve together, dear,
In Childs'.
We'll go to Coney
And eat baloney
On a roll.
In Central Park we'll stroll,
Where our first kiss we stole,
Soul to soul.
Our future babies
We'll take to "Abie's
Irish Rose."
I hope they'll live to see
It close.
The city's clamor can never spoil
The dreams of a boy and goil.
We'll turn Manhattan
Into an isle of joy.

4th REFRAIN

We'll have Manhattan,
The Bronx and Staten
Island too.
We'll try to cross
Fifth Avenue.
As black as onyx
We'll find the Bronnix
Park Express.
Our Flatbush flat, I guess,
Will be a great success,
More or less.
A short vacation
On Inspiration Point
We'll spend,
And in the station house we'll end.
But Civic Virtue cannot destroy
The dreams of a girl and boy.
We'll turn Manhattan
Into an isle of joy.

June Cochrane and Sterling Holloway, introducing "Manhattan." "Manhattan" was originally written for one of Larry and Dick's unproduced early efforts, a show called *Winkle Town*, which made the rounds for years without arousing the interest of the reigning producers. Three of the other *Winkle Town* leftovers were to be used in *The Girl Friend*; two in *One Dam Thing After Another*; and four in *Dearest Enemy* and the second *Gaieties*. This from a show nobody would produce!

Sentimental Me
(And Romantic You)

*{ Originally sung by June Cochrane, James Norris,
Edith Meiser and Sterling Holloway }*

1st VERSE

Look at me again, dear.
Let's hold hands and then, dear,
Sigh in chorus.
It won't bore us,
To be sure.
There's no meaning to it,
Yet we overdo it
With a relish
That is hellish
To endure.
I am not the kind that merely flirts.
I just love and love until it hurts.

REFRAIN

Oh, sentimental me
And poor romantic you.
Dreaming dreams
Is all that we can do.
We hang around all day and ponder,
While both of us grow fonder.
The Lord knows where we're wandering to!
I sit and sigh.
You sigh and sit
Upon my knee.
We laugh and cry and never disagree.
A million kisses
We'll make theft of

Until there's nothing left of
Poor romantic you
And sentimental me.
Oh, me.

2nd VERSE

Darling, you're so handsome
Strong and clever, and sometimes
You seem, dear
Like a dream, dear
That came true.
That's why I picked you out.
Better men I threw out
Of my living room
While giving room
To you.
I would rather read of love in books.
Love is much more painful than it looks.

1926

Dearest Enemy

*Opened September 18, 1926, at the Knickerbocker Theatre
for a run of 286 performances*

Music by Richard Rodgers
Book by Herbert Fields
Directed by Charles Sinclair and Harry Ford
Choreographed by Carl Hemmer
Settings by Clark Robinson
Costumes by Mark Mooring, Hubert Davis and James Reynolds

"Sweet Peter," the comedy highlight of *Dearest Enemy.* The lyric was about the woes of Peter Stuyvesant, who "had a wife
but couldn't cheat her," because the noise made by his wooden leg would wake her up whenever he tried to sneak in late.

Helen Ford as the patriot Betsy Burke and Charles Purcell as the redcoat captain Sir John Copeland in *Dearest Enemy.* She's wearing a barrel because he's made off with her clothes while she was taking a dip. (Helen had all her clothes back on by the time the two of them sang "Here in My Arms.")

1926

The Girl Friend

Opened March 17, 1926, at the Vanderbilt Theatre for a run of 301 performances

Music by Richard Rodgers
Book by Herbert Fields
Directed by John Harwood
Choreographed by Jack Haskell
Settings by P. Dodd Ackerman
Costumes by Booth, Willoughby and Jones

The Blue Room

{ Originally sung by Sammy White and Eva Puck }

1st VERSE

All my future plans, dear,
Will suit your plans—
Read the little blueprints.
Here's your mother's room.
Here's your brother's room.
On the wall are two prints.
Here's the kiddies' room,
Here's the biddy's room,
Here's a pantry lined with shelves, dear.
Here I've planned for us,
Something grand for us,
Where we two can be ourselves, dear.

Here in My Arms

{ Originally sung by Helen Ford and Charles Purcell }

1st VERSE

I know a merry place
Far from intrusion;
It's just the very place
For your seclusion.
There you can while away
Days as you smile away.
It's not a mile away
But it's new to you.

REFRAIN

Here in my arms
It's adorable!
It's deplorable
That you were never there.
When little lips
Are so kissable,
It's permissible
For me to ask my share.
Next to my heart
It is ever so lonely.
I'm holding only air,
While here in my arms,
It's adorable!
It's deplorable
That you were never there.

2nd VERSE

I know a pretty place
At your command, sir;
It's not a city place
Yet near at hand, sir.
Here, if you loll away,
Two hearts can toll away.
You'd never stroll away
If you only knew!

The Girl Friend played all over the world, and eventually it was the most profitable of all Larry's twenties shows. The great dance team of Eva Puck and Sammy White—they had also appeared in *The Melody Man*—played a bicycle racer and his trainer. (Unlike the heroines of the popular operettas of the period, Rodgers and Hart heroines always had spirit.)

1st REFRAIN

We'll have a blue room,
A new room,
For two room,
Where ev'ry day's a holiday
Because you're married to me.
Not like a ballroom,
A small room,
A hall room,
Where I can smoke my pipe away
With your wee head upon my knee.
We will thrive on,
Keep alive on,
Just nothing but kisses,
With Mister and Missus
On little blue chairs.
You sew your trousseau,
And Robinson Crusoe
Is not so far from worldly cares
As our blue room far away upstairs.

2nd VERSE

From all visitors
And inquisitors
We'll keep our apartment.
I won't change your plans—
You arrange your plans
Just the way your heart meant.
Here we'll be ourselves
And we'll see ourselves
Doing all the things we're scheming.
Here's a certain place
Cretonne curtain place
Where no one can see us dreaming.

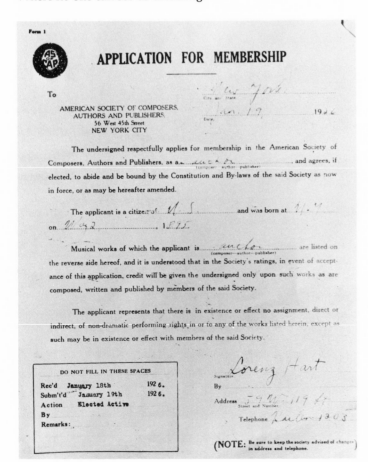

The symbol of an arrived songwriter: Larry's application to ASCAP.

The Girl Friend

{ Originally sung by Sammy White and Eva Puck }

1st VERSE

Lenny: My girl's the kind of girl
For steady company.
It's steady company
That I prefer.
When in the Charleston dance
I want to bump a knee,
I want to bump a knee
With her.
Homely wrecks appeal
When their checks appeal,
But she has sex appeal.
Yes, sir!

1st REFRAIN

Isn't she cute?
Isn't she sweet?
She's gentle
And mentally nearly complete.
She's knockout,
She's regal,
Her beauty's illegal.
She's the girl friend!
Take her to dance!
Take her to tea!
It's stunning
How cunning this lady
Can be.
A look at this vision
Will cause a collision.
She's the girl friend!
She is smart,
She's refined.
How can she be real?
She has heart,
She has mind.
Hell, the girl's ideal!
Isn't she cute?
Isn't she sweet?
An eyeful you'd die full
Of pleasure to meet.
In my funny fashion
I'm cursed with a passion
For the girl friend!

2nd VERSE

Mollie: He's very short on looks
But long on decency.
He's long on decency,
He's very tame.
But he has made an awful hit with me since he—
A hit with me, since he first came.
I have seen so well
He won't screen so well,
But that boy means so well.
He's game!

2nd REFRAIN

Mollie: Isn't he cute?
Isn't he sweet?
He's gentle and mentally

Nearly complete.
He's warm as
An oven.
He knows how
To love an'
I'm the girl friend!

Lenny: Take her to dance,
Take her to tea.
It's stunning
How cunning this lady
Can be.
She ain't got
No culture.
She's keen as
A vulture.
She's the girl friend!

Mollie: He is smart,
He's refined.
How can he be real?
He has heart,
He has mind.
Hell, the boy's ideal!

Lenny: Isn't she cute?
Isn't she sweet?
An eyeful you'd die full
Of pleasure to meet.

Both: In my [his] funny fashion
I'm [he's] cursed with a passion
For the girl friend.

1926

The Garrick Gaieties

*Opened May 10, 1926, at the Garrick Theatre
for a run of 174 performances*

Music by Richard Rodgers
Sketches by Benjamin M. Kaye, Newman Levy, Marion Page
Johnson, Herbert Fields, Chester D. Haywood, Edward Hope
and Philip Lord
Directed by Philip Loeb
Choreographed by Herbert Fields
Settings and costumes by Carolyn Hancock

Mountain Greenery

{ *Originally sung by Bobbie Perkins and Sterling
Holloway* }

VERSE

On the first of May
It is moving day.
Spring is here, so blow your job—
Throw your job away.
Now's the time to trust
To your wanderlust.
In the city's dust you wait.
Must you wait?
Just you wait.

REFRAIN

In a mountain greenery
Where God paints the scenery,
Just two crazy people together.
While you love your lover let
Blue Skies be your coverlet;
When it rains
We'll laugh at the weather.
And if you're good
I'll search for wood,
So you can cook
While I stand looking.
Beans could get no keener
Reception in a beanery.
Bless our mountain greenery home.

TRIO-PATTER

He: When the world was young
Old Father Adam
With sin would grapple.
So we're entitled
To just one apple.
She: You mean to make apple sauce.
He: Underneath the bough
We'll learn a lesson
From Mister Omar
Beneath the eyes of
No pa and no ma.
She: Old Lady Nature is boss.
Washing dishes, catching fishes
In the running stream.
We'll curse the smell o'
Citronella
Even when we dream.
He: Head upon the ground,
Your downy pillow
Is just a boulder.
I'll have new dimples
Before I'm older.
But life is peaches and cream.

1st ENCORE

It's quite all right
To sing at night.
I'll sit and play
My ukulele.
You can bet its tone
Beats a Jascha Heifetz tone.
Bless our mountain greenery home.

2nd ENCORE

In a mountain greenery
Where God paints the scenery
With the world we haven't a quarrel.
Here a girl can map her own
Life without a chaperone.
It's so good it must be immoral.
It's not amiss
To sit and kiss.
For me and you
There are no blue laws.
Life is more delectable
When it's disrespectable.
Bless our mountain greenery home.

Queen Elizabeth

⟨ *Originally sung by Edith Meiser* ⟩

VERSE

I'm Elizabeth, the Virgin Queen.
Don't laugh!
On my title I stand firm,
Though it's just a technical term.
My royal bed was only used by half!
I have never been a prude, or
I had not been born a Tudor.
A royal marriage is a mockery.
A husband's just a piece of crockery!
There's not much I haven't seen.
But I'm still the Virgin Queen!

1st REFRAIN

But even a queen has her moments,
And I see no reason to rue it.
A venial sin
Is no menial sin—
In fact, it's quite a congenial sin,
If nobody sees you do it.
Behind my portal
I am mortal
And the court'll still be blind.
Though there's urge in
Me to burgeon,
I'm a virgin in my mind.
The rumors you heard about Shakespeare
Are vulgar as they are untrue.
I was his inspiration
To help out the nation,
And one must have a moment or two.
Yes, two.

2nd REFRAIN

But even a queen has her moments
When regal wild oats need their sowing
I'd be alone
Drink my tea alone
And make England queen of the sea alone.
For sailors are well worth knowing.
All my gallants
Had their talents—
They were balance for my nerves.
When my army
Failed to charm me
I would call out the reserves.
You think Mary Stuart was naughty
The blonde with the big eyes of blue.
But no royal redhead
Was ever a deadhead,
And one must have a moment or two.
Yes, two.

ENCORE

But even a queen has her moments,
Though duty is stern as a Tartar.
A tall he-man.
And an all he-man,
Was that handsome Sir Walter Raleigh man.
And what a knight—of the Garter!
When 'twas floody
O'er the mud, he
Threw his mantle down for me!
In his shirt, he
Proved a flirt; he
Was more daring vis-à-vis.
They say he discovered tobacco.
And I made him smoke, it is true.
For my tresses so titian
Gave him the ignition,
And one must have a moment or two.
Yes, two.

The Theatre Guild hadn't had a very successful 1926, so, for the opening number of *The Second Garrick Gaieties*, Larry had representatives of the Guild's various recent flops come out and warn Sterling Holloway that he wasn't going to do much better: "You can't be as good as last year!" Androcles's Lion is Romney Brent (second from right); the goat (from *Goat Song)* is William M. Griffith.

Edith Meiser as the Queen who ''has her moments.'' Describing the first-night response to the new *Gaieties,* George Jean Nathan wrote, ''The audience at the opening night applauded everything but the hat holders under the seats.'' They certainly cheered for this number.

Helen Ford

One of the loveliest musical-comedy actresses of the twenties, Helen Ford starred in three of the Rodgers and Hart shows. Petite and adorable, she shone in Dearest Enemy *and then had her greatest triumph in 1926, with the wonderful* Peggy-Ann. *Two years later, a disaster called* Chee-Chee *would end her affiliation with Rodgers and Hart. But she renewed it, when, almost five decades after* Dearest Enemy, *she appeared at the University of Southern California's 1973 tribute to the lyrics of Lorenz Hart. She sang "Here in My Arms."*

I first met Dick Rodgers and Herbert Fields when they came to me at the Algonquin Hotel with a script of the American Revolution. They asked me to read it, and if I liked it, Larry and Dick would play the score for me. The show was *Dearest Enemy.* There was a very good part for me and I loved the music. At that time I wasn't as appreciative of Larry's lyrics as I am now.

We auditioned for every Tom, Dick and Harry, for every cloak-and-suiter. Finally, after getting only half the money for the show—$25,000—we were doing it for gangsters, who were beginning to put money in the theatre. We got the money.

Larry always thought he was very naughty and liked to tease me by offering me a dirty lyric, pretending it was a new lyric for the show. I was young, kind of strait-laced at the time, and that brought out his high school humor. He was like a child.

One night, after a year's run in *Peggy-Ann,* he came rushing in to me and said, "We've got to have a new lyric for 'A Little Birdie Told Me So,' " which was my song. In those days it was considered a little risqué. After the show Larry came back and said, "I've got the lyric." He handed me some toilet paper with a carefully written-out lyric, watching me from the corner of his eye to get my reaction. He always tried to shock me. He was a darling. Everybody loved him.

Helen Ford, singing "Here in My Arms," November 2, 1973.

1926

Peggy-Ann

Opened December 27, 1926, at the Vanderbilt Theatre for a run of 333 performances

Music by Richard Rodgers
Book by Herbert Fields
Directed by Robert Milton
Choreographed by Seymour Felix
Settings by Clark Robinson
Costumes by Mark Mooring

Where's That Rainbow?

{ *Originally sung by Helen Ford* }

1st VERSE

Troubles really are bubbles, they say,
And I'm bubbling over today!
Spring brings roses to people, you see,
But it brings hay fever to me!
If I have ever had luck,
It's bad luck, that's sure.
That Pollyanna stuff, too,
Is tough to endure!

REFRAIN

Where's that rainbow you hear about?
Where's that lining they cheer about?
Where's that love nest,
Where love is king, ever after?
Where's that blue room they sing about?
Where's that sunshine they fling about?
I know morning will come,
But pardon my laughter!
In each scenario
You can depend on the end
Where the lovers agree.
Where's that Lothario?
Where does he roam, with his dome
Vaselined as can be?
It is easy to see all right
Ev'rything's gonna be all right—
Be just dandy for ev'rybody but me.

2nd VERSE

Fortune never smiles, but in my case,
It just laughs right in my face.
If I looked for a horseshoe, I s'pose,
It would bop me right in the nose.
My luck will vary surely,
That's purely a curse.
My luck has changed—it's gotten
From rotten to worse!

A Little Birdie Told Me So

{ Originally sung by Helen Ford }

1st VERSE

Mother said, "My darling, if you're going to New York,
I must tell you of the mysteries of life.
In towns like that, a little friendly visit from the stork
Is rather awkward if you're not a wife!
Although he's not invited, he'll always be delighted
To fly in at a weekend.
Where will that fellow's cheek end?"
But I replied, "I know just what to do, dear, while I roam—
I'll simply tell the stork I'm not at home."

1st REFRAIN

How did I come to know which way the wind would blow?
A little birdie told me so!
A little word called "yes" can make an awful mess.
The answer to "Giddap" is "Whoa."
Don't pity mother Eve, her weakness was detestable,
And soon she learned forbidden fruit was indigestible!
But how did I find out what it was all about?
A little birdie told me so!

2nd VERSE

When a handsome stranger says, "I think we've met before,"
There's more than conversation on his mind.
When he says, "Our souls should meet," just show him the
        door!
For the meeting that he means is not refined!
He'll say his love is mental,
And very transcendental.
His talk will soon get boorish,
And very ostermoorish.
He will use poetic words that no one understands,
And illustrate the meaning with his hands.

2nd REFRAIN

How did I come to know which way the wind would blow?
A little birdie told me so!
So look before you leap—the narrow path is steep.
One little push and down you go!
Of very pure young girls I wouldn't say there's none that's
        left—
The well-known statue called Miss Liberty's the one that's
        left!
But purest driven snow will sometimes drift, you know.
A little birdie told me so!

In the second act of *Peggy-Ann*, a giant silver fish appeared to tow the shipwrecked wedding party to shore. The fish also talked: "I hope I didn't intrude, but I saw that you were having some difficulty." (Left to right, Lulu McConnell, Lester Cole, Helen Ford, Betty Starbuck.)

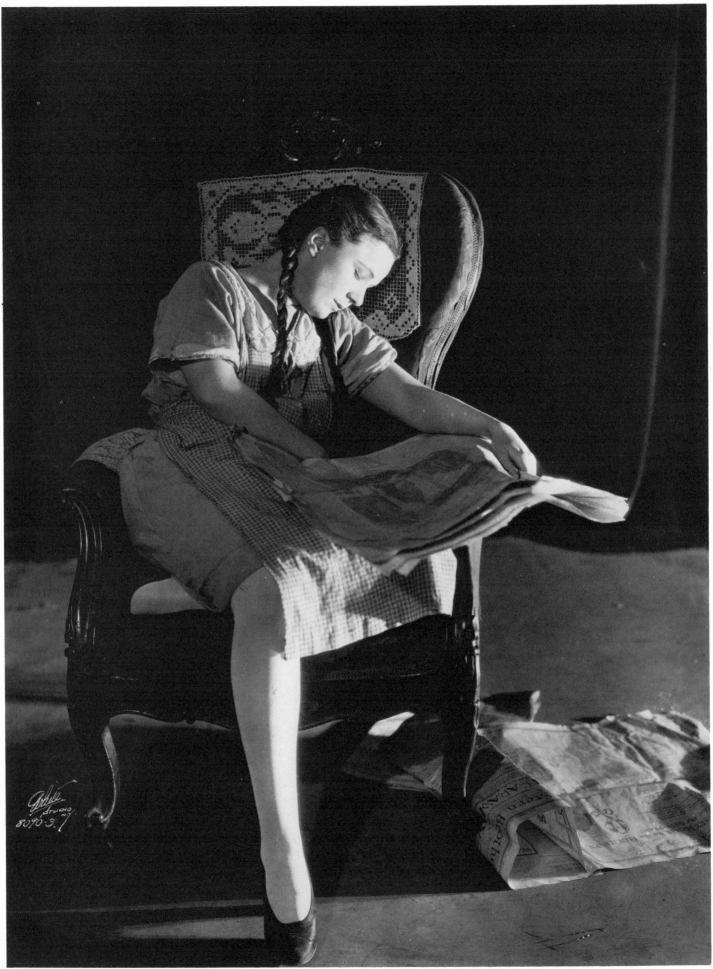

"You bet your life I'd have two hats and a fresh egg once in a while." Helen Ford, in the prologue of *Peggy-Ann,* as the little girl who falls asleep reading the New York papers and dreams of wonderful adventures in Manhattan, Havana and all the other places that girls in the sticks once dreamed of visiting.

1926

Betsy

Opened December 28, 1926, at the New Amsterdam Theatre for a run of 39 performances

Music by Richard Rodgers
Book by Irving Caesar, David Freedman and William Anthony Maguire
Directed by William Anthony Maguire
Choreographed by Sammy Lee
Settings by Frank E. Gates, E. A. Morange, Bergman Studios and Joseph Urban
Costumes by Charles LeMaire

This Funny World

⊰ *Originally sung by Belle Baker* ⊱

VERSE

A mop,
A broom, a pail!
The stuff my dreams are made of!
You hope,
You strive, you fail!
The world's a place you're not afraid of.
But soon you're brought down to earth
And you learn what your dream was worth.

REFRAIN

This funny world
Makes fun of the things that you strive for.
This funny world
Can laugh at the dreams you're alive for.
If you're beaten, conceal it!
There's no pity for you.
For the world cannot feel it.
Just keep to yourself.
Weep to yourself.
This funny world
Can turn right around
And forget you.

A Ziegfeld production, *Betsy* opened the night after *Peggy-Ann*. It was nowhere near as successful, nor as good, and Larry and Dick were especially incensed when Ziegfeld added songs by other writers to their score. Belle Baker (seated, second from left) had the title role. But her big number, *Blue Skies*, was by Irving Berlin.

Larry wrote this admiring letter to Ira Gershwin in 1926. The show of the Gershwins' he's referring to is Tip-Toes, *which starred Jeanette MacDonald, whom he would later write for, and Queenie Smith.*

Dear Mr. Gershwin:

When, the other night at the Guild's Menagerie, Joe Meyer told me a departing guest was Ira Gershwin, I should have brushed aside your friends, grasped you by the hand, and told you how much I liked the lyrics of *Tip-Toes*, but probably because the circus-clowns inspired a speedy retreat from a too acute consciousness, I had imbibed more cocktails than is my wont, and so, when the coffee-loving Mr. Meyer pointed you out, all I could say was "Zat so!"

Your lyrics, however, gave me as much pleasure as Mr. George Gershwin's music, and the utterly charming performance of Miss Queenie Smith. I have heard none so good this many a day. I wanted to write you right after I had seen the show, but—well, I didn't rush up to you at the Guild circus either.

It is a great pleasure to live at a time when light amusement in this country is at last losing its brutally cretin aspect. Such delicacies as your jingles prove that songs can be both popular and intelligent. May I take the liberty of saying that your rhymes show a healthy improvement over those in *Lady Be Good*.

You have helped a lot to make an evening delightful to me—and I am very grateful. Thank you! And may your success continue!

Lorenz Hart

Rodgers and Hart had had a mild success in England in 1926, with a show called *Lido Lady,* which they wrote for the popular British star Cicely Courtneidge. But in 1927, they conquered London with the score of *One Dam Thing After Another,* a Charles Cochran revue, in which Jessie Matthews and Richard Dolman introduced ''My Heart Stood Still.'' Larry and Dick returned to America in triumph—traveling first class, of course.

1927

A Connecticut Yankee

Opened November 3, 1927, at the Vanderbilt Theatre for a run of 418 performances

Music by Richard Rodgers
Book by Herbert Fields, from the novel *A Connecticut Yankee in King Arthur's Court*, by Mark Twain
Directed by Alexander Leftwich
Choreographed by Busby Berkeley
Settings and costumes by John Hawkins, Jr.

Thou Swell

⊰ *Originally sung by William Gaxton and Constance Carpenter* ⊱

1st VERSE

Babe, we are well met,
As in a spell met—
I lift my helmet.
Sandy,
You're just dandy
For just this here lad.
You're such a fistful
My eyes are mistful—
Are you too wistful
To care?
Do say you care
To say, "Come near, lad."
You are so graceful—
Have you wings?
You have a face full
Of nice things.
You have no speaking voice, dear.
With ev'ry word it sings.

REFRAIN

Thou swell!
Thou witty!
Thou sweet!
Thou grand!
Wouldst kiss me pretty?
Wouldst hold my hand?
Both thine eyes are cute, too—
What they do to me.
Hear me holler I choose a
Sweet lollapalooza in thee.
I'd feel so rich in
A hut for two.
Two rooms and kitchen
I'm sure would do.
Give me just a plot of
Not a lot of
Land, and,
Thou swell!
Thou witty!
Thou grand!

2nd VERSE

Thy words are queer, sir,
Unto mine ear, sir.
Yet thou'rt a dear, sir,
To me.
Thou couldst woo me.
Now couldst thou try, knight.
I'd murmur, "Swell," too,
And like it well, too.
More thou wilt tell to Sandy.
Thou art dandy.
Now art thou my knight.
Thine arms are martial,
Thou hast grace.
My cheek is partial
To thy face.
And if thy lips grow weary
Mine are their resting place.

My Heart Stood Still

⊰ *Originally sung by William Gaxton and Constance Carpenter* ⊱

1st VERSE

I laughed at sweethearts
I met at schools.
All indiscreet hearts
Seemed romantic fools.
A house in Iceland
Was my heart's domain.
I saw your eyes—
Now castles rise in Spain!

REFRAIN

I took one look at you,
That's all I meant to do,
And then my heart stood still!
My feet could step and walk,
My lips could move and talk,
And yet my heart stood still!
Though not a single word was spoken,
I could tell you knew;
That unfelt clasp of hands
Told me so well you knew.
I never lived at all
Until the thrill of that moment when
My heart stood still.

2nd VERSE

Through all my school days
I hated boys.
Those April Fool days
Brought me loveless joys.
I read my Plato,
Love I thought a sin.
But since your kiss,
I'm reading Missus Glyn!

On a Desert Island With Thee

{ Originally sung by Jack Thompson and June Cochrane }

VERSE

Galahad: Come, sit thee near,
Place thyself upon my knee.
Make an end of thy fear,
For I love but thee in Camelot.

Evelyn: Oh, no not here,
Where observed of all we'll be.
Should thy father appear,
He would surely scold and damn a lot.

Galahad: Care not a jot.
Harken to my plot:
Soon we'll retreat to a sweet spot!

1st REFRAIN

Oh, for a year on a desert island with thee,
Out in the sheer middle of the sea.
We'll sing tra-la; wouldn't we be happy and gay,
With thy mama many miles away?
In the morning air murmur a blessing;
First we'll eat, then we will dress.

If it's fair, we'll be caressing,
If it rains, we'll caress!
Who knows next year what the population will be
Out in the middle of the sea?

TRIO-PATTER

Evelyn: I'll pack each little thing for thee.
What ten books shall I bring for thee?
We'll need some books to read.

Galahad: Thou needst not bring ten books along.
If thou wilt bring thy looks along,
'Twill be enough for me.
If the heat begins to swelter,
We won't have to fear the sun.
We will lie beneath a shelter
Only big enough for one.

Evelyn: Let the prudish people quarrel—
We'll forget them for the nonce.
If they think our love immoral,
"Honi soit qui mal y pense."

Galahad: I'll dress the way that Adam did.
Evelyn: And I the way his madam did.
Galahad: I'll see enough of thee!

Lew Fields produced five of Larry and Dick's twenties shows: *The Girl Friend, Peggy-Ann, A Connecticut Yankee, Present Arms* and *Chee-Chee.* In this publicity still, taken at the time of *A Connecticut Yankee,* Lew (seated center) is flanked by Herb (directly to his left) and by Dick, Larry, and Busby Berkeley (all at his right).

"Wouldst kiss me pretty? Wouldst hold my hand?" William Gaxton and Constance Carpenter, on the road to Camelot, as the Yankee Martin and the Demoiselle Alisande. Several of the critics compared Constance Carpenter to Gertrude Lawrence, who had just scored a smash hit in *Oh, Kay!* But Billy Gaxton was incomparable, and *A Connecticut Yankee* established him as the top musical-comedy leading man of the next decade.

Give This Little Round Table a Big Round Hand

Musical Version of "A Connecticut Yankee" Sets Up King Arthur's Knights for Life.

By FRANK VREELAND.

A FINE, strapping young musical comedy, yclept "A Connecticut Yankee," came to town at the Vanderbilt Theatre last night, when that most delectable of all existing musical triumvirates, composed of Richard Rodgers, Lorenz Hart and Herbert Fields, gave King Arthur's Round Table a gay run-around. Boyishly spontaneous and merry, this piece was an ideally captivating transcription of Mark Twain's grand old fantasy on which most of us cut our literary milk teeth.

Much has been expected of this production by Lew Fields and Lyle D Andrews, and nobody in the uncommonly knowing and elect audience of first nighters appeared last night to have the slightest expectation jarred. Why should they? The show has some of the most talented principals ever corralled in a musical show, bouncing book and lyrics, and music that you could almost play on a typewriter.

The sprightly scudding chorus in their tripping, saltatory numbers drew at least two bonafide whistles from the gallery. And if two whistles from the gallery don't stamp a musical show as an enormous hit, then I'm badly off on my whistles.

The show is funny even between the acts when the curtain is down, for the front drop then reveals a splendidly dotty map of King Arthur's castle at Camelot and environs, designed by that sterling old master at lunatic maps and tapestries, Robert Benchley. Indeed, I surmise that this production would even meet with the approval of H. L. Mencken, that great dragon of literature who stands guard at Mark Twain's tomb and occasionally belches fire in his praise.

The best notice I can give it is to emulate the advertising signs which the Boss stuck on the plumed knights who were to act as his mailed traveling salesmen, bearing sandwich boards announcing soap and other noble articles. In this vein let me urge you:—

GO, THOU SLUGGARD,
AND ENJOY
"A CONNECTICUT YANKEE"
AND TELL
YE COCKE-EYED WORLDE
THOU HAST HAD
YE HELUVA TIME.

This prodigally profuse offering bids fair to join the memorable ranks of "Peggy-Ann" and "Irene" and other musical shows stationed at this house, and probably will splinter some records. In fact, it almost looked last night when the cheering was at its height as if this piece had set up King Arthur's knights for life.

Last night the youthful collaborators, not being film wiseacres,

Summary of "A Connecticut Yankee" for Busy Readers.

Musical adaptation of Mark Twain's book, presented by Lew Fields and Lyle D. Andrews. Libretto by Herbert Fields, music by Richard Rodgers, lyrics by Lorenz Hart.

Another step forward by this excellent trio, living up to their reputation. The piece, with its ludicrous contrast between modern talk and ideas in a mediaeval court, has been capably staged by Alexander Leftwich, with lively dances by Busby Berkeley. Outstanding in the cast are William Gaxton. in the title role; Constance Carpenter as Sandy, Nana Bryant, June Cochrane and William Norris.

AT THE VANDERBILT THEATRE.

succeeded because they skipped lightly from page to page of the book in a spirit of modest fun, not seeking the ornate dazzlement of an Alice in Movieland. You could almost see the deferential small boys approach for a romp with a jovial, fanciful old gentleman. Dropping his sociological satire, they fondly retained much of his quaint touch in the first act, doing the famous eclipse "miracle" with a great hurrah and hallelujah.

The second act they brisked up with modern solecisms of speech, for which "The Road to Rome" and its clan have prepared us, and also changed the talkative Sandy into a speechifying suffragette and Lucy Stoner—quite naturally. They took particular delight in showing how the old gags of today were hoary chestnuts 1,400 years ago, thus being the only musical show to wring a new twist of laughter from the standard wheezes by shamelessly admitting their antiquity.

One of the most markedly enchanting features of the evening were the remarkably harmonious and striking costumes by John F. Hawkins, Jr., who also did droll dream sets which suggested stained glass windows gone cuckoo. The songs had all the unescapable pulse of "Mountain Greenery" and all the other "Garrick Gaieties" hits, and were conducted by Rodgers himself, mostly with the spine and hips. Occasionally the collaborators seemed to remember that they had been identified as modern Savoyards, and this seemed to please the attendant representatives of Gilbert and Sullivan, who were respectively Alexander Woollcott and Frank Sullivan. But if they want my advice, it's "Be yourselves, kiddoes."

Frank Vreeland's famous review of *A Connecticut Yankee* in the New York *Telegram,* in which he adapted Herb Fields's Jazz Age version of medieval speech to urge his readers to see the show.

I Feel at Home With You

{ *Originally sung by Jack Thompson and June Cochrane* }

1st VERSE

This used to be a grumpy, crabbed old lad—
Look at your beamish boy now.
This used to be a jumpy, silly and sad—
What is simply joy now.
Life was a canyon too dark to view,
Till a companion was found like you.

1st REFRAIN

I feel at home with you.
You always fit on the
Knees that you sit on.
That's why I feel at home with you.
I love to roam with you.
Each place that we go,
You flatter my ego.
That's why I feel at home with you.
I've a sensible, comprehensible,
Great respect for you.
There's a dash in it
Of a passionate, tender feeling, too.
You are a part of me,
Something that's giving me
Reason for living—
That's why I feel at home with you.

2nd VERSE

I used to be a hoyden—
Boys were my hate.
I was a lady hermit—
I couldn't be annoyed in
Making a date.
Silly I would term it.
You seemed so daring, my heart grew frail.
Now I like wearing my coat of male.

2nd REFRAIN

I feel at home with you.
Your brain is dumber
Than that of a plumber.
That's why I feel at home with you.
I'll match my dome with you.
Your brain needs a tonic—
It's still embryonic.
That's why I feel at home with you.
Our minds are featherweight—
Their together weight
Can't amount to much.
You use no better words
Than three-letter words,
"Dog" and "cat" and such.
You have no head at all.
Something like your knob
Is used as a doorknob.
That's why I feel at home with you.

1928

She's My Baby

Opened January 3, 1928, at the Globe Theatre
for a run of 71 performances

Music by Richard Rodgers
Book by Guy Bolton, Bert Kalmar and Harry Ruby
Directed by Edward Royce
Choreographed by Mary Read
Settings by Raymond Sovey
Costumes by Raymond Sovey and Francillon, Inc.

When I Go on the Stage

⊰ *Originally sung by Beatrice Lillie* ⊱

VERSE

Tilly: Do you think I look like Marilyn Miller?
They say my looks will kill 'er
All: Poor little Marilyn Miller
Tilly: Others say I look like Marion Davies.
All: Whom else would you suggest?
Tilly: I look like sweet Mae West!
I know I show great promise as an actress
And you can bet I'll get one yet.
All: Is that a promise? Is that a promise?
Tilly: That's not a promise, that's a threat!

1st REFRAIN

Tilly: I'll follow my ambition
And take up my position.
All: You'll be a star when you go on the stage.
Tilly: I'll make Irene Bordoni
Look like a poor baloney,
And Fannie Ward will start to look her age.
All: To hear your voice and cheer your voice
We'll track the globe.
Tilly: As a willing ham for Dillingham
I'll pack the Globe.
Charles King and Louise Groody
Will look like Punch and Judy.
But I don't care—
I'm going on the stage.

2nd REFRAIN

Tilly: That youthful star Miss Talley
Will yodel in an alley.
My voice will ring
When I go on the stage.

That statue called Jeritza
Will shiver when it hits 'er.
While Galli-Curci sings off key with rage,
Poor Schumann-Heink will hear
The fame my voice enjoys.
She'll come to earth
And then give birth to six more boys.
When I sing for Casazza,
He'll fall on his piazza.
But I don't care—
I'm going on the stage!

Even with Bea Lillie and Clifton Webb (above) as a very elegant butler and maid, and a supporting cast that included Irene Dunne, William Frawley and Jack Whiting (all of whom are seen on the following two-page spread), *She's My Baby* was not a hit. Everyone agreed that the book—about impostors and an aspiring Broadway producer—was to blame.

1928

Present Arms

*Opened April 26, 1928, at Lew Fields's Mansfield Theatre
for a run of 155 performances*

Music by Richard Rodgers
Book by Herbert Fields
Directed by Alexander Leftwich
Choreographed by Busby Berkeley
Settings by Ward and Harvey
Costumes by Milgrim

You Took Advantage of Me

⊰ *Originally sung by Busby Berkeley and Joyce Barbour* ⊱

1st VERSE

Douglas: In the spring when the feeling was chronic
And my caution was leaving you flat,
I should have made use of the tonic
Before you gave me *that!*
A mental deficient you'll grade me.
I've given you plenty of data.
You came, you saw and you slayed me,
And that-a is that-a!

REFRAIN

I'm a sentimental sap, that's all.
What's the use of trying not to fall?
I have no will,
You've made your kill
'Cause you took advantage of me!
I'm just like an apple on a bough
And you're gonna shake me down somehow.
So what's the use,
You've cooked my goose
'Cause you took advantage of me!

I'm so hot and bothered that I don't know
My elbow from my ear.
I suffer something awful each time you go
And much worse when you're near.
Here am I with all my bridges burned,
Just a babe in arms where you're concerned,
So lock the doors and call me yours
'Cause you took advantage of me.

2nd VERSE

Edna: When a girl has the heart of a mother
It must go to someone, of course;
It can't be a sister or brother
And so I loved my horse.
But horses are frequently silly—
Mine ran from the beach of Kalua
And left me alone for a filly,
So I-a picked you-a.

Act One, Scene One of *Present Arms.* Charlie King (center) is hatching some sort of scheme or other with Joyce Barbour and Busby Berkeley.

Present Arms was choreographed by a bright young hoofer named Busby Berkeley, and his dances for the show were an indication of the mad miracles he would one day work in the movies. Not content just to stage the *Present Arms* numbers, Bus Berkeley, in the role of Marine Sergeant Douglas Atwell, also introduced "You Took Advantage of Me" with Joyce Barbour.

It was only when the doctor advised Larry that three flights of stairs were too much for his ailing father to climb that he moved the Hart household to a penthouse on 101st Street and Central Park West. Larry left the by-then famous house on 119th Street reluctantly, and would have been content to stay on. The Harts had a strong feeling for home, and once they burrowed in, they were not movers.

As in the early years, they went on maintaining an open house, where the unknowns of Broadway, as well as the established, were given a warm welcome. Morrie Ryskind, Bob Coleman of the *Daily Mirror*, Billy Rose, Sigmund Romberg and so many others found the atmosphere stimulating and encouraging as they climbed the theatrical ladder.

While Larry started to move up in the theatrical world, Max continued to walk up two flights of stairs for his nightly pinochle game in the Cayuga Club, a Democratic clubhouse that was his favorite hangout and interest. Max fancied himself a lawyer without a degree, and indeed his close friend Max Steuer, a famous lawyer of the period, was not above coming to him for counsel. Max Hart's political friendships were helpful in his various business deals, and though the explosive personality of Max Hart could create terror in his employees at times, he was also generous and kind, and the tenants of the tenements he owned loved him. He not only conversed intimately with them in Irish, Italian or Yiddish dialect; he also did not dispossess them if they could not pay their rent on time.

It was fortunate that Larry's income was growing to sizable proportions as Max's was running down. He was soon forced into bankruptcy, and during the rest of Larry's lifetime Larry was hounded and pursued by his father's creditors. Even when Larry made his will, he had to insert spendthrift clauses in the trusts to keep these claims and claimants from bothering Frieda and Teddy.

Though Larry gave his father two hundred and fifty dollars weekly as "spending money," Max managed to lose it regularly in one or another scheme that he thought might enable him to get back in the business world on a substantial basis. But hardening of the arteries, a bad heart and a complication of degenerative diseases prevented Max from functioning with his old-time skill.

Max died in 1928, at the age of sixty-one, with his two sons holding his hands. The night he died, he called Larry and Teddy into his room. He was having difficulty breathing and Larry propped up several pillows to support his back. "I'm going to die tonight. Don't wake your mother. Let her sleep. She doesn't have to know until morning." Max paused to catch his breath. His final words were "Don't grieve for me. I didn't miss anything." He'd loved his family and his last thoughts were of them. The boys never did understand how their father knew he was about to die. Services were held for Max Hart at Mount Sinai temple in the Bronx.

1928

Chee-Chee

*Opened September 25, 1928, at the Mansfield Theatre
for a run of 31 performances*

Music by Richard Rodgers
Book by Herbert Fields, from the novel *The Son of the
    Grand Eunuch,* by Charles Petit
Directed by Alexander Leftwich
Choreographed by Jack Haskell
Settings by Jack Hawkins, Jr.
Costumes by John Booth

Moon of My Delight

{ *Originally sung by Betty Starbuck and Stark Patterson* }

1st VERSE

Moon of moons, when you are mine,
Bright the night will be.
But remember, when you shine,
Concentrate on me!
Moon of moons, be mine alone,
Mine alone—don't laugh, moon!
I would never care to own
A quarter or a half moon.

REFRAIN

Moon of my delight,
I'm going to put a ring around you—
You'll stay home tonight,
Scintillating where I found you.
When you were a little crescent,
Your manners were as soft as wool.
Now you're getting effervescent—
But maybe that's because you're full.
Moon of my delight,
If you'd only treat me right,
We could have a satellite or two,
Moon of my delight.

2nd VERSE

You're my moon and I'm your earth,
Bless me with your gaze.
What are lovely evenings worth
If I lose your rays?
If you ever should depart,
I would be a mean cheese.
If you leave me, then your heart
Must be made of green cheese.

Chee-Chee (Helen Ford) and Li-Pi Tchou (William Williams) flee Peking, so that Li-Pi can escape the "operation" that would render him Most Noble and August Grand Eunuch. *Chee-Chee* was probably the worst disaster of the Rodgers and Hart partnership, and after it closed, Larry and Dick never worked with Helen Ford or Lew Fields again. But at least the sets and costumes were amusing—and lavish.

The New Play
By St. John Ervine

NASTY! NASTY!

"CHEE-CHEE," a musical narrative by Fields, Rodgers and Hart, based on "The Son of the Grand Eunuch," a novel by Charles Petit. Staged by Alexander Leftwich and presented Tuesday evening by Lew Fields at the Mansfield.

THE CAST

A Eunuch.....................Ralph Clover
Another......................Alan Lowe
Prince Tao-Tee...............Stark Patterson
Li-Li-Wee....................Betty Starbuck
Li-Pi Siao...................George Hassell
Miss Smile of a Rose.........Dorothy Roye
Li-Pi Tchou..................William Williams
Chee-Chee....................Helen Ford
San Toy......................George Ali
A Very Narrow-Minded Owl.....William Griffith
Innkeeper....................Philip Loeb
The Tartar Chief.............George Houston
Leader of Khonghouses........Marshall Bradford
Radiance and Felicity........William Griffith
Profundity and Meditation....Philip Loeb
Holy Emperor.................Ralph Glover

This dull and, in most respects, nasty piece contains two jokes which are incessantly repeated: the first, a reference to enforced sterility, and the second, a reference to the heroine's seduction. The humor, in short, is of the kind that causes small boys to run into corners and titter. The word "eunuch" seemed to throw the auditors into convulsions of laughter, but after it had been mentioned for what seemed to be the millionth time it began to pall upon the audience.

There can rarely have been a play so ornately produced to so little effect. All the mind there is in "Chee-Chee" seems to have been put into the decorations—a little of it might have been put into some disinfectant. The quality of the dialogue may be estimated by those who are unlikely to see the piece by the following sample: Chee-Chee, to a man: "You are never likely to be a mother!" Roars of raucous silence in the audience! . . . Compared with this piece "The New Moon" is not only a good entertainment—it is a work of genius!

I did not believe that any act could possibly be duller than the first act of "Chee-Chee"—until I saw the second act. Then I knew that an act could. Miss Helen Ford, whose dress in the first act must surely be the ugliest that any actress has ever worn on any stage, sang nicely, and so did Mr. William Williams and Mr. George Houston. Their acting, however, scarcely stirs one, although Mr. Houston, if he can contrive to put some authority into his manner, may become an actor. Mr. George Hassell's fruity voice and unctuous manner reminded me of the Widow Twankey in old-fashioned pantomime.

Mr. William Griffith was tolerably amusing, and Mr. Ralph Glover as the Holy Emperor made the greatest hit in the play, so far as I am concerned, by saying nothing at all. A clever girl, Miss Betty Starbuck, might have been given better lines to speak. But if Miss Starbuck wishes to be a fine actress she must take some trouble with her speaking voice, which is harsh and ugly. There are a number of actors and actresses in the plays I have seen since my arrival in New York who would be all the better for a course of voice-production. The price of a stall for the first performance of "Chee-Chee" was $11. That was exactly $11 too much.

St. John Ervine's review of *Chee-Chee* in the New York *World* was typical of his colleagues' feelings about the show. If anything, the other critics hated it even more.

1929

Spring Is Here

Opened March 11, 1929, at the Alvin Theatre
for a run of 104 performances

Music by Richard Rodgers
Book by Owen Davis
Directed by Alexander Leftwich
Choreographed by Bobby Connolly
Settings by John Wenger
Costumes by Kiviette

With a Song in My Heart

{ *Originally sung by John Hundley and Lillian Taiz* }

1st VERSE

Though I know that we meet ev'ry night
And we couldn't have changed since the last time,
To my joy and delight,
It's a new kind of love at first sight.
Though it's you and it's I all the time,
Ev'ry meeting's a marvelous pastime.
You're increasingly sweet,
So whenever we happen to meet
I greet you . . .

REFRAIN

With a song in my heart
I behold your adorable face.
Just a song at the start,
But it soon is a hymn to your grace.
When the music swells
I'm touching your hand;
It tells that you're standing near, and . . .
At the sound of your voice
Heaven opens its portals to me.
Can I help but rejoice?
That a song such as ours came to be?
But I always knew
I would live life through
With a song in my heart for you.

2nd VERSE

Oh, the moon's not a moon for a night
And these stars will not twinkle and fade out,
And the words in my ears
Will resound for the rest of my years.
In the morning I'll find with delight
Not a note of our music is played out.
It will be just as sweet,
And an air that I'll live to repeat:
I greet you . . .

1929

Heads Up!

Opened November 11, 1929, at the Alvin Theatre
for a run of 144 performances

Music by Richard Rodgers
Book by John McGowan and Paul Gerard Smith
Choreographed by George Hale
Settings by Donald Oenslager
Costumes by Kiviette

A Ship Without a Sail

{ *Originally sung by Jack Whiting* }

VERSE

I don't know what day it is,
Or if it's dark or fair.
Somehow that's just the way it is,
And I don't really care.
I go to this or that place,
I seem alive and well.
My head is just a hat place,
My breast an empty shell!
And I've a faded dream to sell.

REFRAIN

All alone, all at sea!
Why does nobody care for me,
When there's no love to hold my love?
Why is my heart so frail,
Like a ship without a sail?
Out on the ocean
Sailors can use a chart.
I'm on the ocean
Guided by just a lonely heart.
Still alone, still at sea!
Still there's no one to care for me.
When there's no hand to hold my hand
Life is a loveless tale.
For a ship without a sail.

Betty Starbuck and Victor Moore in the galley scene from *Heads Up!* Moore is explaining that he times eggs by singing arias, and that if Betty wants them very hardboiled, he'll recite "Gunga Din."

In *Spring is Here*, Charlie Ruggles played a strict Long Island father who disliked his daughter's suitor, Glenn Hunter. Here you can see them shooting dirty looks at one another, surrounded by twenty-one of the show's twenty-four chorus girls.

1930

Simple Simon

Opened February 18, 1930, at the Ziegfeld Theatre
for a run of 135 performances

Music by Richard Rodgers
Book by Ed Wynn and Guy Bolton
Directed by Zeke Colvan
Choreographed by Seymour Felix
Settings by Joseph Urban
Artistic direction by John Harkrider

Ten Cents a Dance

⊰ *Originally sung by Ruth Etting* ⊱

VERSE

I work at the Palace Ballroom,
But gee, that Palace is cheap;
When I get back to my chilly hall room
I'm much too tired to sleep.
I'm one of those lady teachers,
A beautiful hostess, you know,
The kind the Palace features,
For only a dime a throw.

1st REFRAIN

Ten cents a dance—
That's what they pay me;
Gosh, how they weigh me down!
Ten cents a dance—
Pansies and rough guys,
Tough guys who tear my gown!
Seven to midnight, I hear drums.
Loudly the saxophone blows.
Trumpets are tearing my eardrums.
Customers crush my toes.
Sometimes I think
I've found my hero,
But it's a queer romance.
All that you need is a ticket.
Come on, big boy, ten cents a dance!

PATTER

Fighters and sailors and bowlegged tailors
Can pay for their tickets and rent me!
Butchers and barbers and rats from the harbors
Are sweethearts my good luck has sent me.
Though I've a chorus of elderly beaux,
Stockings are porous with holes at the toes.
I'm here till closing time
Dance and be merry, it's only a dime.

TAG

Sometimes I think
I've found my hero
But it's a queer romance.
All that you need is a ticket.
Come on, big boy, ten cents a dance!

Most of the story of *Simple Simon* was supposed to be the dream of Simon Eyyes (Ed Wynn, left), the self-confessed grandson of Harmon Eyyes. Simon's dream was a cockeyed nightmare that borrowed stories and characters from the Arabian Nights, fairy tales, the Bible and Greek mythology. In the end, the true love of Cinderella and Prince Charming (played by Doree Leslie and Alan Edwards) conquered all. Things didn't turn out so well for Sal White (Ruth Etting, right), the tragic dance-hall girl who sang "Ten Cents a Dance"—in a drugstore!

He Was Too Good to Me*

VERSE

There goes my young intended.
The thing is ended.
Regrets are vain.
I'll never find another half so sweet
And we'll never meet again.
I was a good sport,
Told him goodbye, eyes dim,
But why complain?

REFRAIN

He was too good to me—
How can I get along now?
So close he stood to me—
Ev'rything seems all wrong now!
He would have brought me the sun.
Making me smile—
That was his fun!
When I was mean to him,
He'd never say, "Go 'way now."
I was a queen to him.
Who's goin' to make me gay now?
It's only natural I'm blue.
He was too good to be true.

    * This song was originally written for Lee Morse, but both the number and Miss Morse were dropped from *Simple Simon* during the tryout.

1930

Ever Green

Opened December 3, 1930, at the Adelphi Theatre, London, for a run of 254 performances

Music by Richard Rodgers
Book by Benn W. Levy
Directed by Frank Collins
Choreographed by Buddy Bradley and Billy Pierce
Settings by Ernest Stern
Costumes by Reville, Ltd.

Dancing on the Ceiling*

{ *Originally sung by Jessie Matthews and Sonnie Hale* }

VERSE

The world is lyrical
Because a miracle
Has brought my lover to me!
Though he's some other place,
His face I see.
At night I creep in bed
And never sleep in bed,
But look above in the air.

    * This song was written for *Simple Simon*, but was removed at Florenz Ziegfeld's insistence.

Jessie Matthews triumphed in *Ever Green*. The show, a revue with a narrative linking the different episodes, was about a cosmetic hoax. Jessie posed as her own grandmother, supposedly kept young and beautiful by a miraculous beauty product. (In the movie, made four years later, Jessie only had to pass herself off as her mother.)

And to my greatest joy,
My boy is there!
It is my prince who walks
Into my dreams and talks.

REFRAIN

He dances overhead
On the ceiling, near my bed;
In my sight
Through the night.
I try to hide in vain
Underneath my counterpane;
There's my love
Up above.
I whisper, "Go away, my lover,
It's not fair."
But I'm so grateful to discover
He's still there.
I love my ceiling more
Since it is the dancing floor
Just for my love.

Je m'en Fiche du Sex-Appeal

{ Originally sung by Leon Morton }

VERSE

I'm completely surrounded by beauty;
Girls are camping upon my doormat.
Now I must be a man—that's my duty
(I have twenty chaise longues in my flat).
A vision of Venus each night meant
That my temperature surely would fall;
The man who has too much excitement,
He can't get excited at all.

1st REFRAIN

The milkman he do not drink milk.
The butcher he do not eat veal.
The silkworm he never wear silk.
And *je m'en fiche du sex-appeal.*
The first little sweetheart is charming;
The second, ah well, she is *belle;*
The third is a little alarming;
As for the fourth, the fourth is hell!

Too many curves are bad for the nerves.
Too much chicken just ruins the meal.
I have drained the whole cup.
J'en ai marre—I'm fed up.
Je m'en fiche du sex-appeal.
Je m'en fiche du sex-appeal!

2nd REFRAIN

The fisherman never eat trout.
The furrier never wear seal.
The Guinnesses never drink stout.
Et je m'en fiche du sex-appeal.
I am sick of their laughter so rippling,
From chorus girl up to the star.
You have said the mouthful, Monsieur Kipling—
And I prefer the good cigar.
Too much whoopee can give you ennui—
I am growing as thin as an eel.
Greta Garbo is great—
She give me *mal de tête.*
Je m'en fiche du sex-appeal.
Oh, to *hell* with sex-appeal!

In 1929, Larry and Dick appeared in a Paramount two-reeler, called *Masters of Melody;* it was about two young fellows explaining how to write songs. At one point in the film, Larry wore a top hat—and he looked quite handsome in it.

Nanette Guilford

Larry was a passionate operagoer, and one of his favorite people was Nanette Guilford, an American-born, American-trained Metropolitan soprano. A star before she was twenty, Nanette sang roles ranging from Lohengrin *to* La Bohème, *and was continually praised for her beauty and her great gifts as an actress, as well as for her wonderful voice.*

Larry was somebody I loved very dearly. We had first met during the run of *America's Sweetheart*. I was singing at the Metropolitan Opera. We remained very friendly until my marriage to the violinist Max Rosen.

I was some years younger than Larry. He was fun to be with and we used to go to the D'Oyly Carte shows that came over from England so often in those days. He loved Gilbert and Sullivan. We went often to the opera, opening nights at the theatre, Sunday night concerts at the Winter Garden. Those were dress-up days, and you wore formal clothes almost everywhere. Larry stopped wearing a top hat because of an incident that happened as we were leaving the opera one night. As we waited for a cab, a couple of rowdies ridiculed and taunted him. Though he appeared to ignore them, he never wore a top hat again. It made an impression on me so that I remembered it all these years.

My marriage didn't last very long. Larry was the first one to call when he heard of my separation. It was a traumatic one for me because I still loved my husband. Larry came over immediately, so sweet, tender and devoted. I was always "Baby" to him. We resumed going out together. I spent several months in Beverly Hills readying a Mexican divorce, which seemed terribly complicated. Larry and Dick Rodgers were out there making some pictures. Dick and Dorothy asked us to help them receive, at a big party they were throwing. Larry picked me up early and we went to a restaurant for dinner. We became utterly oblivious to time. That is the way Larry and I were when we were together. We had that kind of rapport. Suddenly I looked up. The chairs were stacked on empty tables. Larry and I were the only guests in the place—it was three o'clock in the morning! We hurried over to Dick and Dorothy's house, but of course the party was long since over. The Hollywood crowd didn't keep late hours.

About his height: I was with Larry at a party when all those glamour men—the handsomest men in Hollywood, Clark Gable and Cary Grant among them—were present. Larry held everyone there in almost spellbinding attention. At that moment, he was the giant and they were pygmies. His wonderful mind was overwhelming at times.

One night I had to appear on the radio for *The Catholic Hour*. I was expected to sing, but at the last minute the Metropolitan refused permission. I could only speak. With just a few hours to go, I called Larry in a panic. I explained my dilemma. He asked, "When do you have to

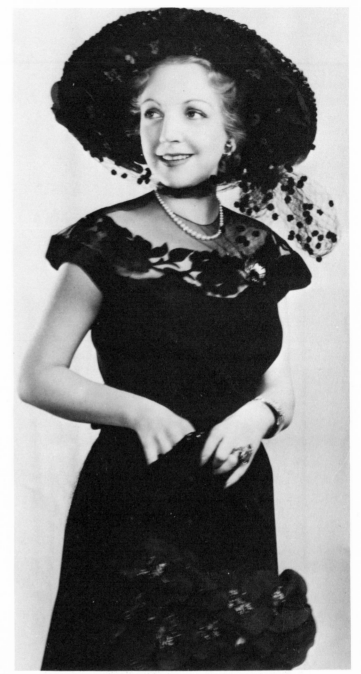

A contemporary photograph of Nanette

go on the air, Baby?" "Nine o'clock," I replied, frantic. I thought the situation hopeless. After promising, "All right, Baby, I'll be right down," Larry arrived at seven o'clock. He said, "Let me go into the library and close the door." Only ten minutes later he was back with pages and pages of a marvelous script explaining in verse form why I was unable to sing. Still in verse, he said what I wanted to say to the public about the Paulist fathers. It set the town on fire, it was so talked about. Only two or three years ago someone called and asked if I had that wonderful thing Lorenz Hart wrote for me years ago.

Unfortunately, I don't keep things. Larry asked me to marry him. After my miserable marital experience with one genius, I decided never to marry again. Though I knew Larry hadn't stopped loving me, and I adored him, we drifted apart after a time.

1931

America's Sweetheart

Opened February 10, 1931, at the Broadhurst Theatre
for a run of 135 performances

Music by Richard Rodgers
Book by Herbert Fields
Directed by Monty Woolley
Settings by Donald Oenslager
Costumes by Charles LeMaire

I've Got Five Dollars

{ Originally sung by Ann Sothern and Jack Whiting }

1st VERSE

Michael: Mister Shylock was stingy.
I was miserly, too.
I was more selfish
And crabby than a shellfish.
Oh, dear, it's queer what love can do!
I'd give all my possessions for you.

1st REFRAIN

I've got five dollars;
I'm in good condition;
And I've got ambition—
That belongs to you.
Six shirts and collars;
Debts beyond endurance
On my life insurance—
That belongs to you.
I've got a heart that must be spurtin'!
Just be certain I'll be true!
Take my five dollars!
Take my shirts and collars!
Take my heart that hollers,
"Ev'rything I've got belongs to you!"

2nd VERSE

Gerry: Peggy Joyce has a bus'ness;
All her husbands have gold.
And Lilyan Tashman
Is not kissed by an ashman.
But now, somehow, wealth leaves me cold.
Though you're poor as a church mouse, I'm sold!

2nd REFRAIN

I've got five dollars;
Eighty-five relations;
Two lace combinations—
They belong to you!
Two coats with collars;
Ma and Grandma wore 'em;
All the moths adore 'em—
They belong to you!

I've got two lips that care for mating,
Therefore waiting will not do!
Take my five dollars!
Take my coats and collars!
Take my heart that hollers,
"Ev'rything I've got belongs to you!"

We'll Be the Same

{ Originally sung by Ann Sothern and Jack Whiting }

VERSE

They say a person changes ev'ry seven years:
I've been three diff'rent persons with one name.
My years with you will all be made-in-heaven years,
So love's a thing that will remain the same!
In the future when styles and customs seem strange,
My love is the one thing that won't change!

REFRAIN

The sun may rise and shine at night;
Birds swim and fish take flight—
Heigh-ho, it's still all right,
We'll be the same!
They may have thirteen months in the year;
Nations may disappear—
Heigh-ho, no need to fear,
We'll be the same!
Though Hollywood's screenless, Boston beanless!
And the sea turn into land!
The country may tumble. I won't grumble—
I'll be holding your hand!
Though love no longer is in style,
Heigh-ho, we'll only smile!
We've got that flame,
We'll be the same!

America's Sweetheart starred Harriette Lake (who later became Ann Sothern) as a small-town girl who made it big in silent movies but bellyflopped when talkies came in. In this scene, the heroine was still at the top, and her former boyfriend (Jack Whiting), sick of her tantrums, had just tossed her into a fountain: "Sit there and you'll cool off."

A Lady Must Live

{ *Originally sung by Jeanne Aubert* }

VERSE

Some women are colder than steel—
From such a fate heaven preserve us!
Some women repress what they feel,
And that's why some women are nervous.
A woman is just like a plum
That ripens and falls very soon.
But should she refuse to succumb,
She swiftly dries up like a prune.

1st REFRAIN

Life is love and know that
Love is life, and so that
Should make you forgive,
For a lady must live!
When no love is callin',
All your joys start fallin'
Like sand through a sieve,
For a lady must live!
I've never thought that holding a hand
Meant throwing your soul away,

Had Mother Eve obeyed that commandment away,
Where would we be today?
We have lips and why waste them?
If you would love to taste them,
You ought to forgive,
For a lady must live!

2nd REFRAIN

How can love be vicious
When it's so delicious?
So you must forgive,
For a lady must live!
With my John and my Max,
I can reach a climax
That's proof positive
That a lady must live!
If she's not a coldblooded person,
What's a girl to do?
But if I looked like Aimée MacPherson,
I'd be a good girl, too.
What's the siren song for?
What's my chaise longue for?
So you must forgive,
For a lady must live!

SO then there was a musical comedy called "America's Sweetheart," by the Messrs. Fields, Rodgers, and Hart, two of whom seem to me to be extraordinarily over-rated young men. This costly and colorful production is a satire on Hollywood, with, running through it in the American manner, a love story of the sort that all our bitter and brilliant young satirists purport to satirize, and then go employ in their works. Mr. Fields has, apparently, compiled his libretto with a pair of scissors, and his poor thumb must be awfully sore after all that clipping of jokes. Lord knows I have lived too long to demand originality in writers of musical-comedy books, but at least I cannot feel that I am asking too much when I implore that while they are stealing gags, they might for goodness' sake steal good gags. Surely it can't be more trouble, after all. One may not demand inspiration in the writers of libretti, but one might put in a prayer for selection. Mr. Hart has donated lyrics the rhymes of which are less internal than colonic; they have also a peculiar, even for Broadway, nastiness of flavor. What, by the way, has ever become of that little thing called taste? And Mr. Rodgers has contributed a truly charming score, each number of which gets better each time you hear it. Employed in the entertainment are Inez Courtney, Jack Whiting, Harriette Lake, and Gus Shy, all of whom do what they can. They are assisted by as pretty and as well-trained a chorus as you ever saw in your life, if that's what makes you go to shows. And there is, besides, Jeanne Aubert, whose husband, if you can believe the papers, recently pled, through the French courts, that he be allowed to restrain his wife from appearing on the stage. Professional or not, the man is a dramatic critic.

Personal: Robert Benchley, please come home. Nothing is forgiven.
—DOROTHY PARKER

America's Sweetheart brought Herb Fields back into the Rodgers and Hart fold. His libretto for the show was a satire on Hollywood in the twenties and thirties. The week the show opened, Dorothy Parker was substituting for Robert Benchley as *The New Yorker*'s drama critic, and she, like several other reviewers, wasn't too impressed. (Many of the early Rodgers and Hart shows were not in the hit class, but every one of them had songs that have survived.)

Mel Shauer

In 1930, Larry went to Hollywood for the first time, to work on The Hot Heiress *with Dick Rodgers and Herb Fields. Then, after the year of stage work in New York and in London that produced* America's Sweetheart *and* Ever Green, *Larry returned to Hollywood, where he wrote exclusively for the movies until 1935. All told, he and Dick worked for five studios—Warners, Paramount, RKO, MGM and United Artists. Larry's housemate in L.A. was his old camp friend Mel Shauer.*

After spending some time in Europe working for Paramount, I went out to California to live in 1930. I was instrumental in bringing Larry and Dick to Hollywood. I had met Maurice Chevalier in Paris, and we became very friendly. When Chevalier was brought out to Hollywood (I was producing at Paramount) I wanted Larry and Dick to do a picture with him. But the consensus was that Larry's lyrics were—I remember the words exactly—"too flip," perhaps even "too good for the screen." It was a tough struggle to sell Rodgers and Hart as a movie songwriting team. I think it was Jesse Lasky who eventually prevailed. That's when the boys came out to California.

At first Larry lived with Dick and Dorothy Rodgers on Linden Drive in Beverly Hills. Dick didn't like Hollywood at all. Larry accepted it matter-of-factly and proceeded to have a good time. I was living alone in a little apartment in Hollywood. It was adequate, since I was at the studio all day; most of the time there were previews at night. And as a bachelor, I was invited out very often. I didn't want an elaborate place. When I suggested to Larry that we take a house together, sharing the expenses, I thought of a small bungalow. But Larry rented a lavish house at 910 North Bedford Drive, a really large place with an Olympic-size swimming pool. In 1932 the Olympics were held in Los Angeles. Having been a swimmer, I knew the coach of the Olympic team and others, and invited the entire Olympic swimming team to a party. We had all the movie stars. It was the party of the year. This was the kind of party that went on constantly during our stay there.

I had insisted to Larry that we split expenses for the house down the middle. He said, "Yeah, yeah," and tried to pay all the bills on the first of the month. Then he brought Mama, Teddy and the two servants and Kiki the chow dog out to join us. He said, "You see, we've got too many here. We can't split expenses." After frustrating arguments, we agreed on my share. That was Larry's attitude to money always. He couldn't care less, and he always seemed to have plenty for his quite profligate spending. He'd remember, almost to the penny, what his checking account balance was, though you'd never think he bothered keeping track. Yet he'd forget his home phone number and have to ask me what it was, time and again.

During that period he was making big money. There

were all kinds of foreign Rodgers and Hart shows and there was no controlling his spending. He'd call anybody, anywhere in the world, on a sudden impulse. Larry went back to New York after the picture was completed. When he returned some months later for another picture, we took a small, unpretentious house. It was obvious to me, after a couple of weeks, that he was miserable in such a little house. He called me all kinds of names and said it was ridiculous not to live well, and one day rushed in rubbing his hands and chuckling. He had re-rented the Bedford Drive house! So we moved back. It was great for entertaining, and entertain Larry did. I used to retire to my beautiful suite upstairs after my studio chores. I had to go to work in the morning. So did Larry. But the whole world dropped in until two, three and four every morning. All the Hollywood famous congregated, or freeloaded—whichever way you look at it. Any new actor came to town, the word got around. Go to Larry Hart's. Everyone's welcome.

I was beginning to worry that it would interfere with his studio work. The required lyrics were not always ready when they were needed for shooting. But then, late at night, after everyone had cleared out, Larry would sit down in his shorts, light up a big cigar, and by seven-thirty or thereabouts the next morning he'd dash into my room and practically knock me out of bed, saying, "Get up, get up! I want you to hear what I wrote!"

It was unbelievable that after all that carousing he could come up so quickly with those beautiful lyrics. It was always a kick to me to watch this kind of creation. In later years, many years later, when I heard those self-same words on the air and everywhere, the marvel of his talent remained with me.

Ernst Lubitsch was at the house a lot. He got a kick

out of Larry because they were both pixies. Had the same kind of humor. He often spoke of Larry's tremendous ability. Maurice Chevalier came to dinner a few times, and Fannie Brice. The conversation between Fannie and Larry was hilarious. Even after dinner, they sat at the dinner table trying to top each other with funny stories and reminiscences. One night around twelve o'clock Larry insisted that we accompany him to a little club on Hollywood Boulevard called The New Yorker. It was a

Groucho Marx was a frequent visitor to the house on North Bedford Drive, on this occasion for a pool party. Mel Shauer, still skinny, is at his left.

Larry, Dick and Herb Fields, departing for Hollywood in 1930. They had a joint contract to write three musical movies for Warners, though, in the end, only *The Hot Heiress* was made. When Larry and Dick returned to Hollywood, to work on *Love Me Tonight* for Paramount, it was without Herb.

smallish place, holding probably forty or fifty patrons. Like everything surrounding Larry at that time, it was fun. At closing time—and it had to be closing time before Larry would give up—Larry called the headwaiter and paid for everyone's check in the place! He didn't know anybody there except me and Fannie and Lew, her brother. This absurd generosity, if it can be called that, was typical of his strange quirks. I believe Larry had to prove himself to be a little above everyone else. Perhaps picking up checks so senselessly gave him a feeling of power. Because very short men are often ignored by maître d's and others in the service areas if they are not recognized as celebrities. I think that was it. He'd never see these people again. They didn't know who he was. Just some crazy little man who had paid their bills. I saw Larry repeat this many times. Yet he didn't have to "buy" friends. Everybody loved this guy.

I know that I pointed this out to him time and again through the years. I'd say, "Larry, how do you ever tell your real friends from the people who just want to stick out their hands and grab?" It was hard to talk to Larry about anything that was intimate or unpleasant. He'd just brush you aside and laugh. This was the way he wanted to live, and he couldn't care less about the money he was spending (that's what it was for, he always said) or whether the hangers-on were taking advantage of his open-handedness.

I never heard Larry discuss the stock market or anything about making money. But about world affairs he knew everything. He spoke German. He spoke French. He seemed to understand what was going on, what was the "in" thing. He just had an amazing mind. I was always astonished that when he wrote his lyrics he knew the verbal expressions that were being used in Greenwich Village, on Park Avenue, or anywhere. I lived in New York also, and got around, but I didn't know them. He knew what was going on currently in France, in Germany, in England. His mind was so alert, so active; I believe he needed to drink to relax from its incessant activity.

Back in New York, I had accompanied Larry many times when he was dating Nanette Guilford. I know he was in love with Nanette. I retain a vivid picture of Larry when he, Nanette and I went to Reuben's after attending an opera. Larry wore evening clothes and top hat. (We really dressed in those days for a special occasion.) The impression I took from that evening was that Larry, even with the top hat on, was only slightly higher than Nanette's head. Nanette was beautiful, but like most prima donnas of that day, buxom. I think if Nanette had been more petite, and they had made less of an odd pair, he would have married her. The women he was attracted to later, like Vivienne Segal, were closer to his size.

If you were with him in New York he might suddenly say, "Let's go up to George Gershwin's." Gershwin would play for us the score of his latest show in rehearsal. And wasn't that a thrill for a frustrated composer! Larry loved to discuss show business. He spoke with such enthusiasm, brilliance and conviction. He was so *alive* then, had such dynamic energy.

Mel and his lovely wife, the dancer Rosita Moreno, whom he married in the mid-thirties

The Hot Heiress didn't do much to advance the cause of movie musicals. The plot concerned the love affair of a riveter (Ben Lyon) and a debutante (Ona Munson). Ona Munson and the young Walter Pidgeon, who was also in the cast, are seen here.

1932

Love Me Tonight

Released by Paramount Pictures on August 13, 1932

Music by Richard Rodgers
Screenplay by Samuel Hoffenstein, Waldemar Young and
    George Marion, Jr., based on a play by Leopold Marchand
    and Paul Armont
Directed by Rouben Mamoulian
Art direction by Hans Dreier
Settings by A. E. Freudeman
Costumes by Travis Banton
Photographed by Victor Milner

Isn't It Romantic?

*{ Originally sung by Maurice Chevalier
and Jeanette MacDonald }*

1st VERSE

Maurice: My face is glowing;
I'm energetic.
The art of sewing
I find poetic.
My needle punctuates the
Rhythm of romance:
I don't give a stitch
If I don't get rich.
A custom tailor
Who has no custom
Is like a sailor:
No one will trust 'em.
But there is magic in the
Music of my shears.
I shed no tears.
Lend me your ears.

1st REFRAIN

Isn't it romantic?
Starting out the day
A citizen of France.
Isn't it romantic?
In the month of May
To sew a pair of pants.
My business is a honey:
Goods on every shelf.
We make so little money
I can't pay myself.
Isn't it romantic?
When each millionaire
Is broke and has the blues,
Why should I be frantic,
Pulling out my hair?
I've nothing left to lose.
I'd borrow from myself now,
But I can't afford to take a chance.
Isn't it romance?

2nd REFRAIN

Isn't it romantic?
Soon I will have found
Some girl that I adore.
Isn't it romantic?
While I sit around,
My love can scrub the floor.
She'll kiss me ev'ry hour
Or she'll get the sack,
And when I take a shower
She can scrub my back.
Isn't it romantic?
On a moonlight night
She'll cook me onion soup.
Kiddies are romantic
And if we don't fight
We soon will have a troupe.
We'll help the population:
It's a duty that we owe to France.
Isn't that romance?

Some scenes from *Love Me Tonight*. Left, Maurice Chevalier as Maurice Courtelin, the romantic tailor who goes to a castle to collect an overdue bill and ends up winning the heart of the bored Princess Jeanette. Right, Hollywood royalty: Myrna Loy as the Countess Valentine; at her left, Charlie Ruggles as the foppish Vicomte de Vareze; at her right, C. Aubrey Smith, as Charlie's uncle, the Duke.

2nd VERSE

Jeanette: I've never met you,
Yet never doubt, dear,
I can't forget you.
I've thought you out, dear.
I know your profile
And I know the way you kiss.
Just the thing I miss
On a night like this.
If dreams are made of imagination,
I'm not afraid of my own creation.
With all my heart,
My heart is here
For you to take.
Why should I quake?
I'm not awake.

3rd REFRAIN

Isn't it romantic?
Music in the night:
A dream that can be heard.
Isn't it romantic?
Moving shadows write
The oldest magic word.
I hear the breezes playing
In the trees above,
While all the world is saying,
"You were meant for love."
Isn't it romantic?
Merely to be young
On such a night as this.
It is so romantic.
Every note that's sung
Is like a lover's kiss.
Sweet symbols in the moonlight,
Do you mean that I will fall
In love, perchance?
Isn't it romance?

4th REFRAIN

Isn't it romantic?
Music in the night:
A dream that can be heard.
Isn't it romantic?
That a hero might
Appear and say the word.
Brought by a secret charm or
By my heart's command,
My prince will ride in armor
Just to kiss my hand.
Isn't it romantic?
He will hear my call
And bend his royal knee.
Isn't it romantic?
He'll be strong and tall
And yet a slave to me.
Sweet lover of my fancy,
Will you ever come to life:
To love, perchance?
Isn't it romance?

Lover

⋅{ *Originally sung by Jeanette MacDonald* }⋅

VERSE

Dear, you did something grand to my heart.
And we played the scene to perfection
Though we didn't have time to rehearse.
Since you took control of my life
You have become the whole of my life.
When you are away, it's awful,
And when you are with me, it's worse.

REFRAIN

Lover, when I'm near you
And I hear you speak my name
Softly, in my ear
You breathe a flame.
Lover, when we're dancing
Keep on glancing in my eyes,
Till love's own entrancing music dies.
All of my future is in you.
You're ev'ry plan I design.
Promise me that you'll continue to be mine.
Lover, please be tender,
When you're tender fears depart.
Lover, I surrender to my heart.

ORIGINAL LYRIC

Lover,
When you find me,
Will you blind me
With your glow?
Make me cast behind me
All my . . .
"Whoa!"
Kiss me,

Hear me saying—
Gently swaying—
"I'll obey."
Like two children playing
In the . . .
"Hey!"
He'll be my lord and my master,
I'll be a slave to the last.
He'll make my heartbeat go faster—
"Not too fast!"
Lover,
When you take me
And awake me,
I will know,
Lover, you can make me
Love you so.

Love Me Tonight

{ *Originally sung by Maurice Chevalier
and Jeanette MacDonald* }

VERSE

There's a glistening ring around the moon—
Are you listening? It is not too soon—
Must we sleep tonight all alone?
Let us keep tonight as our very own.

REFRAIN

Your heart and my heart were made to meet.
Don't make them wait—love me tonight!
Why should our lips be afraid to meet?
Love me tonight.
Who knows what tomorrow brings
With the morning light?
Dear, I am here with a heart that sings—
Love me tonight.

Mimi

{ *Originally sung by Maurice Chevalier* }

VERSE

My left shoe's on my right foot,
My right shoe's on my left.
Oh! Listen to me, Mimi,
Of reason I'm bereft!
The buttons of my trousers
Are buttoned to my vest.
Oh! Listen to me, Mimi,
There's passion in my breast!

REFRAIN

Mimi,   You've got me
You funny little   Sad and dreamy.
Good-for-nothing Mimi,   You could free me,
Am I the guy?   If you'd see me.
Mimi,   Mimi,
You sunny little honey   You know I'd like to
Of a Mimi,   Have a little
I'm aiming high.   Son of a Mimi, by and by.
Mimi,

A very welcome visitor to the garden at Larry's Beverly Hills home. Maurice Chevalier, with Frieda (right) and Larry's Aunt Rachen (Frieda's sister).

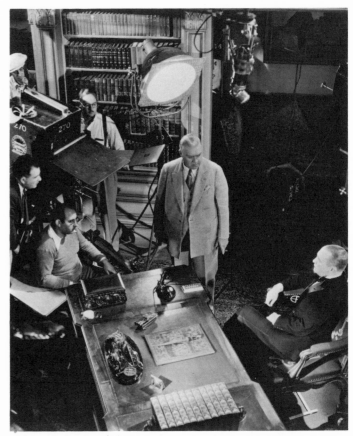

Shortly after Metro released *Love Me Tonight*, Paramount released Rodgers and Hart's *The Phantom President*, an *Of Thee I Sing!* spinoff about shady politics. George M. Cohan (seen in the production still above) starred in a dual role. He wasn't at all pleasant to work with, constantly wanting to change lyrics and do everything his own way. The movie marked the first time Larry and Dick crossed swords with Cohan, but not the last. They would have far worse trouble three years later, when Cohan starred as FDR in *I'd Rather Be Right*.

1933

Hallelujah, I'm a Bum

Released by United Artists on January 27, 1933

Music by Richard Rodgers
Screenplay by S. N. Behrman, from a story by Ben Hecht
Directed by Lewis Milestone
Art direction by Richard Day
Costumes by Milo Anderson
Photographed by Lucien Andriot

You Are Too Beautiful

{ *Originally sung by Al Jolson* }

VERSE

Like all fools, I believed
What I wanted to believe.
My foolish heart conceived what
Foolish hearts conceive.
I thought I found a miracle,
I thought that you'd adore me.
But it was not a miracle,
It was merely a mirage before me.

REFRAIN

You are too beautiful, my dear, to be true
And I am a fool for beauty.
Fooled by a feeling that
Because I had found you
I could have bound you, too.
You are too beautiful for one man alone,
For one lucky fool to be with,
When there are other men
With eyes of their own to see with.
Love does not stand sharing
Not if one cares.
Have you been comparing
My ev'ry kiss with theirs?
If, on the other hand,
I'm faithful to you,
It's not through a sense of duty.
You are too beautiful
And I am a fool for beauty.

What Do You Want With Money?

{ *Originally sung by Al Jolson* }

VERSE

Friends, Rummies, Countrymen—well, anyway, jes' friends—
We find a thousand dollars, and friendship ends.
If you divide the thousand, what each gets is a joke.
A little less than nothing. You're better off just broke.

Some movie cultists have seen *Hallelujah, I'm a Bum* as many as twenty times. By now they must recognize the two young unknowns who have small walk-on roles: Richard Rodgers as a photographer and Lorenz Hart as a bank teller.

REFRAIN

You got the grass,
You got the trees.
What do you want with money?
You got the air,
You got the breeze.
What do you want with money?
Look at the birds, hear how they sing;
They have no rent to pay in the spring.
You've won the world when you don't own a thing.
What do you want with money?
What do you want with dough?

TRIO-PATTER

Frankie, you got your shine box! Sam, you got your fiddle!
Egghead, you got your principles, and you're richer than
        Ford or Biddle.
You know you can't take money; you know you hate the rich!
Be consistent, Egghead, you stupid son of a which.
One of you is unhappy right now?
What do you want with money?
What do you want with dough?
What do you want with dough?

To make Larry completely happy, all you had to do was ask him to do his impersonation of Al Jolson. His Jolie came complete with knee drops—"Shine on, Harvest Moon" performed in the living room to an audience of two—and the resultant applause seemed more satisfying to him than a great Brooks Atkinson review. But in *Hallelujah,* Jolson, as the king of Central Park's bums, never got down on bended knee once. He didn't even wear blackface makeup.

Richard Rodgers

Larry and Dick never believed in letting a song go to waste. "The Pipes of Pansy," dropped from Dearest Enemy, *found its way into the early drafts of* The Girl Friend, Peggy-Ann *and* She's My Baby—*and in every instance, the song was thrown out of the show before it opened. But no Rodgers and Hart tune ever led as many lives as the one that finally became "Blue Moon." Richard Rodgers explains the whole complicated story below.*

We arrived in California on the twenty-third day of December, 1932, and we stayed there until April 1933, without coming east at all.

During this period, Eddie Goulding, who had directed such pictures as *Grand Hotel*, came into my office at Metro with an idea for a picture called *Hollywood Party*, in which he wanted to use as many of the stars on the MGM lot as possible. One of the ideas was that of a telephone operator, to be played by Jean Harlow, anxious to break into moving pictures and become a star. Eddie wanted her to sing a song just as she was going to bed, talking about her ambitions and desires as far as the moving picture business was concerned. I, in turn, suggested that it be a prayer—this little girl praying because she was a kind of a "jazz" kid. But I wanted the melody played on a solo trumpet because Jean Harlow had such a small voice, with the reiterated verse. I wrote this tune because it seemed to fit the requirements. I played it for Larry, who then wrote the lyric. But Jean never signed for *Hollywood Party,* and the song was dropped.

Then, not much after that, we tried the song another way. New lyrics were written and the song was called "Manhattan Melodrama," to be put in the picture of the same name. That didn't work out either, and the lyrics were again rewritten, this time as "The Bad in Ev'ry Man." It was shot and sung with that lyric and that title and is still in the print of that picture. Shirley Ross sang it.

Our contract was up with MGM in April 1933. When we were in California in July 1933, working for Paramount, we received a telegram from Jack Robbins suggesting that we take the melody of "Prayer," "Manhattan Melodrama" and "The Bad in Ev'ry Man" and write for it what was called a "commercial" lyric, and let him publish it.

Sometime within the next three months, a new lyric was written, the song being called "Blue Moon." When Larry Hart showed the lyrics to Jack Robbins, Robbins personally suggested changes in the last three lines of the chorus.

1934

Hollywood Party

Released by MGM on May 25, 1934

Music by Richard Rodgers
Other music and lyrics by Walter Donaldson and Gus Kahn, Walter Donaldson and Howard Dietz, and Nacio Herb Brown and Arthur Freed
Choreographed by Seymour Felix, George Hale and Dave Gould
Photographed by James Wong Howe
Mickey Mouse sequence by Walt Disney

Hollywood Party

⊰ *Originally sung by Frances Williams* ⊱

VERSE

Phones busy! We're dizzy!
It's that affair.
He's going! She's going!
Put on your bib and tucker.
Put on your soup and fish.
I'm going! You're going!
This is our dish.

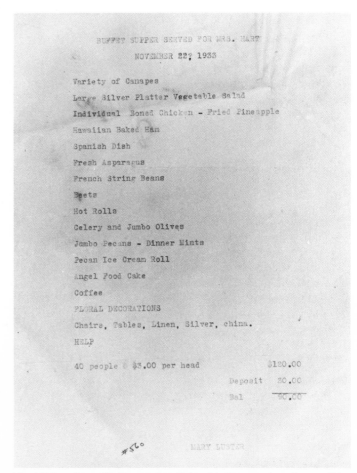

The bill for a large "Hollywood Party" that Frieda gave when she was living in Hollywood with Larry. Mary Luster was a top Hollywood caterer—and for this whole feast, she charged a grand total of 120 dollars!

REFRAIN

Hollywood Party!
Get up! Get out! Get in it!
Hollywood Party!
Nobody sleeps tonight.
Bring along your girl!
Go home with someone else's,
Forget about your girl.
She's gonna do all right.
We'll be kicking our heels up
Till the rooster is crowing.
Bring the automobiles up.
Ev'rybody is going Hollywood Party,
Going a mile a minute,
Hollywood Party!
Nobody sleeps tonight.

Prayer

REFRAIN

Oh, Lord, if
You ain't busy up there,
I ask for help with a prayer,
So please don't give me the air.
Oh, hear me, Lord.
I must see Garbo in person
With Gable when they're rehearsin'
While some director is cursin'.
Please let me open up my eyes at seven
And find I'm looking through the Golden Gate,
And walking right into my movie heaven,
While some exekative tells me I'll be great.
Oh, Lord,
I know how friendly you are.
If I'm not going too far
Be nice and make me a star.

Manhattan Melodrama

VERSE

All New York's a stage
And all its men and women are very bad actors.
How they rant and rage
For food and drink and money, for those are the factors.
Out of the Bronx and Yonkers
Rushing to earn a wage—
He must be strong who conquers
On the Manhattan stage.

REFRAIN

Act One
You gulp your coffee and run;
Into the subway you crowd.
Don't breathe—it isn't allowed.

Act Two:
The boss is yelling at you;
You feel so frightened and cowed.
Don't breathe—it isn't allowed.

The rows of skyscrapers are like a canyon,
The sun is hidden 'neath a stony shroud,
Eight million people and not one companion:
Don't speak to anyone—it's not allowed.

Act Three:
You hate the sight of Broadway.
It's just that kind of a play—
"Manhattan Melodrama."

The Bad in Ev'ry Man

VERSE

Sitting all alone
In moving picture theatres
Is ev'ry night's pleasure!
Walking on my own
When working hours are over,
I've nothing but leisure.
Am I a fool, I wonder?
Marriage is one way out.
But I'm afraid to blunder,
I sit home and doubt.

REFRAIN

Oh, Lord!
What is the matter with me?
I'm just permitted to see
The bad in ev'ry man.
Oh, hear me, Lord!
I could be good to a lover,
But then I always discover
The bad in ev'ry man.
They like to tell you that they love you only.
And you believe it though you know you're wrong.
A little hallroom can be awfully lonely
And the nights can be so very long.
Oh, Lord!
Perhaps I'll alter my plan
And overlook if I can
The bad in ev'ry man!

Blue Moon

1st VERSE

Once upon a time,
Before I took up smiling,
I hated the moonlight!
Shadows of the night
That poets find beguiling
Seemed flat as the moonlight.
With no one to stay up for,
I went to sleep at ten.
Life was a bitter cup for
The saddest of all men.

REFRAIN

Blue Moon,
You saw me standing alone,
Without a dream in my heart,
Without a love of my own.

Blue Moon,
You knew just what I was there for,
You heard me saying a prayer for
Someone I really could care for.
And then there suddenly appeared before me,
The only one my arms will ever hold.
I heard somebody whisper, "Please adore me."
And when I looked,
The moon had turned to gold!
Blue Moon,
Now I'm no longer alone,
Without a dream in my heart,
Without a love of my own.

2nd VERSE

Once upon a time,
My heart was just an organ.
My life had no mission.
Now that I have you,
To be as rich as Morgan
Is my one ambition.
Once I awoke at seven,
Hating the morning light.
Now I awake in heaven
And all the world's all right.

Larry and Herb in Hollywood, sometime around 1935.

Shirley Ross, singing the only lyric of the "Blue Moon" melody that ever made it to the screen: "The Bad in Ev'ry Man" from *Manhattan Melodrama*

Larry's experience as a translator for United Plays came in handy when, in 1934, MGM assigned him to write the lyrics for his friend Ernst Lubitsch's new production of *The Merry Widow*. The movie, starring Maurice Chevalier and Jeanette MacDonald, is one of the most glorious of all Metro musicals. It's often said that Larry's translations of the lyrics are the best that exist in English.

1934

The Merry Widow

Released by MGM on October 12, 1934

Additional lyrics by Gus Kahn
Music by Franz Lehár
Screenplay by Ernest Vajda and Samson Raphaelson from
  Franz Lehár's operetta
Directed by Ernst Lubitsch
Choreographed by Albertina Rasch
Settings by Cedric Gibbons, Gabriel Scognamillo,
  Frederic Hope and Edwin B. Willis
Costumes by Adrian and Ali Hubert
Photographed by Oliver T. Marsh

Maxim's

⊰ *Originally sung by Maurice Chevalier* ⊱

REFRAIN

I'm going to Maxim's,
Where all the girls are dreams.
Each kiss goes on the wine list
And mine is quite a fine list.

Lo-lo, Do-do, Jou-jou, Clo-clo, Margot, Frou-frou,
We promise to be faithful until the night is through.
Goodbye to you, Maxim's,
I don't believe in dreams.
The evening was splendid,
But now the play is ended.
I give you to Jou-jou, Clo-clo, Margot, Frou-frou.
The wine has lost its flavor.
I leave Maxim's to you.

Frances Manson

Larry saw a lot of different girls when he was in Hollywood. But Frances Manson, a long-time friend, was one of his favorites, and a co-worker in the movie industry.

Larry and I remained friends for a long time. I was story editor for Columbia Pictures for many years. Before that I was an instructor at Columbia University. I saw a lot of Larry when he and Dick came out to Hollywood to do a couple of pictures.

I adored Larry and was never bothered by his short stature. He was so dynamic and energetic, his presence was so magnetic, that I honestly never gave a thought to his being shorter than I was, though I am not at all tall. From time to time he asked me to marry him—many times, as a matter of fact. I had an invalid mother I was caring for. But my real fear was that I might wind up drinking as much as Larry!

We went to Tijuana one weekend to stand up for Gertie Purcell, a well-known writer, who was getting married. During the ceremony Larry sat on a window sill singing "Hallelujah, I'm a Bum." I guess the odd atmosphere of the place didn't lend itself to sentiment.

We went to the Clover Club one night, a gambling place, on the Strip in Hollywood. Money poured out of every pocket as he placed his bets. In a short while he had won quite a bundle. Back the bills went, crumpled up, in every pocket! He never seemed to carry a wallet. He left me at my door and continued on with some friends.

The next day he called me.

"I must have lost a lot of money last night at the Clover Club. I haven't a cent on me!"

He didn't remember winning at the tables. . . .

Not too long before he died I went to the hospital to see him. He was there to dry out. His manager had asked me to visit him to see if I could get him to give up drinking. But of course it was no use.

1935

Mississippi

Released by Paramount Pictures on April 2, 1935

Music by Richard Rodgers
Screenplay by Francis Martin, Jack Cunningham, Herbert
    Fields and Claude Binyon, from a play by Booth Tarkington
Directed by A. E. Sutherland
Art direction by Hans Dreier and Bernard Herzburn
Photographed by Charles Lang

It's Easy to Remember

‑{ *Originally sung by Bing Crosby* }‑

VERSE

With you I owned the earth.
With you I ruled creation.
No you, and what's it worth?
It's just an imitation.

REFRAIN

Your sweet expression,
The smile you gave me,
The way you looked when we met—
It's easy to remember,
But so hard to forget.
I hear you whisper,
"I'll always love you,"
I know it's over, and yet—
It's easy to remember,
But so hard to forget.
So I must dream
To have your hand caress me,
Fingers press me tight.
I'd rather dream
Than have that lonely feeling
Stealing through the night.
Each little moment
Is clear before me,
And though it brings me regret—
It's easy to remember
But so hard to forget.

In 1935, Larry and Herb were professionally reunited. Herb and Claude Binyon adapted the screenplay of *Mississippi* from Booth Tarkington's much-filmed *Magnolia*. Larry and Dick wrote the score, half of which was cut—the usual fate of R & H movie scores. But the movie wasn't too bad, and the cast included (left to right) Queenie Smith, W.C. Fields, Joan Bennett, Bing Crosby (with a mustache) and Gail Patrick. Bing insisted on inserting Stephen Foster's "Swanee River" into the movie. Larry tried to block the insertion, wanting an all Rodgers and Hart score, but the superstar crooner won out.

By 1935, Larry and Dick had pretty much had it with Hollywood. They returned to New York for good, where they were to write a series of the greatest musicals ever—*Jumbo, On Your Toes, Babes in Arms, I'd Rather Be Right, I Married an Angel, The Boys from Syracuse, Too Many Girls* and *Pal Joey.* Some of these shows were produced at the rate of two a year.

Teddy Hart and I met sometime in 1935 and it was through Teddy that I met his brother Larry. I was introduced to Larry in Hollywood, and I was impressed at this first meeting by his constant good humor, his intensity, his warmth and friendliness—so that I felt I had known him for a long time. He was heavily tanned and looked very fit, no doubt from the Beverly Hills Hotel pool and patio, so popular with the movie crowd. Larry was living in a bungalow at the hotel.

He had asked to see Teddy's apartment before going on to a party, so we had picked him up in Teddy's Plymouth, walking to the car from the hotel. (Teddy was only a few inches taller than his brother. He never wore lifts on his shoes, though in Hollywood actors, even some fairly tall ones, wore them. You couldn't be too tall for the movies, though it never seemed to matter that much on the stage.)

I was immediately fascinated by Larry's constant patter. He talked in quick, staccato phrases with nervous gestures. But he was always vital and with an air of authority and self-assurance that were magnetic. At Teddy's apartment, a modest one by Larry's standards, he looked around approvingly, satisfying himself that it was comfortable. After the hotels ("schlock houses," as Teddy called them) that he had lived in when touring in vaudeville, Teddy considered his accommodations in Hollywood top-drawer.

Larry patted Teddy's cheek affectionately, and said, "See you," and he was gone. I realized that Teddy was in awe of his famous brother, and I was thrilled to meet the man who had written the lyrics to "Manhattan," "Sentimental Me" and "Mountain Greenery." I had seen *The Garrick Gaieties* of 1925 and 1926 and had been a Rodgers and Hart fan ever since.

The wife of Larry's best friend asked me, when I mentioned this meeting some years later, "But didn't you notice that his head was too big for his small body? That's the first thing I noticed when I met him. Teddy, on the other hand, is perfectly proportioned."

Of course, I'd never noticed! And only when I looked over some photographs for this book did I notice. When I was with Larry, I was always so involved with what Larry was saying, so overwhelmed by his presence.

THE GREAT SHOWS 1935-1940

1935

Jumbo

Opened November 16, 1935, at the Hippodrome
for a run of 233 performances

Music by Richard Rodgers
Book by Ben Hecht and Charles MacArthur
Directed by John Murray Anderson and George Abbott
Choreographed by Allan K. Foster
Settings by Albert Johnson
Costumes by Raoul Pène du Bois

The Most Beautiful Girl in the World

{ *Originally sung by Donald Novis and Gloria Grafton* }

VERSE

We used to spend the spring together
Before we learned to walk;
We used to laugh and sing together
Before we learned how to talk.
With no reason for the season,
Spring would end as it would start.
Now the season has a reason
And there's springtime in my heart.

REFRAIN

The most beautiful girl in the world
Picks my ties out,
Eats my candy,
Drinks my brandy—

The most beautiful girl in the world.
The most beautiful star in the world
Isn't Garbo, isn't Dietrich,
But the sweet trick
Who can make me believe it's a beautiful world.
Social—not a bit,
Nat'ral kind of wit,
She'd shine anywhere,
And she hasn't got platinum hair.
The most beautiful house in the world
Has a mortgage—
What do I care?
It's goodbye care
When my slippers are next to the ones that belong
To the one and only beautiful girl in the world!

TRIO-PATTER

She: Climb off your perch and go home
with your dreams.
He: No, ma'am, I'm in love.
She: Where did you think of such elegant schemes?
He: Here, ma'am, up above.
She: Do you think that kind of blarney
Will win a woman's heart?
He: Little daughter of Killarney,
That heart was mine from the start.
She: I'd slap your face if I had you down here.
He: Presto, here I come.
She: Careful, dear.
He: Have no fear.
She: Darling, look out,
Or you'll fall on your ear.
He: Which side?
She: Outside.
He: Which side?
She: This side.

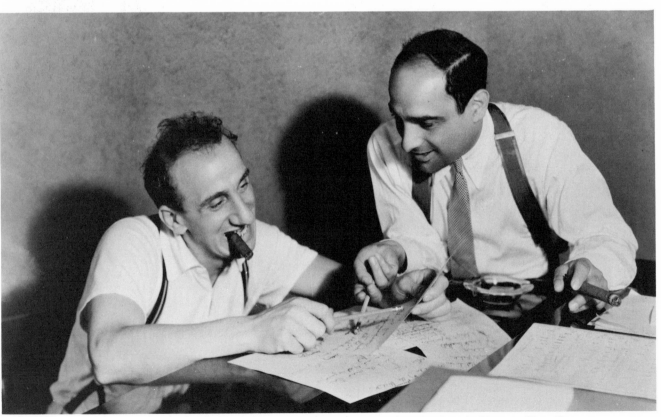

Larry's first Broadway show in four years was *Jumbo*, produced by his old associate Billy Rose. But Larry had been working with Jimmy Durante far more recently. Jimmy had leading roles in both *The Phantom President* and *Hollywood Party*.

Jimmy Durante, as Claudius Bowers, with Rosie, the elephant. At one point in the show, a sheriff who was repossessing the circus asked Jimmy, "Hey, where are you going with that elephant?" His reply was serene: "What elephant?" Billy Rose had to tear up the Hippodrome for *Jumbo*'s armies of aerial acts, bareback riders and jugglers—and for Paul Whiteman's band. But, for an effect like the Circus wedding finale (shown on the following two pages), it was all worth it.

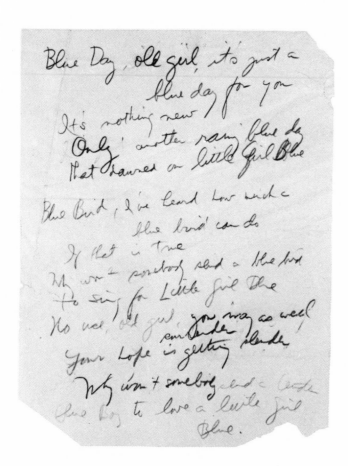

My Romance

{ *Originally sung by Donald Novis and Gloria Grafton* }

VERSE

I won't kiss your hand, madam,
Crazy for you though I am.
I'll never woo you on bended knee.
No, madam, not me.
We don't need that flow'ry fuss.
No, sir, madam, not for us.

REFRAIN

My romance
Doesn't have to have a moon in the sky.
My romance
Doesn't need a blue lagoon standing by.
No month of May,
No twinkling stars.
No hideaway,
No soft guitars.
My romance
Doesn't need a castle rising in Spain.
Nor a dance
To a constantly surprising refrain.
Wide awake,
I can make
My most fantastic dreams come true.
My romance
Doesn't need a thing but you.

Little Girl Blue

{ *Originally sung by Gloria Grafton* }

REFRAIN

Sit there
And count your fingers.
What can you do?
Old girl, you're through.
Sit there
And count your little fingers.
Unlucky little girl blue.
Sit there
And count the raindrops
Falling on you.
It's time you knew
All you can count on
Is the raindrops
That fall on little girl blue.
No use, old girl,
You may as well surrender.
Your hope is getting slender.
Why won't somebody send a tender
Blue Boy, to cheer
Little girl blue?

TRIO-PATTER

When I was very young
The world was younger than I,
As merry as a carousel.
The circus tent was strung
With ev'ry star in the sky
Above the ring I loved so well.
Now the world has grown old.
Gone are the tinsel and gold.

George Balanchine

George Balanchine was maître de ballet of the American School of Ballet and director of the Metropolitan Opera corps de ballet when he signed on to choreograph On Your Toes. *His only previous musical-comedy experience had been on the belated Ziegfeld Follies of 1936. But his association with the musicals of Rodgers and Hart resulted in some of the most brilliant and innovative show dancing in theatre history.*

It was Larry who first wanted me for *On Your Toes.* I was newly arrived from Europe and it was not easy getting started in a new country. His friend Doc Bender introduced us. This led to my doing four Rodgers and Hart shows: *On Your Toes, Babes in Arms, I Married an Angel* and *The Boys from Syracuse.* The "Slaughter on Tenth Avenue" ballet was Larry's idea. He was so full of wonderful ideas and worked very hard. What no one realized about Larry was that he was so quick; his mind worked so fast that in a few minutes whatever you needed —a suggestion, a lyric—he would do it very fast. Then he was off away somewhere. I'd say, "Larry, is this all right?" He would look quick, very quick, nod his head and then turn to do something else. All in a minute.

In *I Married an Angel* I had trouble with the producer, Dwight Wiman, and everyone else connected with the show, about the Surrealist ballet. I wanted a slow-motion, Daliesque effect. Nobody understood. Everybody was against it. Except Larry. He was the only one who knew what I was trying to do. He fought for me and insisted that they let me have my way. Larry discovered

Monty Woolley for *On Your Toes.* Woolley was a professor at Yale and had no professional experience. He was a perfect type with his beard, which very few people wore at that time. He made a big hit and remained an actor and a star.

I always considered Larry the Shelley of America. I thought at the time that Larry's lyrics should be published without the music as a book of verse or poetry.

We were very friendly all this time. Larry had no chauffeur then and he didn't drive. I would drive him around in his Cadillac. We went to the country and everywhere. He always appeared happy and laughing. He was so full of fun and energy, throwing his money around. From every pocket would come money and he paid everyone's bills wherever he went. I never got the feeling that Larry was not as happy as he appeared. But Bender told me that he was despondent because a woman he loved had turned him down. He felt that no woman could love him. But to me he never talked about these things. I knew he was depressed sometimes, but never when he was with me. I think maybe when he was alone. With me he always had the façade, the appearance that nothing ever bothered him. There was never any mention of his height, though he called the built-up heels in his shoes "the two-inch liars."

After he and Dick separated, about a year before he died, I was to do *Miss Underground,* which Larry was working on with Paul Gallico and Emmerich Kálmán, a famous European composer. The story was very interesting, about the French underground, and I thought the score was beautiful. This was during the war, and it was hard to get money for shows. Unfortunately, it was never produced because they could never get the money.

On Your Toes was one of the first shows in which dancing was fully integrated into the story. Above is the "Princess Zenobia" ballet, which closed the play's first act. It was a wicked parody of such glamorous Russian ballets as "Aurora's Wedding." When Balanchine was asked how he could make fun of the art form he was raised on, he knew just what to say. "The answer, I suppose, is that an artist need not be without a sense of humor. Buffoonery is still among the greatest of arts."

1936

On Your Toes

Opened April 11, 1936, at the Imperial Theatre
for a run of 315 performances

Music by Richard Rodgers
Book by Richard Rodgers, Lorenz Hart and George Abbott
Directed by Worthington Miner
Choreographed by George Balanchine
Settings by Jo Mielziner
Costumes by Irene Sharaff

On Your Toes

⊰ *Originally sung by Doris Carson, Ray Bolger*
and David Morris ⊱

VERSE

Remember the youth
'Mid snow and ice,
Who bore the banner
With the strange device:
"Excelsior."
This motto applies to those who dwell
In Richmond Hill or New Rochelle,
In Chelsea or in Sutton Place.

You've got to reach the heights
To win the race.

REFRAIN

See the pretty apple,
Top of the tree!
The higher up,
The sweeter it grows.
Picking fruit, you've got to be
Up on your toes.
See the pretty penthouse,
Top of the roof!
The higher up,
The higher rent goes.
Get that dough, don't be a goof,
Up on your toes.
They climb the clouds
To come through with airmail.
The dancing crowds
Look up to some rare male.
Like that Astaire male.
See the pretty lady,
Top of the crop!
You want to know
The way the wind blows!
Then, my boy, you'd better hop
Up on your toes,
Up on your toes!

Ray Bolger, Doris Carson and David Morris performing the original "On Your Toes" number. Larry and Dick had first thought of *On Your Toes* as a movie for Fred Astaire and Ginger Rogers, but the studios turned it down (among other things, they objected that the story would give Astaire no opportunities to wear a top hat and tails!). But Ray Bolger was a smash, and his dance style and personality were perhaps better suited to the role of Phil Dolan III than Astaire's would have been.

It's Got to Be Love

{ Originally sung by Ray Bolger and Doris Carson }

VERSE

I love your eyes, but I wouldn't know the color—
Aquamarine or em'rald green?
And if your hair couldn't possibly be duller,
The shade I see
Looks gold to me.
That's how naïve I've grown to be.
Mais oui!

1st REFRAIN

It's got to be love.
It couldn't be tonsillitis.
It feels like neuritis,
But nevertheless it's love.
Don't tell me the pickles and pie à la mode
They served me
Unnerved me
And made my heart a broken-down pump.
It's got to be love.
It isn't the morning after
That makes ev'ry rafter
Go spinning around above.
I'm sure that it's fatal, or why do I get
That sinking feeling?
I think that I'm dead,
But nevertheless it's only love.

2nd REFRAIN

It's got to be love.
It could have been fallen arches
Or too many starches,
But nevertheless it's love.
Don't tell me the lamp in the barbershop
Gave me sunstroke.
With one stroke,
You made me feel like yesterday's hash.
It's got to be love.
It couldn't be indigestion.
Beyond any question,
I'm fluttery as a dove.
I've heard people say it's no worse than a cold.
But oh, that fever!
I'm burned to a crisp,
But nevertheless it's only love.

Too Good for the Average Man

{ Originally sung by Monty Woolley and Luella Gear }

VERSE

When Russia was white
It was white for the classes
And black for the masses.
Unfortunate asses!
All wealth belonged to few.
When England was Tudor
The king and his cronies
Had cocktails at Tony's.
The poor had baloneys,
And that's how England grew!

Luella Gear and Monty Woolley, as the ballet master and the society lady, singing "Too Good for the Average Man."

Sing "La and huzzah" for the poor folks
As long as the poor folks are your folks.

1st REFRAIN

Finer things are for the finer folk.
Thus society began.
Caviar for peasants is a joke.
It's too good for the average man.
Supper clubs are for the upper folk,
Packed like sardines in a can.
Through the smoke you get your check and choke.
It's too good for the average man.
Each poor man has a wife he must stick to.
Men of fashion can be cocky.
To be caught in flagrante delictu
Is much too good for the average mockey!
All-night parties,
Drinking like a lord,
Fit into our social plan.
Waking in the alcoholic ward
Is too good for the average man.

2nd REFRAIN

Fancy nerves are for the fancy class
Since psychiatry began.
Neurasthenia isn't for the mass.
It's too good for the average man.
Patriotic talk against the Red
Is a plutocratic plan.
Sleeping with a bomb beneath his bed
Is too good for the average man.
Lots of kids for a poor wife are dandy.
Girls of fashion can be choosy.
Birth control and the modus operandi
Are much too good for the average floozy!
Psychoanalysts are all the whirl.
Rich men pay them all they can.
Waking up to find that he's a girl
Is too good for the average man.

Al Hirschfeld's marvelous caricature of Ray Bolger, Luella Gear, Tamara Geva and Monty Woolley

The Heart Is Quicker than the Eye

{ *Originally sung by Luella Gear and Ray Bolger* }

VERSE

Peggy: Dear old mother was as wise as ten folks
And she knew her way about the menfolks.
Once she said to me, "Daughter, you're quite a pup.
Daughter, dear, it's time to wise you up."
She said, "Love has always been my hoodoo.
Though I've lived, I know much less than you do."

1st REFRAIN

Mother told me there's no use asking why
He loves she
And she loves he.
The heart is quicker than the eye.
Mother warned me that fair play doesn't apply.
Turn your back
And love goes whack!
The heart is quicker than the eye.
Love can kill you off, baby, faster than Flit.
It finds its mark, and, toots, you're *it!*
Dear sweet Mother was careful and so sly!
But, my dear,
You see I'm here.
The heart is quicker than the eye.

PATTER

In December, nineteen-five, Mother got a little
    snootful.
In September, nineteen-six, I was born alive and
    beaut'ful.
I recall a few years later,
I was taken with the measles
And my darling little mater
Just sat up all night—
With a good-looking guy!
Phil: Oh me! oh my!
Peggy: We would travel quite a lot, but we always went to
    Reno.
She'd remarry like a shot—
Not for long, but how could she know?
Number Four was a musician
Who could swing it sweet and hot.
Whistler's Mother is a classic,
Mother's whistler was not—
He was dropped like the rest.
Phil: Mother always knows best.
It may seem strange to you—
I have a mother, too.

2nd REFRAIN

Phil: Mother told me, "Be good until you die."
She meant well, but could she tell
The heart is quicker than the eye?
Mother warned me my instincts to deny.
Yet I fail.
The male is frail.
The heart is quicker than the eye.
She said, "Love one time, Junior.
Look at the Lunts!"
I've fallen twice, with two at once.
Passion's plaything—that's me, oh me, oh my!
But at least
I'm quite a beast.
The heart is quicker than the eye.

PATTER

Phil: Miss Porterfield, I want to
Thank you for your advice.
Peggy: You're welcome.
Phil: But it didn't do me any good.
Peggy: I didn't think it would.
Phil: Well, *c'est la vie!*
Peggy: The same goes for me.
Phil: I don't know which way to turn
Or which is which.
Peggy: That's why I just told you
The heart is quicker than the eye.

TAG

Peggy: You say love is blind.
I say love's cockeyed, too.
The gift of gab obscures the view.
Mother begged me, "Don't drink with any guy."
So I was made on lemonade.
The heart is quicker than the Rye!

Before they went into their classic "Heart Is Quicker than the Eye" routine, Ray Bolger and Luella Gear exchanged a peerless bit of dialogue. Confused about love, he asked her if a good man could love two women at the same time. She paused and then responded, "If he's very good."

Glad to Be Unhappy

{ *Originally sung by Doris Carson* }

VERSE

Look at yourself.
If you had a sense of humor,
You would laugh to beat the band.
Look at yourself.
Do you still believe the rumor
That romance is simply grand?
Since you took it right
On the chin,
You have lost that bright
Toothpaste grin.
My mental state is all a jumble.
I sit around and sadly mumble.

REFRAIN

Fools rush in, so here I am,
Very glad to be unhappy.
I can't win, but here I am,
More than glad to be unhappy.
Unrequited love's a bore.
And I've got it pretty bad.
But for someone you adore,
It's a pleasure to be sad.
Like a straying baby lamb
With no mammy and no pappy,
I'm so unhappy,
But oh, so glad!

"Slaughter on Tenth Avenue," on stage (left) and on film. Ray Bolger's partner was Tamara Geva (they're also shown in the picture on the following two pages). In the movies, Eddie Albert danced with Vera Zorina. But, both on stage and on screen, George Church was the heavy in the outlandish jacket and cap.

There's a Small Hotel*

⦃ *Originally sung by Ray Bolger and Doris Carson* ⦄

VERSE

Frankie: I'd like to get away, Junior,
Somewhere alone with you.
It could be oh, so gay, Junior!
You need a laugh or two.

Phil: A certain place I know, Frankie,
Where funny people can have fun.
That's where we two will go, darling,
Before you can count up
One, two, three,
For . . .

REFRAIN

There's a small hotel
With a wishing well.
I wish that we were there
Together.
There's a bridal suite,
One room bright and neat,
Complete for us to share
Together.
Looking through the window you
Can see a distant steeple.
Not a sign of people.
Who wants people?

* This song was originally written for *Jumbo*, but was dropped.

When the steeple bell
Says, "Good night, sleep well,"
We'll thank the small hotel
Together.

INTERLUDE

Pretty window curtains made of chintz
In our make-believe land.
On the wall are sev'ral cheerful prints
Of Grant and Grover Cleveland.
Go down into the parlor and feast your eyes
On the moosehead on the wall.
Perhaps you'd like to play the organ—
They tune it ev'ry other fall.
The garden will be like Adam and Eve land.
No, they never did go in for carriage trade;
They get what is known as marriage trade.

CODA

When the steeple bell
Says, "Good night, sleep well,"
We'll thank the small hotel,
We'll creep into our little shell,
And we will thank the small hotel together.

COMIC REPRISE

⦃ *Originally sung by Luella Gear and
Monty Woolley* ⦄

There's a small hotel
Which we loved so well—
From there we'll get the air tomorrow.
One big bill to pay,
One old jazz ballet,
Is all we'll have to share tomorrow.
Looking through the window is
A man with a subpoena.
If you lose that meanie
You're Houdini.
When the steeple bell
Says, "Good night, sleep well,"
We'll miss that small hotel
Together.

1937

Babes in Arms

*Opened April 14, 1937, at the Shubert Theatre
for a run of 289 performances*

Music by Richard Rodgers
Book by Lorenz Hart and Richard Rodgers
Directed by Robert Sinclair
Choreographed by George Balanchine
Settings by Raymond Sovey
Costumes by Helene Pons

The Lady Is a Tramp

{ *Originally sung by Mitzi Green* }

VERSE

I've wined and dined on Mulligan stew
And never wished for turkey.
As I hitched and hiked and drifted, too,
From Maine to Albuquerque.
Alas, I missed the Beaux Arts Ball,
And what is twice as sad,
I was never at a party
Where they honored Noël Ca'ad.
But social circles spin too fast for me.
My Hobohemia is the place to be.

1st REFRAIN

I get too hungry for dinner at eight.
I like the theatre, but never come late.
I never bother with people I hate.
That's why the lady is a tramp.
I don't like crap games
With barons and earls.
Won't go to Harlem
In ermine and pearls.
Won't dish the dirt
With the rest of the girls.
That's why the lady is a tramp.
I like the free, fresh wind in my hair,
Life without care.
I'm broke—it's oke.
Hate California—it's cold and it's damp.
That's why the lady is a tramp.

2nd REFRAIN

I go to Coney—the beach is divine.
I go to ball games—the bleachers are fine.
I follow Winchell and read ev'ry line.
That's why the lady is a tramp.
I like a prize fight that isn't a fake.
I love the rowing on Central Park Lake.
I go to opera and stay wide awake.
That's why the lady is a tramp.
I like the green grass under my shoes.
What can I lose?
I'm flat, that's that.
I'm all alone when I lower my lamp.
That's why the lady is a tramp.

REPRISE

Don't know the reason for cocktails at five.
I don't like flying—I'm glad I'm alive.
I crave affection, but not when I drive.
That's why the lady is a tramp.
Folks go to London and leave me behind.
I'll miss the crowning, Queen Mary won't mind.
I don't play Scarlett in "Gone With the Wind."
That's why the lady is a tramp.
I like to hang my hat where I please.
Sail with the breeze.
No dough—heigh-ho!
I love La Guardia and think he's a champ.
That's why the lady is a tramp.

ADDITIONAL LYRICS

Girls get massages, they cry and they moan.
Tell Lizzie Arden to leave me alone.
I'm not so hot, but my shape is my own.
That's why the lady is a tramp!
The food at Sardi's is perfect, no doubt.
I wouldn't know what the Ritz is about.
I drop a nickel and coffee comes out.
That's why the lady is a tramp!
I like the sweet, fresh rain in my face.
Diamonds and lace,
No got—so what?
For Robert Taylor I whistle and stamp.
That's why the lady is a tramp!

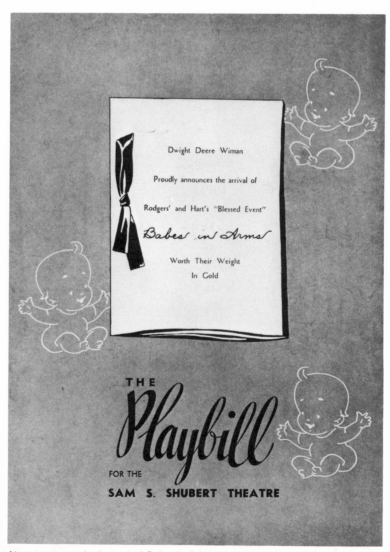

Almost everyone in the cast of *Babes in Arms* was a teen-ager, and the show's play-bill took the form of a birth announcement from the producer, Dwight Deere Wiman. Wiman also produced three other Rodgers and Hart shows—*On Your Toes*, *I Married an Angel* and *Higher and Higher*—and always with impeccable taste.

Johnny One-Note

{ *Originally sung by Wynn Murray* }

VERSE

Johnny could only sing one note
And the note he sang was this:
Ah-h-h-h-h!

REFRAIN

Poor Johnny One-Note
Sang out with gusto
And just overlorded the place.
Poor Johnny One-Note
Yelled willy-nilly
Until he was blue in the face—
For holding one note was his ace.
Couldn't hear the brass,
Couldn't hear the drum.
He was in a class
By himself, by gum.
Poor Johnny One-Note
Got in "Aïda"—
Indeed a great chance to be brave.
He took his one note
Howled like the North Wind—

Brought forth wind that made critics rave,
While Verdi turned round in his grave.
Couldn't hear the flute
Or the big trombone.
Ev'ryone was mute.
Johnny stood alone.

Cats and dogs stopped yapping,
Lions in the zoo all were jealous of Johnny's big trill.
Thunderclaps stopped clapping,
Traffic ceased its roar,
And they tell us Niag'ra stood still.
He stopped the train whistles,
              Boat whistles,
              Steam whistles,
              Cop whistles,
All whistles bowed to his skill.
Sing, Johnny One-Note,
Sing out with gusto
And just overwhelm all the crowd.
Ah-h-h-h-h!
So sing, Johnny One-Note, out loud!
Sing, Johnny One-Note!
Sing, Johnny One-Note, out loud!

The "got in 'Aïda'" lyric of "Johnny One Note" gave Balanchine the idea to stage a ballet after the number in which the cast dressed as ancient Egyptians, wearing towels, bath mats and wash cloths. The ballet also had a plot—in which Mitzi Green (center) played "The Singer" and Alfred Drake (not pictured) was "The High Priest."

Wonderful Wynn Murray, introducing ''Johnny One Note,'' in the climactic amateur-show sequence. The idea was that Wynn was a young mother telling her baby a bedtime story about Johnny One Note, the show-off opera star whose leading lady had her fairy godmother put a curse on him.

Way Out West

{ *Originally sung by Wynn Murray, Alex Courtney, Robert Rounseville, James Gillis and Ted Gary* }

VERSE

I've traveled the plains.
In mountain streams I've paddled.
Over the Rockies I would trail.
I'd hark to the strains
Of cowboys in the saddle—
Not very musical, but male.
I've roamed o'er the range with the herd,
Where seldom is heard an encouraging word.

1st REFRAIN

Git along, little taxi, you can keep the change.
I'm riding home to my kitchen range
Way out west on West End Avenue.
Oh, I love to listen to the wagon wheels
That bring the milk that your neighbor steals
Way out west on West End Avenue.
Keep all your mountains
And your lone prairie so pretty,
Give me the fountains
That go wrong at Rodeo City.
I would trade your famous deer and antelope
For one tall beer and a cantaloupe.
Way out west on West End Avenue.
Yippee-aye-ay!

2nd REFRAIN

Git along, little elevator,
Climb once more
To my lone shack on the fourteenth floor
Way out west on West End Avenue.
When the sun's a-rising over Central Park
I pull the blinds and it's nice and dark
Way out west on West End Avenue.
Redskins may battle with their tomahawks and axes.
I'll join the cattle
In the big corral at Saks's.
Oh, the wild herd gathers when the moon is full.
There's not much buffalo, but lots of bull
Way out west on West End Avenue.

My Funny Valentine

{ *Originally sung by Mitzi Green* }

VERSE

Behold the way
Our fine feathered friend
His virtue doth parade.
Thou knowest not,
My dim-witted friend,
The picture thou hast made.
Thy vacant brow
And thy tousled hair
Conceal thy good intent.
Thou noble, upright
Truthful, sincere
And slightly dopey gent—you're . . .

REFRAIN

My funny Valentine,
Sweet comic Valentine,
You make me smile with my heart.
Your looks are laughable,
Unphotographable,
Yet you're my fav'rite work of art.
Is your figure less than Greek?
Is your mouth a little weak?
When you open it to speak
Are you smart?
But don't change a hair for me,
Not if you care for me,
Stay, little Valentine, stay!
Each day is Valentine's Day.

Where or When

{ *Originally sung by Mitzi Green* }

VERSE

When you're awake, the things you think
Come from the dreams you dream.
Thought has wings, and lots of things
Are seldom what they seem.
Sometimes you think you've lived before
All that you live today.
Things you do come back to you,
As though they knew the way.
Oh, the tricks your mind can play!

REFRAIN

It seems we stood and talked like this before,
We looked at each other in the same way then,
But I can't remember where or when.
The clothes you're wearing are the clothes you wore.
The smile you are smiling you were smiling then,
But I can't remember where or when.
Some things that happen for the first time
Seem to be happening again.
And so it seems that we have met before,
And laughed before, and loved before,
But who knows where or when!

I Wish I Were in Love Again

{ *Originally sung by Grace McDonald and Rolly Pickert* }

VERSE

You don't know that I felt good
When we up and parted.
You don't know I knocked on wood,
Gladly broken-hearted.
Worrying is through,
I sleep all night,
Appetite and health restored.
You don't know how much I'm bored.

1st REFRAIN

The sleepless nights,
The daily fights,
The quick toboggan when you reach the heights—
I miss the kisses and I miss the bites.
I wish I were in love again!
The broken dates,
The endless waits,
The lovely loving and the hateful hates,
The conversation with the flying plates—
I wish I were in love again!
No more pain,
No more strain,
Now I'm sane, but . . .
I would rather be gaga!
The pulled-out fur of cat and cur,
The fine mismating of a him and her—
I've learned my lesson, but I
Wish I were in love again.

2nd REFRAIN

The furtive sigh,
The blackened eye,
The words "I'll love you till the day I die,"
The self-deception that believes the lie—
I wish I were in love again.
When love congeals
It soon reveals
The faint aroma of performing seals,
The double-crossing of a pair of heels.
I wish I were in love again!
No more care.
No despair.
I'm all there now,
But I'd rather be punch-drunk!
Believe me, sir,
I much prefer
The classic battle of a him and her.
I don't like quiet and I
Wish I were in love again!

The stars of *Babes in Arms*, romping for photographers before the show went into rehearsal: Rolly Pickert, Grace McDonald, Mitzi Green, Ray McDonald and Wynn Murray (left to right).

1937

I'd Rather Be Right

*Opened November 2, 1937, at the Alvin Theatre
for a run of 290 performances*

Music by Richard Rodgers
Book by George S. Kaufman and Moss Hart
Directed by George S. Kaufman
Choreographed by Charles Weidman and Ned McGurn
Settings by Donald Oenslager
Costumes by Irene Sharaff and John Hambleton

Off the Record*

{ *Originally sung by George M. Cohan* }

VERSE

It's really a wonderful job
For fellows like George, Abe and me, too.
It's great to shake hands with the mob,
And to hold every kid on your knee, too.
Ev'ry word that I speak goes into headlines;
When I speak, all the papers hold their deadlines.
But I've found a way of dropping a hint,
Or a glint of the truth
That the boys cannot print.
For instance. . . .
For instance. . . .

1st REFRAIN

When I was only governor, and just a good-time Charlie,
A certain party came to me—he said his name was Farley.
Don't print this—it's strictly off the record.
He sat right down and talked to me till I was in a stupor,
And ended up by selling me the works of Fenimore Cooper.
Don't print it—it's strictly off the record.
I said, "You're quite a salesman;
You've been sent here by the fates.
If you can sell these dreary books,
Which ev'rybody hates,
Then maybe you can sell me to the whole United States!"
But that's off the record.

2nd REFRAIN

My messages to Congress are a lot of boola-boola.
I'm not so fond of Bankhead, but I'd love to meet Tallulah.
Don't print it—it's strictly off the record.
I sit up in my bedroom reading books like "Silas Marner,"
And Sears and Roebuck catalogues to get away from Garner.
Don't print it— it's strictly off the record.
If I'm not re-elected and the worst comes to the worst,
I'll never die of hunger and I'll never die of thirst.
I've got one boy with Du Pont and another one with Hearst.
But that's off the record.

3rd REFRAIN

When I go up to Hyde Park, it is not just for the ride there.
It's not that I love Hyde Park, but I love to park and hide there.
Don't print that—it's strictly off the record.
Oh, sing a song of Boulder Dam, but what's a little song
 worth?
We'll use it to throw razor blades, and maybe Alice Longworth.
Don't print it—it's strictly off the record.
And now I'd like to talk about some folks I used to know—
Mr. John L. Lewis and his famous CIO.
"Frankie and Johnnie were sweethearts"—
But that's off the record.

4th REFRAIN

My speeches on the radio have made me quite a hero.
I only have to say "My friends" and stocks go down to zero.
Don't print it—it's strictly off the record.
The radio officials say that I'm the leading fellow.
Jack Benny can be President and I'll go on for Jell-O.
Don't print it—it's strictly off the record.
It's pleasant at the White House, but I'll tell you how I feel:
The food is something terrible—just sauerkraut and veal.
If Eleanor would stay at home, I'd get a decent meal—
But that's off the record.

Movie lyrics*

When I was courting Eleanor
I told her Uncle Teddy
I wouldn't run for president
Unless the job was steady.
Don't print it—it's strictly off the record.
We entertained the royalty
But we were never flustered
We gave them Yankee hot dogs
With Coleman's English mustard.
Don't print it—it's strictly off the record.
I sit up in my study
Writing gags for Mr. Ickes
And insults for the gentlemen
Who'd love to slip him mickeys.
Don't print that—it's off the record.
I scrapped the Prohibition Act
When we required a bracer
And finished up the Boulder Dam
To give the boys a chaser.
Don't print it—it's strictly off the record.
And for my friends in Washington
Who complain about the taxes
Who cares as long as we cannot be axed
Out of the Axis?
Don't print it—it's strictly off the record.
I can't forget how Lafayette
Helped give us our first chance
To win our fight for liberty
And now they've taken France.
We'll take it back from Hitler
And put ants in his Japans
And that's off the record.

* The lyrics of "Off the Record" appeared on the front page
of the New York *Sun*, November 2, 1937.

* These additional lyrics were written for James Cagney to
sing as George M. Cohan in *Yankee Doodle Dandy* (1942).

People came to *I'd Rather Be Right* to see and be surprised by the agility of George M. Cohan, who came out of retirement to play a tap-dancing FDR. (The opening was very glamorous, attended by society, the theatrical elite, and the politically prominent.) But Cohan still considered Larry and Dick upstarts, and at the first out-of-town performance, he tampered with some lyrics about his friend Al Smith. Larry, however, remained adamant about the original lyric, telling the papers, "You understand that a writer must take a firm stand that no one collaborate with him."

Have You Met Miss Jones?

{ Originally sung by Austin Marshall and Joy Hodges }

REFRAIN

"Have you met Miss Jones?"
Someone said as we shook hands.
She was just Miss Jones to me.
Then I said, "Miss Jones,
You're a girl who understands;
I'm a man who must be free."

And all at once I lost my breath,
And all at once was scared to death,
And all at once I owned the earth and sky!
Now I've met Miss Jones,
And we'll keep on meeting till we die—
Miss Jones and I.

I'd Rather Be Right was probably the most highly publicized of all the Rodgers and Hart shows—chiefly because it satirized a still-presiding President. At the climax of the show, George M. Cohan, as FDR, pleaded for a third term for Roosevelt. And every night, the speech drew boos from the orchestra and cheers from the balcony.

Joshua Logan

Young, tremendously talented, and about to direct his first musical, Joshua Logan entered Rodgers and Hart's professional life with I Married an Angel, *a lavish, beautifully produced show with a great score sung by a very talented cast. Josh had already distinguished himself with earlier productions of O'Neill and other writers, and as this interview shows, he understood Larry with great sensitivity.*

About Larry: he was a will-o'-the-wisp. He would disappear while you were watching him. We often had to walk from one theatre to another when two companies were rehearsing, or two parts of a company, and I'd be walking along planning the next scene or a song with Larry. I'd suddenly look around and he wasn't there. How he disappeared without my knowing it, I don't know, because we were talking. I would look up and down the street. I couldn't find him! It was almost as though he had dropped through a manhole, or had been spirited up to the sky. I'd stay there a second and look around. I usually located him in a cigar store. He just stopped into a cigar store to buy a cigar. He'd never say Goodbye, Wait a minute, anything.

I found he was a perfectionist on lyrics. He didn't want one extra syllable or the wrong syllable. Larry and Dick drove me crazy because we went into rehearsal and they wrote no second act. We'd be rehearsing only the first act. There was one song, "Spring Is Here," that had a bit in the second act. I went to Larry and Dick and said, "We must have it. We have to plan the scenery. This is impossible," and Larry said, "All right, come up to my house tonight and we'll write it." So I went up to his apartment at the Ardsley. Dick was there.

The scene was laid in Budapest. It hadn't been written; it was just kind of a general plan. We did stay up all night. I wrote it down while they paced and dictated. The next night Dick and Larry stayed up all night again and wrote the score for the second act, which included the Radio City Music Hall takeoff scene.

I said, "My God, how are you going to get this into Budapest?" and Larry said, "That's all right. Just write a line and go right into it." He said, "It's got to be a *divertissement*. I must give all the actors a chance to be funny, to clown around, and then go back to the plot. Because the plot gets kind of heavy in the second act and I've done enough German operettas to know you need a *divertissement*." So it was that. It was crazy, and it was funny, but it just didn't fit Budapest. So the boys said, "Just write a line and lead into it." But I said, "No, I'm not going to write any line to lead into it. Larry's going to write a lyric to lead into it. He's clever and they'll listen to him." So he put a little prologue to the song: "You've got to come to New York. It would be such a pity for anyone to go through life without seeing Roxy City. The first thing foreigners do in New York is to look at Roxy City. Come

with me . . ." and he went into it. And it worked. It worked beautifully.

Now, when we put it in we had to work on it. We were having a dress rehearsal at the Wilbur Theatre in Boston. We were opening in Boston. Audrey Christie started to sing "Now come with me." All of a sudden I heard this screaming sound. I looked over to the aisle and there was this little windmill; Larry was flinging his arms around and screaming and yelling. He was very full of liquor. I said, "What is it, Larry, what is it?" He kept on making screaming sounds. I said, "What, what? Slow down. I can't understand you." And he said, "No 'Now' singers in this show!"

A "Now" singer was a singer who put "Now" in front of the chorus. It cheapened it to Larry and, tight as he was, he knew it. He felt he had to stop this kind of shenanigans going on with his lyrics. So he sat up on the stage right in front of the proscenium, and very seriously and quietly watched the rest of the show. Walter Slezak came over to me and said, "I don't like this scenery. You should have another little Larry Hart over on the other side!"

Larry hated law and order. He hated to be told to sit down and write a lyric, or write anything. That's why he didn't have any second act. When I was hired to direct *Angel* I met Dick Rodgers and he said, "You've got to go down to Atlantic City. Larry's there writing the book, but I don't think he's getting very far. Go down and see if you can help him." I did go down. Larry met me at the station in a big limousine. He was terribly nice, terribly voluble. I had never seen him before.

"I'm so glad you're here. You're going to enjoy it here. We have some good food, but first we have to go to the suite and get set."

We got there and I thought he was going to say, "Let's sit down and work on a scene," but he didn't. He pulled out a deck of cards and started playing rummy. Well, I played rummy for four days and ate—that's all we did! Nothing was written until one hour before we took the train back to New York. I said, "Larry, what are we going to do? How are we going to face Dick?" He said, "Don't worry. I'll have a second act by the time we get to New York!" He took a sheet of foolscap and pencils. We had a drawing room and Larry wrote faster than any man who's ever written. But the trouble was, he didn't put down words. He put down scratches on every page. There were about three lines on each page. He'd throw them on the floor and continue to write. There were an awful lot of pages. I kept trying to read them, but I just couldn't work it out. "That's all right," Larry said, "Dick can read it." So we saw Dick. Dick, you know, can have a very sour face. There is an unfortunate thing about Dick. When he's serious, and when he's efficient, he looks a little disapproving, which drove Larry wild. Larry kept calling him "The Principal," a school principal. And when you asked Dick a question about taste—you know, should we have the chorus come in here—he'd turn slightly away from you, wince, as though it was the

"At the Roxy Music Hall," the one song from *Angel* that Josh was doubtful about, ended up the hit of the show. *I Married an Angel* brought Vivienne Segal (left) out of the ingenue class forever, revealing her in full bloom as a comedienne of sophistication. In the Balanchine ballet that followed this number, she and Audrey Christie played *all* of the Rockettes. Of Audrey, Brooks Atkinson wrote, "she sings with that metallic exuberance that comes as close as anything can to being the true voice of Broadway."

worst idea in the world. What he's really doing when he winces is going into his little private thought chamber. Then he says, "Great," and you're fooled. But in the meantime you think he's going to kick you.

Larry handed him this mess of papers. I felt sorry for Dick because Dick tried to read it. Larry said, "Go on, read it. Yeah, yeah, try." Dick finally handed back the papers and said, "Larry, there's nothing on them, you know that." Larry shrugged. "Well, we can do it later."

He really invented the word "hooky." I think he just played hooky, like a schoolboy. It was a question of the school principal telling him what to do and he just couldn't stand doing it. Larry hated work and yet he loved the theatre and loved the play once it was on.

When he was working on *Pal Joey*, he called me up. He knew how I loved his lyrics. I was mad about them. You know, "Couldn't sleep until I could sleep where I shouldn't sleep." He howled with laughter as he sang those lyrics over the phone. It was enchanting.

Just before the war we did *By Jupiter*. Larry was seldom there. He just kind of appeared once in a while. We just had to go on without him. But finally Dick said, "I just can't do this without the ballad." Somehow he got to Larry and Larry came and finished the song right there

with Dick. He'd written a marvelous song, "Wait Till You See Her." Unfortunately, we found it almost impossible to stage. The right person wasn't there to sing it. But we pushed it in because we loved the song. After the show opened in New York, we took it out. It didn't belong in it.

I think his being so very small had a lot to do with his writing those bittersweet lyrics, but I never discussed it with him. I am positive, though, that Larry found himself a romantic figure, embarrassingly ugly, dwarfed. Everything he did was related to that. I think he was mad about Vivienne Segal. Mad about her. He may have been mad about others. I think that the drinking and the disappearing was all a kind of escape. He never accepted any social engagements, ever. I don't think he wanted anybody to point and say, "There's Larry Hart." It's so touching, it's so pitiful. And yet it's an emotion that causes writers to write. Yet I never heard him complain, except about Dick making him work. I never heard him say one personal thing about himself, though I was at his apartment many times, in many bars and hotels during the times we worked together. He seemed to save everything for the songs.

Conferring over their newest project at Dinty Moore's: (clockwise) George Balanchine, Larry, Josh Logan, Bob Alton (who later choreographed *Pal Joey)*, Dwight Wyman and Dick.

1938

I Married an Angel

*Opened May 11, 1938, at the Shubert Theatre
for a run of 338 performances*

Music by Richard Rodgers
Book by Lorenz Hart and Richard Rodgers, from a play by
    James Vasarzy
Directed by Joshua Logan
Choreographed by George Balanchine
Settings by Jo Mielziner
Costumes by John Hambleton

Spring Is Here*

{ *Originally sung by Dennis King and
    Vivienne Segal* }

VERSE

Once there was a thing called spring,
When the world was writing
Verses like yours and mine.
All the lads and girls would sing
When we sat at little tables
And drank May wine.
Now April, May and June
Are sadly out of tune.
Life has stuck the pin in the balloon.

REFRAIN

Spring is here!
Why doesn't my heart go dancing?
Spring is here!
Why isn't the waltz entrancing?
No desire,
No ambition leads me.
Maybe it's because
Nobody needs me.
Spring is here!
Why doesn't the breeze delight me?
Stars appear!
Why doesn't the night invite me?
Maybe it's because
Nobody loves me.
Spring is here, I hear!

* Larry actually wrote two songs called "Spring Is Here." The
first was in the 1929 show *Spring Is Here*. But the second, and more
famous, was this one, from *I Married an Angel*.

At the Roxy Music Hall

{ *Originally sung by Audrey Christie* }

VERSE

You've got to come to New York.
It would be such a pity
For anyone to go through life
Without seeing Roxy City!
The first thing foreigners do in New York
Is to look at Roxy City!

1st REFRAIN

Come with me
And you won't believe a thing you see.
Where an usher puts his heart in what he ushes,
Where a fountain changes color when it gushes,
Where the seats caress your carcass with their plushes,
At the Roxy Music Hall.
Hold my hand,
Don't be frightened when you hear that band:
They come up, like Ali Baba from the cellar,
Through the courtesy of Mr. Rockefeller.
Then they play the overture from "William Tell"-er,
At the Roxy Music Hall.
You don't have to read the ads.
It's always worth the dough.
Any week you go,
It's the same old show!
Don't be shy
If a naked statue meets your eye.
Where the ballet is so sweet with birds and roses,
That you break out in a rash before it closes,
At the Roxy Music Hall.

2nd REFRAIN

Step this way
Hear the super-duper organ play.
Where the stage goes up and down when they begin it.
Where they change the lights a hundred times a minute.
It's a wonder Mrs. Roosevelt isn't in it,
At the Roxy Music Hall.
Come along,
Hear them sing a "Volga Boatman" song.
Where the acrobats are whirling on their digits,
Where the balcony's so high you get the fidgets,
Where the actors seem to be a lot of midgets,
At the Roxy Music Hall.
If you're lost while climbing up
And find the going hard,
They are on their guard:
They send a Saint Bernard!
Come with me
Where the drinking cups are always free.
It's a Wonderland where ev'ryone is Alice,
Where the ladies' room is bigger than a palace,
At the Roxy Music Hall!

The Angel of *I Married an Angel* was one of the most beautiful stars ever to appear on Broadway—Vera Zorina. Dennis King, her handsome leading man, sang "Spring Is Here," the show's love song, and the song most closely associated with Larry. Zorina and King were a romantic sensation, but the romance wasn't a real-life one: during the show's run, Balanchine and Zorina were married.

Marcella Wallace

A good friend of Larry's, Teddy's and mine, Marcella Wallace was a contributing writer to Dell and Fawcett Publications in the thirties. Her remarks here bring back the New York of that day, and the stars we all had in our eyes then. For Marcella, a girl from North Dakota, the Stork Club (where Larry frequently threw his Sunday night parties) was an incredible place. Especially when Sherman Billingsley sent over perfume and magnums of champagne, and Tallulah was talking your ear off, and Ethel Merman was sparkling in a corner, and a handsome Vernon Duke was flirting with a sixteen-year-old Wynn Murray—two hundred pounds of loveliness.

The first time I went to Larry's home, the apartment surpassed my expectations of glamour, even for New York. The scene was *gemütlich*, with Mrs. Hart senior making motherly inquiries as to the progress of the decoration in Dorothy Hart's new apartment and the maid, Mary, passing things on a tray.

Then Larry entered. Some people come into a room. Some make an entrance. Without trying, Larry was one of those people who generate excitement in a room when they open the door.

What I remember is his eyes, rapt, brilliant with a sort of triumph.

"I've just finished it," he said. "Do you want to hear it?" Then, half singing, half reciting, mouthing each word as if it were something precious, he started: "Have you heard, I married an angel . . .'"

I knew I was in the presence of greatness and that I was experiencing a moment I would never forget. A creative artist in his excited realization of a conception.

The next morning in the Fawcett fan-magazine office, I mentioned that I had heard a new Larry Hart lyric, sung by Larry Hart himself. There was respectful attention. Even my editor was (temporarily) respectful. Then questions: What was he like? Someone said, "He's a short man, isn't he?" I was indignant. "Of course not. Teddy's the short one! Larry's tall!" "Tall?" "Well—maybe average. . . .'"

I believed I was telling the truth. Later, seeing Larry, I realized that he *was* short. But in his presence, like many of the people who knew him, I was always too conscious of his stature to be really aware of his height.

Larry's Sunday night parties at the Stork Club captured all the glamour of the era—celebrities, debutantes, fun people, music and laughter. The evening's feature was the balloon dance. In the middle of a dance, the music stopped and the gentlemen were asked to leave the dance floor. Then colorful balloons filled the air, each with the promise of a prize on a slip of paper inside. While the swing orchestra swung, the girls vied with each other to gather as many balloons as possible. Larry's eyes sparkled with delight when we used to return to the table with our booty—perfume, cards for free dinners, liquor. . . . Once, when Dorothy came back

triumphantly bearing a bottle of a famous champagne, Larry was overwhelmed. "Why, Dorothy! That's wonderful!" He seemed as admiring of her accomplishment as if she'd grown, picked and pressed the grapes with her own hands. I couldn't understand his enthusiasm—after all, his check at the end of the evening would pay for quite a few bottles of vintage wine. But later I understood. Money was an abstraction that Larry could never quite grasp. It was the things money bought that were important. It was fun to buy things, but greater fun to win them, and the greatest fun of all was to have someone he cared for be the winner. He was a giver.

It was Larry's couldn't-care-less attitude toward money that led, eventually, to a business manager whose money attitude was, quite properly, couldn't-care-more. And this, in turn, led to a game of Larry's called Running Away From Kron. Mr. Kron, the business manager, was a seemingly meek accountant type, who scanned a check efficiently, laughed a little too loudly at Larry's wisecracks—the laughter seemed loudest when his blank look revealed that he hadn't got the point, which at times was just as well. He had the habit of appearing at Larry's early in the evening with some business matter to discuss, and to join whatever party might be on the program later.

It became a challenge to Larry to leave before Mr. Kron appeared. "Kron!" Larry would cry out suddenly, and drinks would be set down, there would be a scramble for wraps, and out! Sometimes Mr. Kron was encountered in the hall, and then Larry would always invite him to join the group; sensitive himself, Larry could never deliberately hurt anybody's feelings. But often the exodus was successful, and then Larry's eyes would sparkle with the mischievous triumph of a small boy who had eluded the truant officer.

Larry in a night club, during the late thirties.

Teddy (way over on left) re-creating his hilarious role as the impish tinhorn in the movie of *Three Men on a Horse*. Sitting is Frank McHugh; next to him Sam Levene and Allen Jenkins.

When I met Teddy in 1935, I was a struggling writer, and Teddy was an actor-comedian who had been in vaudeville with Jimmy Cagney and knocked around in half a dozen other vaudeville skits. Once Teddy, who was about to be booked into the Palace, was replaced by a very youthful Phil Silvers. Teddy had also toured with the road company of *The Gingham Girl*, a hit musical; then he returned to vaudeville in a two-act with a woman who remained his partner for as long as booking in the small-time was available. There were a couple of Broadway flops in between.

In 1934 Teddy completed a comedy role in Paramount's *Million Dollar Legs*, starring W.C. Fields, which has since become a comedy classic. At this time Teddy met Alex Yokel, who was trying to get *Three Men on a Horse* produced on Broadway. Yokel told Teddy there was a good part in it for him, and when George Abbott showed a serious interest in the play, Teddy went on to New York and fought his way into the cast.

Sam Levene had a friend he was secretly rehearsing in Teddy's part, and when Teddy used Larry's famous habit of rubbing his hands together as part of his "Frankie" characterization, Sam complained, "What are you doing that for? You crazy or something?" But Teddy wasn't crazy. He was a very good actor, as well as an excellent comedian, and he got the part and made a smash hit with the audiences and critics. Mervyn LeRoy signed him to repeat his role in the Warner screen production, along with Sam, and Warners picked up his option for the following year. Teddy did *After the Thin Man* on loan to MGM, and some minor productions.

At the end of 1936, Teddy and I drove back to New York with the idea that we would be married when finances permitted. George Abbott had already contacted Teddy for *Room Service*, which turned out to be an even greater smash, and Teddy in the meantime had received the Screen Actors Guild award for best supporting performance. But he was far happier on Broadway. He never liked working in front of the camera. He needed the reaction of live audiences.

We had decided to marry during the run of *Room Service*, in January 1938, instead of waiting until March as planned. Teddy would tell his former girlfriend (who had been the straight woman in his act for so many years) that their relationship was ended. I knew that Teddy had strong sentiments for the woman who had struggled with him for years to build up a small-time act, and he was reluctant to break the news to her that we were to be married shortly. We decided that we would be married without fanfare at City Hall and that then as a *fait accompli* one of us would tell her.

We had taken an apartment in a new building on West Fifty-fifth Street. Teddy wasn't as bound to the old neighborhood on the Upper West Side as Larry. We had no furniture, but as his wedding present, Larry had retained Dorothy Rodgers, Dick's wife, as decorator. But it would take several months for her to complete the furnishings. We decided that Teddy would go back to Larry's apartment that night and I would stay at what was to be our home, sleeping on an army cot that I had purchased at Rexall's. We got married in the morning, and I met Teddy at the theatre after his show that evening. Following our usual routine, we went to Ralph's for dinner. Then we parted, Teddy taking a cab to Larry's apartment. Larry asked him, "Where's Dorothy?" Teddy explained and Larry said in indignation, "How can you leave your wife alone in an apartment? Don't you know that's dangerous? Go right back to her."

That was like Larry. Though I was well into my twenties and had lived alone for ever so many years, Larry was proper and old-fashioned about family affairs. So Teddy came "home" and spent his first night of marriage on the floor! The next day we bought a sofa bed for two. Some weeks later there was an item in the paper to the effect that Teddy had forgotten he was married and had gone back to his old home! Teddy had his absent-minded moments, but he never, in our thirty-four years together, forgot for a moment that he was a married man. He was the responsible, not the forgetful, one. He had the Harts' concern with family.

One time Teddy and I wanted to give Larry a party in the beautiful apartment he was so proud of and

In 1937, Larry and Dick gave Hollywood one more try, to work on a picture with Mervyn LeRoy of *I Am a Fugitive* fame. LeRoy is the tough guy with the cigar in this picture. The movie, *Fools for Scandal*, was to have featured Ethel Merman and a complete Rodgers and Hart score. Instead, it had Carole Lombard and Fernand Gravet, and almost no songs at all!

that Dorothy Rodgers had decorated for us. I told him to draw up a list of the people he wanted to attend, and he did. Then he gave me a list of Bender's friends as well. Then day after day he called and added more names. At week's end I found myself in a difficult position. There were hundreds of names and we had a three-room apartment, and knowing Larry, I knew that by the actual date of the event there would be dozens more unfamiliar faces pouring in. Not until the very night of the affair would Larry end his "Come to the Party" routine.

It was an embarrassment. Larry's duplex could hold an expanded guest list, but neither our little flat nor our pocketbook could include everybody. So I called the party off, to Larry's obvious disappointment. Had I been older and more experienced in playing the hostess, I would have said, "Come one, come all," opened the door to the hall, and let everyone take care of himself. But never having been hostess to more than a few dinner guests, I was terrified. Too bad. Larry loved parties if he was the host, or almost the host. I know now what little difference it would have made to have had wall-to-wall people. Larry's pride and delight would have made it all memorable.

Frieda, without Max, ran her household just as she had for fifty years. From brownstone to brownstone, from penthouse to the Beresford, from the Beresford to the Ardsley, a man came twice weekly to wind the grandfather's clock in the foyer. During the warm months, slipcovers went over the upholstered furniture, the drapes were taken down by Mr. Seligman, the drapery man, and the rugs were taken up and stored for the duration. The result was a drab, away-for-the-summer look, which Larry protested each summer, to no avail. Since the warm months were usually new-production time, it was Larry's stay-at-home time. But Frieda remained unruffled. This had been her routine for all these years; this was the way nice, respectable homes were run. This was her security in the world she lived in with her unpredictable son.

Frieda's maid, black Mary, had come as a young girl from Jamaica to the Hart family when they were living at 119th Street. She was taught to cook German style and was expected to ignore the good-natured jibes of Max and Larry and remain calm in the midst of the constant tempests that shook Max's business and Larry's theatre world. That her good nature remained constant and her loyalty to the Harts undiminished made her a member of the family from the beginning, and when her attractive daughter, Lillie, came of age, she went to work for the Harts, too.

Mary's rise-and-shine eye-opener was the inevitable "Get up, Mr. Larry, Mr. Teddy, you bums, time for dinner already." When they were long into their thirties, to Mary they were still "the boys." To Frieda, any man who slept late was a "bum." Teddy insisted piously, after years of non-jobs, that a man who worked wasn't a "bum," and that all show people slept late. Teddy was as much of a night owl as Larry, and since sharing a bedroom with Larry meant that even a late-night sleep was interrupted by Larry's conversational ramblings, and his readings with the full light on, sleeping late, Teddy felt, was the privilege of the working (or for that matter nonworking) actor. And Frieda always remained awake until both her boys were ready for bed and had joined her in her room for a little chat and a good-night kiss.

Life at Frieda's was routine, though Larry begged to be surprised some night with a dinner that hadn't been served on a given night practically all his lifetime: Monday sweetbreads, Tuesday pot roast, Wednesday sauerbraten, etc., etc., and chicken every Sunday. Only Uncle Willie and Aunt Rachen showed up for the chicken-every-Sunday meal, which was served exactly at 1 P.M. despite the fact that Larry wasn't even up at that hour, nor were we. Even if there were only three at the table, Frieda continued to prepare enough food for a large family. She never gave up hope that we would one of these days assemble for her favorite meal.

Sunday the young cousins would drop by with a friend or two. Larry enjoyed them as much as they loved spending the afternoon with him—laughing at his stories, trading show-business gossip. He took a special interest in them, and his enthusiasm inspired them all to go into the theatre in some capacity. Around

Take It from Mary, Now, She Can Give the Low-Down on High-Ups in Stage and Film World, and Say, Does She Tell 'em?—and How!

She had to have the broom handy to use on Tyrone Power to keep him out of the kitchen.

Mary sees that Mr. Hart drinks his coffee. Richard Rodgers (at top), Mr. Hart's side-kick, stays home every night. "He's married."

Fannie Brice (above) brought around Josephine Baker, who Mary told to "talk out of the mouth, like you were born."

Lorenzo Hart's Mighty Maid Sketched Into Play and That Roused Her.

Bellows and shouts and "Get up, Mr. Lorenz, you, somebody to see you." Then Lorenz Hart, black with the night's beard, swathed in a black bathrobe, came out and revealed it all.

Hard behind him was the maid, Mary Campbell, buxom, powerful, six inches above the satyr of songwriters. And it was then that Mr. Hart admitted his maid ran he house.

Mary Campbell has a new prescription for success for Mr. Hart this time—and a new way for getting rid of Dr. Milton Bender. Dr. Bender's the ex-dentist who swallowed stage dust and now handles a theatrical agency.

"Mr. Lorenz just isn't Mr. Lorenz any more," said Mary. "He stays out with Dr. Bender all night long, and Dr. Bender, he just eats and eats. He brings Mr. Hart in at 3 in the morning, and they're right for the icebox.

"But I fix them. Now I take all the meat out every night. I bring it into my room. I lock the door, and I open the window and I put the meat on the windowsill. And they can bang and bang—all they want."

Life with the Harts after nineteen years—Lorenz; his brother,

Teddy; their mother, Frieda—has unfitted Mary, in her opinion, ever to work for anybody else.

She said it was Mr. Hart's father who turned her to drink, and she a churchgoer and the parish needing a new church up in Harlem, too.

Now she imbibes a rye highball, one and no more, every party. More makes her sleepy. One, Mr. Hart's father being the citation, keeps the cold out of your lungs.

The Harts' guests never fail to plague Mary. There was Tyrone Power out in Hollywood. Mary had to keep the broom out for him. "I have to chase Mr. Power out of the kitchen all the time; he's always after sandwiches. They don't eat in California—just sandwiches and bread."

Mary's reluctant to tell this one now, but the Harts always had counselled her to be forthright. One day she concluded a certain French actor was a pennypincher.

That one took place in Hollywood, too. The actor ignored Mary when he departed, and it had been a considerable stay. She flounced out right after him. She gave him a quarter.

Josephine Baker earned Mary's disapproval another time. Last Follies, Fannie Brice brought the Parisienne hit-ette to the Hart domicile, and Miss Baker pulled a "cafe avec lait, s'il vous plait" on Mary.

"Talk out of the mouth, like you you were born," bellowed Mary.

Phillips Holmes once helped Mary in Hollywood when Mary decided Mr. Hart should be bedded. Mr.

"Kind of Man I Want I Don't Get," and Vice Versa, She Says.

Holmes offered his services, and they stove Mr. Hart into bed.

Mr. Hart didn't like the idea. He kicked and Mr. Holmes grabbed a leg to blanket him down. Mary grabbed another. The one Mary seized turned out to be Mr. Holmes's.

"Hey," shouted Mr. Holmes. "I'm not going to bed."

Mary hadn't thought of that one. But it gave her an inspiration. She finished up Mr. Hart and then started to bed Mr. Holmes. Luckily he escaped.

Moss Hart, one visitor to the menage, wrote Mary into the character of the maid in "You Can't Take It with You." He endowed her with an illicit lover.

That's one thing Mary never has forgiven. She hasn't seen the play, doesn't expect to. "I don't have no man," she protested. "The kind I want I don't get; the kind that want me I don't want."

Lorenz Hart, she thinks, would be a better man if he got married. Take his sidekick, Richard Rodgers. Mr. Rodgers stays home every night. Explained Mary:—"He's married."

"I couldn't work for anybody but the Harts," said Mary. "Once I worked two weeks for a friend of Mrs. Hart, Sam Briskin. I couldn't stand it. It was quiet."

Mary, telling it like it is, to the New York *World Telegram* in 1937.

seven o'clock we would enter the dining room for Larry's favorite meal: sturgeon from Barney Greengrass, "the sturgeon king," and delicatessen from the Tip Toe Inn. It was the most relaxed time, dinner family-style, with Larry presiding as head of the household.

It had often been said that Larry didn't care where he lived. Wrong. True, the Beresford, at 211 Central Park West, where Larry had moved after Max's death, was on the "wrong" side of Central Park. But it was where Larry enjoyed living. The West Side was more convenient to the theatre district, and nothing could mean less than status to Larry. And the Beresford was perhaps the leading apartment house on the West Side and had some distinguished tenants.

Larry did love luxury and all its comforts. All the furniture in the apartment was custom-made in Belgium, and the rugs were hand-loomed, and the dining room had a hand-carved chest from Spain. The apartment included a large den, whose four walls were brick-lined. There was a large bedroom he shared with Teddy. (His devotion to his brother was evidenced by the fact that until Teddy married, they slept in adjoining beds in the same room.) Frieda Hart had a splendid room, and there was a tremendous maid's room, where Mary reigned. (In 1936, Moss Hart increased Mary's fame by making her a character in his play *You Can't Take It with You*.)

People also said that Larry didn't care what he wore. In all the time I knew Larry, his suits and overcoats were made to order. Ruby the shirtmaker, who catered to the profession, made up Larry's shirts with initialed sleeves, and his shorts, and his pajamas with the Peter Pan collars that made him look like a twelve-year-old. He purchased pure Irish linen handkerchiefs at $120 per dozen, which he never kept long enough to be laundered, though once a week a laundress did his personal laundry at the apartment. He usually left the apartment dressed meticulously and beautifully groomed. But because of his nervous mannerisms, and his habit of pacing back and forth, sitting down, jumping up and running a hand over his wisps of hair, he managed a rumpled and untidy look sometimes. At home, Larry remained in pajamas most

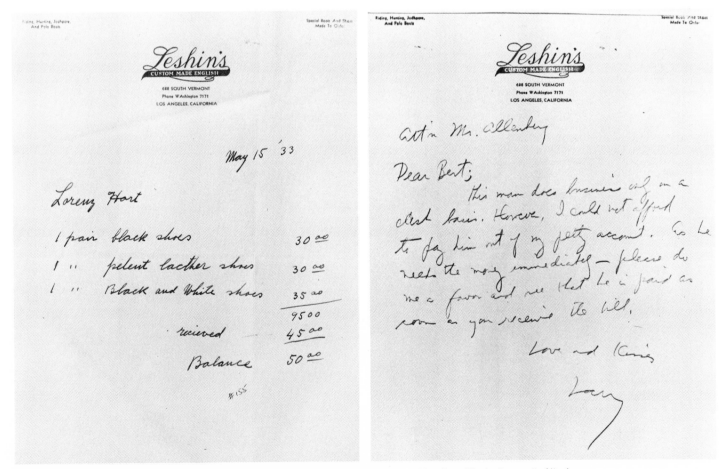

A bill from one of Larry's elegant custom shoemakers, and a frantic note from Larry asking Bert Allenby to pay it. Allenby was Larry's business manager before William Kron.

of the day. He made a scruffy, far from glamorous figure. Despite his made-to-order wardrobe, he somehow never got around to a dressy bathrobe. His bathrobes were the old-fashioned horse-blanket type, flopping loosely, revealing the Peter Pan pajamas. Though he liked to order expensive clothes, he seemed to have no vanity, and if he caught an accidental glimpse of himself in a mirror, he made a face of disapproval if not outright disgust. Looking at his reflection was not one of his favorite things. But dressed up on his way to keeping an appointment, he could primp and fix his pocket handkerchief just so, and pat his freshly shaven cheeks with some approval and leave the apartment standing straight if not tall, for the moment not too dissatisfied with his appearance.

Baldness overtook Larry when he was not yet thirty. Without going to the extreme of donning weird contraptions in an attempt to defy heredity (Max Hart had also lost his hair early), Larry went in for extensive and expensive hair treatments, year after year. With unquenchable optimism, he'd rush home after each visit to the scalp specialist, trying to convince everyone that a bit of fuzz here and there on his scalp was new hair growth. Couldn't we see where the hair was growing back? Indeed we couldn't, but who had the heart to tell him so? To Larry, becoming bald was one more minus in his negative feeling about his appearance. (Teddy kept all his hair throughout his lifetime.)

Meanwhile, every Friday afternoon Frieda had her ladies' day penny poker session. It had been the cause of much hilarity between Teddy and Larry, especially when she said, as she was frequently heard to say, in her gentle but firm voice, "Ladies, this is the *last* time." The "last time" had been going on for fifty years. The ladies were now a little blind, a little deaf, and a little addled. (Teddy had once made a recording mimicking his mother and her familiar remark. Larry, impish as always, would play it loud and clear in the next room while the game was going on, infuriating Frieda.)

Frieda liked her poker, but Larry's card game was pinochle. Sam, the barber from the Dawn Patrol (the twenty-four-hour barbershop next door to the Stage delicatessen), made his daily visit to the Hart household late in the afternoon. He would give Larry a very close shave (though a few hours later Larry looked as though he hadn't shaved for days), then a light facial and possibly a hair trim. After that, Larry and Sam would have their pinochle game. Cards were relaxing to Larry, but he wasn't a gambler. Teddy tried to get him interested in the five-and ten-cent poker games we had at our apartment once in a while, but he went back to solitaire, gin, pinochle and hearts. Whenever I played with them, he had great fun with hearts. Doc Bender and Larry would try to give me the Black Maria card, the queen of spades. He had made up a silly little rhyme beginning "Little Dorothea," which he sang in his cracked voice with childish glee as he knocked me out of the game. Often, when he was working on a show or lyric problem, he played solitaire for hours. But despite his great concentration on the game, I could almost see his mind working.

There were often times when Larry would play operatic records on his Capehart. He would sit hour after hour listening with enjoyment and pleasure. There might be half a dozen people in the living room, and when Larry played the Capehart, after a few minutes Frieda would tiptoe to her room to read her German novels. After an hour most everyone else in the room would be sleeping, more or less silently, but I would be wide awake, sitting next to Larry while he explained, with that special enthusiasm he had, the libretto of the operas, delighted that I shared his appreciation.

Lots of people thought that Larry never ate out anywhere but Ralph's, or Bergen's on West Forty-fifth Street, but that's not so. His favorite dining place was Dinty Moore's, and I went very often with him to Tony's, which was an intimate literary hangout where I was thrilled to meet Vincent Sheean and many top writers of the day. Other places he liked were Henri Soule's Le Pavillon and many, many times he ate at Sardi's and Reuben's.

One night when Teddy was on the road, Larry and I had gone to Reuben's. At about 2:30 A.M., we were suddenly embraced by Humphrey Bogart and his then wife, Mayo. They were a bedraggled pair, but, still laughing and drinking, they told us, "Larry, the Algonquin has just thrown us out on our ass! At this hour. And all because we painted our room black and had a few little fights! We haven't checked into anyplace else yet. Have a drink . . . ."

As a Bogey fan, I was aflutter. Surely Larry would invite them up to his place. Or since Teddy was on the road, perhaps I could invite the battling Bogarts to spend the night with me! But I hadn't reckoned with a very sober, very dignified Larry. He nudged me, all the while edging me to the back of the restaurant, so that before I knew it we had left Bogey and his mate. Larry could be surprising when he wasn't drinking, even a bit aloof, and sometimes not at all gregarious or even friendly.

But Larry's drinking problems had, sadly, already begun. I knew that if Larry was on the wagon, I was supposed to ask him if he wanted a drink as the liquor was passed around, so that it could be his privilege to turn it down. He was strangely sensitive about being on the wagon.

Whatever his problems, Larry could sleep. He often slept through all the activities going on in every part of the apartment, which at this time was at the Ardsley on West Ninety-second Street. Sometimes there would be his business manager, William Kron, right next to him, placing bets on the races over the telephone with Larry's chauffeur. Larry's semiconscious form didn't seem to bother anyone drifting in and out of the room. But the den was an enormous room with an even larger terrace. An uncomfortable sleeping couch in one corner was Larry's bed. The marvelous wall-to-wall bookcases that had been in his previous apartment at the Beresford had not been moved to the Ardsley. Dorothy Rodgers was the interior decorator of the new apartment, but had neglected to build space for his hundreds of books. They remained on the landing outside the room in their moving cartons for a long time.

Larry, Teddy and I at the premiere of the movie of *Three Men on a Horse* in New Jersey. The other two men are the theatre owners.

Larry was the only theatrical personality I have ever known not to have mementos of the famous people he worked with on the walls of his den. There was a large pencil sketch of Larry over the fireplace, a famous photograph of Teddy from *Three Men on a Horse* over the bed.

Barbra Streisand has the apartment today. Even though Larry lived in it over thirty years ago, she still boasts that it is Larry Hart's apartment.

There have been so many press-agented versions of how Rodgers and Hart happened to do *The Boys from Syracuse* that I think I should explain it for the record. Teddy was constantly being mistaken for Jimmy Savo, though Savo was slightly taller and heavier, but often when we went out it was always "Thank you, Mr. Savo," "Good night, Mrs. Savo." One Monday night, after we had spent the previous Sunday evening at the Stork Club, I said to Larry, "How can anyone see any resemblance between Teddy and Savo? At the Stork Club everybody kept calling Teddy Mr. Savo. Do you see any resemblance?" Larry nodded his head. "A little. . . ." Then you could see those wheels turning. "When Teddy had his vaudeville act he did work like Savo. . . ." And that did it. To Larry, a Shakespearean nut since childhood, the Dromios from *The Comedy of Errors* was an immediate inspiration.

During the first rehearsal days of *The Boys from Syracuse* Larry's chauffeur frequently interrupted Larry's concentration on the show's action to give him a race by race report on the horses. It was as though, when Larry reached the age of forty-three, he needed this diversion. It certainly wasn't any gambling fever. He never bet more than a couple of hundred dollars on an afternoon's races. The astonishment I showed while watching Larry conferring with his chauffeur made Larry laugh, as he usually did when confronted with some bizarre behavior on his part. The racing interest seemed to be some extra excitement or stimulation that he was after. I wondered if his work in the theatre was finally becoming merely a routine and too predictable.

Larry and Dick, in Baltimore, October 27, 1939, toasting the success of the out-of-town tryout of *I'd Rather Be Right*. They were right to have such high hopes—even if the show did require Noël Coward to come in and help rewrite some of the book.

Shortly after *I Married an Angel* opened, *The New Yorker* ran a marvelous two-part "profile" of Rodgers and Hart. The author, Margaret Case Harriman, told a story about Larry raising the roof when a hotel newsstand in Khartoum didn't have the latest issue of *Variety*. The above caricature is by *New Yorker* artist William Auerbach Levy.

Was it the theatre itself in which he was losing interest? I attended many shows with him during that time and he rarely remained for the second act and I, of course, dutifully followed. The following year, I don't know that he was drinking more, but he certainly was handling it less well. Too, his eating was sporadic and he was beginning to show signs of malnutrition. At times he was forgetful and vague and had blackouts. He would occasionally allude to these breakdowns, but showed little concern otherwise.

During the second week of rehearsals of *Syracuse*, Larry developed pneumonia. He was ill at home for some weeks, but when a persistent spot remained in one lung, he was sent to the hospital for a week. Convalescing at home was no problem, as Larry was so involved with taking his temperature every hour or so, he didn't seem to miss the *Syracuse* rehearsals. But he was visibly upset when a recitative accompanying a Balanchine ballet was eliminated by Dick Rodgers, especially as Teddy was the narrator. But he calmed down after a bit, and shrugged. After he got better, his physician insisted he go to Florida with Frieda to convalesce further. He spent several weeks there at the Roney Plaza, his favorite Miami spot. His recovery was without incident, except that for another year he continued obsessively to take his temperature every few hours.

But because of his drinking and because of the other problems, it was decided, after a family conference, that I should try to get Larry to enter Doctors Hospital, where he would be admitted as a volunteer patient. (Larry never admitted that he was in any way an alcoholic. He insisted he could stop drinking whenever he wanted to.) When the hospital was mentioned to him, Larry didn't shout me down as I had anticipated. He agreed to go for a week or so, if we could get him the doctor who had treated his pneumonia. That Larry agreed to enter a hospital for any kind of treatment of this nature was a turning point, we felt. Larry's doctor was out of town, but I contacted a young doctor who had treated Larry from time to time and thus began Larry's short stays at Doctors Hospital. They were not long enough to do him any real good. Just a week or so though, at least then he received proper food and care. But too often, he left before he was discharged.

DOROTHY   HART

v11 Cent I'll WKST   December 14. 1938.

Dear Mel:

My sister- in- law is writing for me, as I'm still not quite up and around. Have been ill with pneumonia for the past couple of months. Spent a couple of weeks in the hospital, and am in the convalescent stage. A small spot on my lungs is clearing up nicely. A month or so in Miami should fix me up. I think I will leave sometime next week. Mama is coming along-- don't know yet whether I'll take a nurse along.

Teddy says to tell you he always knew you couldn't keep a steady job. We read in one of the trade papers that you were leaving for England soon. True? Of course, you must stop with us if you get East. Our new show, "Syracuse" is a smash hit. Great for Teddy. I'm getting my first peek at it Saturday matinee. I took sick while it was in rehearsal, you know.

Have you made any plans yet? We read something about Rosita's South American

tour and were glad to hear it was so successful Our love to you both. ama has been under such a strain, she doesn t feel up to writing you just yet. So this will do for us both.

Regards,

Larry

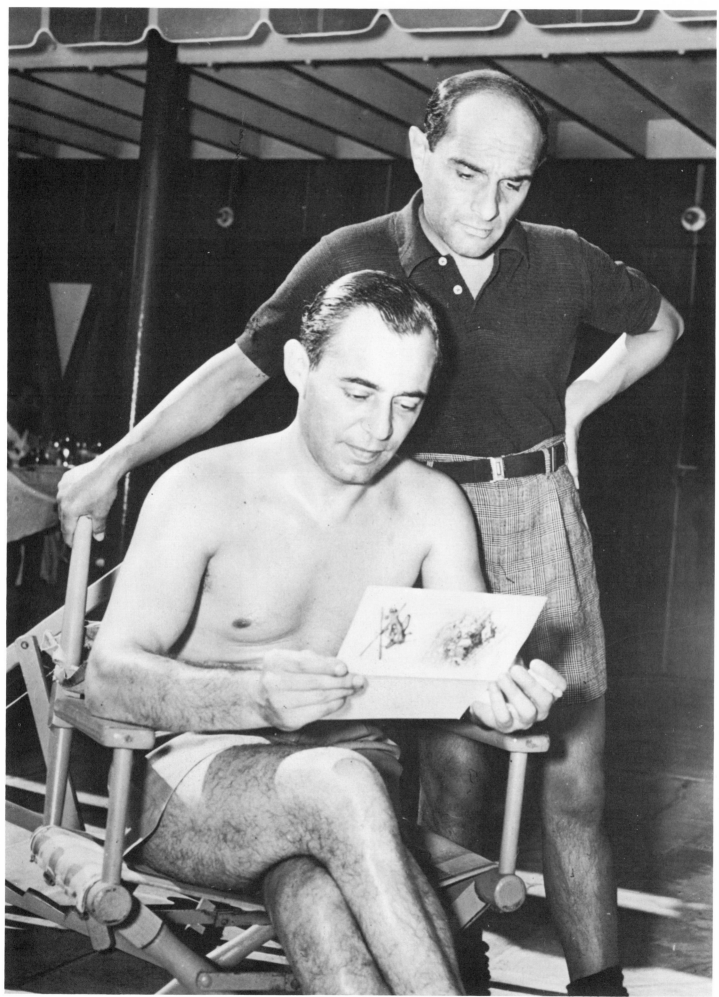

Larry and Dick by the pool at the Roney Plaza.

TIME

The Weekly Newsmagazine

Paul Dorsey

Volume XXXII

MR. RODGERS AND MR. HART
"If it's good enough for Shakespeare, it's good enough for us."
(See THEATRE)

Number 13

1938 was a big year for the ever-rising reputation of Rodgers and Hart. After *I Married an Angel* and *The New Yorker*'s profile came *The Boys from Syracuse* and the cover of *Time. Time* called Larry and Dick "the U.S. Gilbert and Sullivan" and "the Boys from Columbia." It was quite an honor.

1938

The Boys from Syracuse

*Opened November 23, 1938, at the Alvin Theatre
for a run of 236 performances*

Music by Richard Rodgers
Book by George Abbott
Directed by George Abbott
Choreographed by George Balanchine
Settings by Jo Mielziner
Costumes by Irene Sharaff

I Had Twins

*{ Originally sung by Bob Lawrence, Carroll Ashburn
and John O'Shaughnessy }*

Crowd:	Ha-raa, ha-roo—
	There'll be an execution.
	It serves him right.
	The law makes retribution.
	There's going to be a killing.
	Ha-raa, ha-roo—
	It serves him right.
	Ha-raa, ha-roo—
	What did he do?
Policeman:	He came from Syracuse.
Crowd:	No, no, no.
Policeman:	Yes, yes, yes.
	So let him plead,
	For what's the use?
	That man's from Syracuse.
	The man's from Syracuse.
Duke:	He dies tomorrow at sundown.
	Our rigid laws of Ephesus
	Most rightfully refuse
	A visa to any citizen
	Of uncivilized Syracuse.
	If any one of us would dare to go
	To that barbaric city
	He'd get the ax the same as he—
	That's why he gets no pity.
Crowd:	Give him the ax, the ax, the ax—
	Give him the ax, the ax.
Duke:	Unless he can pay a thousand marks.
Policeman:	Or borrow it from the local shark.
Duke:	Why did you come here?
Aegean:	I had twins.
Crowd:	He had twins.
	That's nothing much agin him.
	He had twins.
Policeman:	I never thought he had it in him—
	Ha, ha, ha, ha, ha.
Duke:	Is that why you came here?
Aegean:	I had twins who looked alike—
	Couldn't tell one from the other.
	They had two slaves who looked alike—
	Couldn't tell one from his brother.

	But on one unhappy day
	We went sailing on the sea.
	This was an unlucky blunder,
	For our ship was torn asunder—
	Just like that, just like that,
	Just like that, see.
	One young twin went down with me,
	One went swimming with his mother.
	We were parted by the sea,
	Man and wife and slave and brother.
	Now my one remaining brave boy
	Went a-searching with his slave boy.
	Having lost my sons and wife, too,
	I will gladly give my life, too—
	Just like that, just like that,
	Just like that, see.
	I have searched the isles of Greece
	From my home to far-off Samos.
	Didn't know your local laws—
	I am just an ignoramus.
	I am sinless, I am twinless,
	I am wifeless.
	I am glad to die.
Policeman:	He had twins.
	For them he'd give his life.
	He had twins,
	To say nothing of his wife.
	Ha-raa, ha-roo—
	There'll be an execution.
Crowd:	It serves him right.
Policeman:	The law makes retribution.
Crowd:	There's going to be a killing.
	Ha-raa, ha-roo—
	What did he do?
	He came from Syracuse.
	Yes, yes, yes. Yes, yes, yes.
	Yes, yes, yes.

A month before *The Boys from Syracuse* opened, the *Herald Tribune* ran this caricature of Larry, Dick and George Abbott conferring—where else?—at the Algonquin.

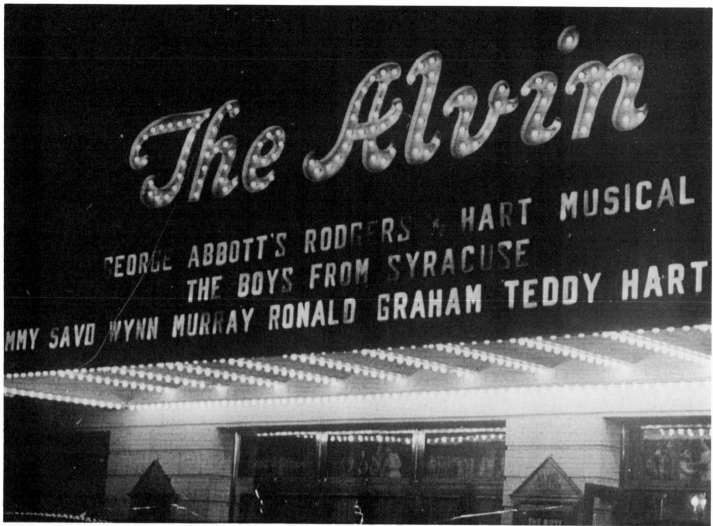

The marquee of the Alvin Theatre, during the *Syracuse* run. At first, there was trouble choosing a title for the show, so Larry, Dick and George Abbott decided to put the matter before the public, asking for their suggestions. Among the many titles offered (and declined) was *Wherefore Art Thou, Dromio?*

Dear Old Syracuse

{*Originally sung by Eddie Albert*}

VERSE

This is a terrible city.
The people are cattle and swine.
There isn't a girl I'd call pretty
Nor a friend that I'd call mine.
And the only decent place on earth
Is the town that gave me birth.

1st REFRAIN

You can keep your Athens,
You can keep your Rome.
I'm a hometown fellow
And I pine for home.
I wanna go back, go back
To dear old Syracuse.
Though I've worn out sandals
And my funds are low,
There's a light that's burning in the patio.
I wanna go back, go back
To dear old Syracuse.
It is no metropolis,
It has no big Acropolis,

And yet there is a quorum
Of cuties in the forum.
Though the boys wear tunics that are out of style,
They will always greet me with a friendly smile.
I wanna go back, go back
To dear old Syracuse.

2nd REFRAIN

I do not agree with Mr. Sparticus—
I was never meant to be a hearty cuss.
I wanna go back, go back
To dear old Syracuse.
When a man is lonely it is good to know
There's a red light burning in the patio.
I wanna go back, go back
To dear old Syracuse.
Wives don't want divorces there,
The men are strong as horses there,
But should a man philander,
The goose forgives the gander.
When the search for love becomes a mania
You can take the night boat to Albania.
I wanna go back, go back
To dear old Syracuse.

The Shortest Day of the Year

{ *Originally sung by Ronald Graham* }

REFRAIN

The shortest day of the year
Has the longest night of the year,
And the longest night
Is the shortest night with you.
The smallest smile on your face
Is the greatest kind of embrace,
And a single kiss
Is a thousand dreams come true.
Your softest sigh—
That is my strongest tie.
There's you, there's I.
What can time do?
The shortest day of the year
Has the longest night of the year.
And the longest night
Is the shortest night with you.

ALVIN THEATRE

ALVIN THEATRE CORP., OWNERS AND MANAGERS
250 WEST 52nd STREET

FIRE NOTICE: The exit, indicated by a red light and sign, nearest to the seat
you occupy, is the shortest route to the street.
In the event of fire or other emergency please do not run—WALK TO THAT EXIT.
JOHN J. McELLIGOTT, Fire Chief and Commissioner

THE · PLAYBILL · PUBLISHED · BY · THE · NEW · YORK · THEATRE · PROGRAM · CORPORATION

BEGINNING
MONDAY EVENING,
DECEMBER 19, 1938

MATINEES
WEDNESDAY AND
SATURDAY

George Abbott

Presents

THE BOYS FROM SYRACUSE

A musical comedy based on Shakespeare's "The Comedy of Errors"

Music by Richard Rodgers   Lyrics by Lorenz Hart

Book and Direction by George Abbott

Scenery and Lighting by Jo Mielziner   Choreography by George Balanchine

Costumes designed by Irene Sharaff

CAST
(In order of appearance)

SINGING POLICEMAN	*Played by*	BOB LAWRENCE
ANOTHER POLICEMAN	" "	JAMES WILKINSON
ANTIPHOLUS OF EPHESUS	" "	RONALD GRAHAM
DROMIO OF EPHESUS	" "	TEDDY HART
DANCING POLICEMAN	" "	GEORGE CHURCH
TAILOR	" "	CLIFFORD DUNSTAN
TAILOR'S APPRENTICE	" "	BURL IVES
ANTIPHOLUS OF SYRACUSE	" "	EDDIE ALBERT
DROMIO OF SYRACUSE	" "	JIMMY SAVO

THE PLAYBILL   37

MERCHANT OF SYRACUSE	*Played by*		BYRON SHORES
DUKE OF EPHESUS	"	"	CARROLL ASHBURN
AEGEON	"	"	JOHN O'SHAUGHNESSY
LUCE	"	"	WYNN MURRAY
ADRIANA	"	"	MURIEL ANGELUS
LUCIANA	"	"	MARCY WESCOTT
SORCERER	"	"	OWEN MARTIN
COURTEZAN	"	"	BETTY BRUCE
SECRETARY TO COURTEZAN	"	"	HEIDI VOSSELER
ASSISTANT COURTEZAN	"	"	DOLORES ANDERSON
ANGELO	"	"	JOHN CLARKE
1st MAID	"	"	FLORINE CALLAHAN
2nd MAID	"	"	CLAIRE WOLF
3rd MAID	"	"	ALICE CRAIG
MERCHANT OF EPHESUS	"	"	CLIFFORD DUNSTAN
SEERESS	"	"	FLORENCE FAIR

SINGERS: Grace Albert, Laura Kellogg, Dolores Anderson, Armonce Wilkins, Mar-
guerite Benton, Margaret Walsh, James Wilkinson, Joseph Scandur, Joe Granville,
Herbert Wood.

DANCERS: Libby Bennett, Ruth Brady, Renee Cettel, Stella Clausen, Alice Craig,
Bee Farnum, Ruth Gormly, Claire Harvey, Lita Lede, Connie Leslie, Vivien Moore,
Florine Callahan, Mildred Solly, Anna Mae Tesslo, Davenie Watson, Betty De
Elmo, Claire Wolf, Micky Alvarez, Sidney Gordon, Dan Karry, Tommy Lynch,
Jack Malis, Edwin Mills, Harry Peterson, Joe Harris, Lee Tannen, Beau Tilden,
Robert Howard.

This Can't Be Love

⊰ Originally sung by Eddie Albert and Marcy Westcott ⊱

1st VERSE

He: In Verona, my late cousin Romeo
Was three times as stupid as my Dromio.
For he fell in love
And then he died of it.
Poor half-wit!

REFRAIN

This can't be love
Because I feel so well—
No sobs, no sorrows, no sighs.
This can't be love,
I get no dizzy spell,
My head is not in the skies.
My heart does not stand still—
Just hear it beat!
This is too sweet
To be love.
This can't be love
Because I feel so well,
But still I love to look in your eyes.

2nd VERSE

She: Though your cousin loved my cousin Juliet
Loved her with a passion much more truly yet,
Some poor playwright
Wrote their drama just for fun.
It won't run!

COMIC REPRISE

⊰ Originally sung by Wynn Murray ⊱

This must be love
For I don't feel so well—
These sobs, these sorrows, these sighs.
This must be love,
Here comes that dizzy spell,
My head is up in the sky.
Just now my heart stood still—
It missed a beat!
Life is not sweet—
This is love.
This must be love
For I don't feel so well.
Alas, I love to look in your eyes.

He and She

⊰ Originally sung by Jimmy Savo and Wynn Murray ⊱

VERSE

She: I was I,
You were you,
And now we're only we.
We are one,
Who were two,
Or we had better be.

He: "I now pronounce you man and wife"
Are magic words like "Open Sesame."
She: But though they made you mine for life,
They also made you think much less of me.
He: It only shows how little you know of it.
She: I know a pair who made quite a go of it.

1st REFRAIN

She: He was a man who was very fond of women.
She was a girl who was very fond of men.
She had a taste for both corpulent and slim men.
He wouldn't look at a lady under ten.
She went abroad just to find a man to marry.
He went abroad just to find himself a wife.
She didn't want any Tom or Dick or Harry.
He sought a mate who'd be true to him for life.
She fell in love with the angle of his eyebrow.
He fell in love with the dimple on her knee.
And when they wed
He went around with other women
And she went with other men.
And that is he and she.

2nd REFRAIN

He: He always said, "I would like to have a daughter."
She always said, "I would like to have a son."
She took to kids like a duckling takes to water.
He always thought having babies would be fun.
He told her this on the very day he met her.
She said the wish is the father to the sport.
He bought a house, in the nursery he set her.
She helped the stork make his annual report.
He won renown as the father of a squadron.
She won awards for her prolificacy.
And just because,
And just because they loved their children
They got married after all.
And that is he and she.

3rd REFRAIN

He: She was as pure as the snow before it's driven.
She: He never smoked and he never touched a drop.
He: When she said "Boo" she would ask to be forgiven.
She: When he would swim he would always wear the top.
He: She wore no rouge though she had a bad complexion.
She: He always prayed ev'ry time he went to bed.
He: She was so kind that she hated vivisection.
She: He loved his ma and he swore he'd never wed.
He: She was so chaste that it made her very nervous.
She: He loved to go to the vicarage for tea.
Both: And when they died,
And when they died and went to heaven
All the angels moved to hell.
And that is he and she.

Dromio of Syracuse (Jimmy Savo, left) and Dromio of Ephesus (Teddy). Before the show opened, Larry told a magazine interviewer, "Teddy had to be star, and this is the first star part that ever fit him."

Come With Me

{ Originally sung by Ronald Graham,
Bob Lawrence and John Clarke }

VERSE

Come with me
Where the food is free,
Where the landlord never comes near you.
Be a guest in a house of rest,
Where the best of fellows can cheer you.
There's your own little room,
So cool, not too much light,
Where you're one man for whom
No wife waits up at night.
When day ends
You have lots of friends
Who will guard you well while you slumber.
Safe from battle and strife,
Safe from wind and gale,
Come with me to jail!

INTERLUDE

You never have to fetch the milk
Or walk the dog
At early morn.
There's no "Get up—you're late for work!"
While you rest in the pearly dawn.
You're never bored by politics,
You're privileged to miss a row
Of tragedies by Sophocles
And diatribes by Cicero.
Your brother's wife will never come
On Sunday noon to bring to you
Her little son who plays the lute
Or little girl to sing to you.
You can commit your little sins
And relatives won't yell "Fie!"
You needn't take that annual trip
To the oracle at Delphi.
You snore and swear and stretch and yawn
In this, our strictly male house;
The only way that sinners go to heaven
Is in the jailhouse!

Some backstage celebrities at *The Boys from Syracuse*. Top is Dorothy Lamour, having as much trouble figuring out who's who as the people of Ephesus did in the show. Below, the Hon. Fiorello H. LaGuardia—everyone said he could have stepped in for Teddy or Jimmy in a pinch.

Falling in Love With Love

⁅ Originally sung by Muriel Angelus ⁆

VERSE

I weave with brightly colored strings
To keep my mind off other things;
So, ladies, let your fingers dance,
And keep your hands out of romance.
Lovely witches,
Let the stitches
Keep your fingers under control.
Cut the thread, but leave
The whole heart whole.
Merry maids can sew and sleep;
Wives can only sew and weep!

REFRAIN

Falling in love with love is falling for make-believe.
Falling in love with love is playing the fool.
Caring too much is such a juvenile fancy.
Learning to trust is just for children in school.
I fell in love with love one night
When the moon was full.
I was unwise, with eyes
Unable to see.
I fell in love with love,
With love everlasting,
But love fell out with me.

For *The Boys from Syracuse* Larry was lucky to have the British soprano Muriel Angelus (center) in the role of Adriana to sing such enchanting lyrics as the ones to "Falling in Love With Love."

GEORGE ABBOTT
presents

THE BOYS FROM SYRACUSE

A MUSICAL COMEDY SENSATION

MUSIC BY
RICHARD RODGERS

LYRICS BY
LORENZ HART

BOOK BY **GEORGE ABBOTT**

SETTINGS BY **JO MIELZINER** ▾ CHOREOGRAPHY BY **GEO. BALANCHINE**

COSTUMES BY **IRENE SHARAFF**

MATINEES
WEDNESDAY & SATURDAY

ALVIN THEATRE

52nd STREET
WEST OF BROADWAY

Sing for Your Supper

‹ *Originally sung by Muriel Angelus, Marcy Westcott and Wynn Murray* ›

VERSE

Hawks and crows do lots of things,
But the canary only sings.
She is a courtesan on wings,
So I've heard.
Eagles and storks are twice as strong.
All the canary knows is song.
But the canary gets along—
Gilded bird!

REFRAIN

Sing for your supper, and you'll get breakfast.
Songbirds always eat
If their song is sweet to hear.
Sing for your luncheon, and you'll get dinner.
Dine with wine of choice,
If romance is in your voice.
I heard from a wise canary
Trilling makes a fellow willing,
So, little swallow, swallow now.
Now is the time to
Sing for your supper, and you'll get breakfast.
Songbirds are not dumb:
They don't buy a crumb of bread, it's said.
So sing and you'll be fed.

Big Brother*

‹ *Originally sung by Teddy Hart* ›

REFRAIN

Where do you wander tonight,
Big Brother?
Is the world treating you right,
Big Brother?
If you are east or west
Listen to my request:
Come to your brother's breast,
Big Brother!
Come to your twin.
I'll treat you like a mother.
Each little twin can have only
One Brother,
Big Brother! Big Brother!

* This book's dedication page is a photo of "Big Brother."

Marcy Westcott, Wynn Murray and Muriel Angelus (left to right) doing "Sing for Your Supper," a number which combined the best of Hart, Rodgers and Balanchine. From the opening night on, this song stopped the show.

1939

Too Many Girls

Opened October 18, 1939, at the Imperial Theatre
for a run of 249 performances

Music by Richard Rodgers
Book by George Marion, Jr.
Directed by George Abbott
Choreographed by Robert Alton
Settings by Jo Mielziner
Costumes by Raoul Pène du Bois

I Like to Recognize the Tune

⊰ *Originally sung by Mary Jane Walsh, Marcy Westcott,*
Hal LeRoy, Eddie Bracken and Richard Kollmar ⊱

VERSE

Some funny folks like to shoot off rockets,
Others like to pick your pockets.
Some of them kill when they feel the urge,
Others go in for perjury.
I, too, have a passion that I can't understand,
It comes out when I hear a band.

1st REFRAIN

I like to recognize the tune,
I want to savvy what the band is playing.
I keep saying,
Must you bury the tune?
I've got to know the answer soon.
Is it a cat meowing in the attic?

Is it static?
Must you bury the tune?
A guy called Krupa plays the drums like thunder,
But the melody is six feet under.
There isn't anyone immune—
They kill the Billy Roses and Puccinis.
Don't be meanies.
Must you bury the tune?

2nd REFRAIN

When that big maestro plays the songs he's written
Poor Tchaikovsky down below starts spittin'.
There isn't anyone immune—
They kill the Irving Berlins and Rossinis.
Don't be meanies.
Must you bury the tune?
When old Ben Bernie starts his band with "Yowser,"
Ole Man Mose is dead, and so's "Tannhäuser."
There isn't anyone immune—
They kill the Georgie Cohans and the Strausses.
Don't be louses.
Must you bury the tune?
When Horace Heidt gives out with rhythm silky
Mrs. Roosevelt starts to dance with Willkie.
There isn't anyone immune—
They kill the Vincent Youmans and the Gounods.
Don't be *you-knows*.
Must you bury the tune?

ENCORE

When she hears those chords of Eddie Duchin's
Elsa Maxwell quivers with her two chins.
There isn't anyone immune.
They kill the Arthur Schwartzes and the Glinkas.
Don't be shtinkers.
Must you bury the tune?

Don Freeman drew this sketch of Larry Hart and Moss Hart (no relation) having a chat by the stage
doors of their respective hits, *Too Many Girls* and *The Man Who Came to Dinner*.

Recognizing the Tune: left to right, Marcy Westcott, Dick Kollmar, Mary Jane Walsh and, yodeling, Eddie Bracken. Larry meant every word of the lyrics of "I Like to Recognize the Tune." At about the time of *Too Many Girls,* he said of swing music, "It's old stuff. Benny Goodman only does better what Ted Lewis did years ago."

Giving It Back to the Indians: Mary Jane Walsh as the student body president of Pottawatomie College, with the male chorus behind her all the way. Van Johnson is second from right. His personality and smile made him stand out, and when the show moved on to Chicago, he was given the role Dick Kollmar had originated.

Give It Back to the Indians

{ *Originally sung by Mary Jane Walsh* }

VERSE

Old Peter Minuit had nothing to lose
When he bought the isle of Manhattan
For twenty-six dollars and a bottle of booze,
And they threw in the Bronx and Staten.
He thought that he had the best of the bargain,
But the poor Red Man just grinned.
And he grunted, "Uh," meaning O.K. in his jargon.
For he knew poor Pete was skinned.
We've tried to run the city,
But the city ran away.
And now, Peter Minuit,
We can't continue it.

1st REFRAIN

Broadway's turning into Coney,
Champagne Charlie's drinking gin,
Old New York is new and phony—
Give it back to the Indians.
Two cents more to smoke a Lucky,
Dodging buses keeps you thin,
New New York is simply ducky—
Give it back to the Indians.
Take all the reds
On the boxes made for soap,
Whites on Fifth Avenue,
Blues down in Wall Street losing hope—
Big bargain today,
Chief, take it away.
Come, you busted city slickers,
Better take it on the chin.
Father Knick has lost his knickers—
Give it back to the Indians!

2nd REFRAIN

Eighty-sixth Street looks like Berlin
And the Giants never win.
No dark park to kiss your girl in—
Give it back to the Indians.
Even Harlem's getting darker,
No more jokes to make us grin.
MGM's got Dotty Parker—
Give it back to the Indians.
Go to the park, see the monkeys in the zoo,
All absolutely free;
But then the city tax comes through—
Whose monkey are you?
Just to make it easy sailin',
Sell the Fair, it's made of tin.
But be sure that they get Whalen—
Give it back to the Indians!

3rd REFRAIN

The Music Hall has presentations,
But you simply can't get in—
Try to jump those excavations.
Give it back to the Indians.
Shakespeare doesn't get a showin'
When those striptease girls begin,
Yet "Tobacco Road" keeps goin'.

Give it back to the Indians.
Bound on the north
By the Bronx—a pretty view.
East
By Long Island—smoke.
West
By New Jersey—pots of glue.
South Brooklyn's asleep—
Chief no wanna keep!
Swing bands give you heebie-jeebies.
Dewey's put an end to sin.
Men wear clothes like Lucius Beebe's—
Give it back to the Indians!

I Didn't Know What Time It Was

{ *Originally sung by Marcy Westcott and
Richard Kollmar* }

1st VERSE

Once I was young—
Yesterday, perhaps—
Danced with Jim and Paul
And kissed some other chaps.
Once I was young,
But never was naïve.
I thought I had a trick or two
Up my imaginary sleeve.
And now I know
I was naïve!

REFRAIN

I didn't know what time it was,
Then I met you.
Oh, what a lovely time it was,
How sublime it was, too!
I didn't know what day it was.
You held my hand.
Warm like the month of May it was,
And I'll say it was grand.
Grand to be alive, to be young,
To be mad, to be yours alone!
Grand to see your face, feel your touch,
Hear your voice say, "I'm all your own."
I didn't know what year it was.
Life was no prize.
I wanted love and here it was,
Shining out of your eyes.
I'm wise,
And I know what time it is now.

2nd VERSE

Once I was old—
Twenty years or so—
Rather well preserved:
The wrinkles didn't show.
Once I was old,
But not too old for fun.
I used to hunt for little girls
With my imaginary gun.
But now I aim for only one!

You're Nearer*

VERSE

Time is a healer,
But it cannot heal my heart.
My mind says I've forgotten you
And then I feel my heart.
The miles lie between us,
But your fingers touch my own.
You're never far away from me,
For you're too much my own.

REFRAIN

You're nearer
Than my head is to my pillow.

Nearer
Than the wind is to the willow.
Dearer
Than the rain is to the earth below.
Precious
As the sun to the things that grow.
You're nearer
Than the ivy to the wall is.
Nearer
Than the winter to the fall is.
Leave me,
But when you're away you'll know
You're nearer,
For I love you so.

 * This song was written specially for the movie of *Too Many Girls*, where Trudy Erwin dubbed it for Lucille Ball.

The movie of *Too Many Girls* was the only film made out of a Rodgers and Hart play over which Larry and Dick had artistic control. In the cast were Richard Carlson, Lucille Ball, Desi Arnaz, Ann Miller, Hal LeRoy, Frances Langford, Eddie Bracken and Libby Bennett.

Too Many Girls was a fun, happy show, rather than a distinguished one, and it had some very amusing songs. The color of Raoul Pène du Bois's costumes and the wonderful youthful zing of the entire proceedings made this production a favorite of many—as did the presence of Desi Arnaz, in his Broadway debut. Desi is seen above, surrounded, clockwise, by Marcy Westcott (Consuela), Diosa Costello (Pepe) and Mary Jane Walsh (Eileen).

I have always considered Larry the good-luck charm in the Desi Arnaz-Lucille Ball super-romance. Larry informed me once that he was to stand up for Lucy and Desi at their marriage in Connecticut. But, years later, Lucy told me that Larry never *showed* up. It seems the ceremony was too early for him, and he didn't get up in time.

Desi was a regular at the Harts', and a favorite of Frieda's. When he was bongo-playing at the night club La Conga, before he was cast in *Too Many Girls,* he had exactly that problem: too many girls. Desi was only twenty-three then, with a natural Latin exuberance and enthusiasm for the pleasures of life. (After one of the Cuban revolutions had deposed his father, the former mayor of Santiago, Desi and his family arrived broke in Miami.)

Right after Desi was signed for the Rodgers and Hart show which led to fame and fortune he sent for his mother. And when Teddy and I headed for the West Coast, he rented our apartment. Desi's mother told me some years later that she still remembered the Hart family in her prayers for giving her son his big opportunity.

THE LAST WORDS

1940-1945

1940

Higher and Higher

Opened April 4, 1940, at the Shubert Theatre
for a run of 108 performances

Music by Richard Rodgers
Book by Gladys Hulburt and Joshua Logan, from an idea
   by Irvin Pincus
Directed by Joshua Logan
Choreographed by Robert Alton
Settings by Jo Mielziner
Costumes by Lucinda Ballard

It Never Entered My Mind

{ *Originally sung by Shirley Ross* }

VERSE

I don't care if there's powder on my nose,
I don't care if my hairdo is in place.
I've lost the very meaning of repose,
I never put a mud pack on my face.
Oh, who'd have thought
That I'd walk in a daze now?
I never go to shows at night,
But just to matinées now.
I see the show and home I go.

1st REFRAIN

Once I laughed when I heard you saying
That I'd be playing solitaire,
Uneasy in my easy chair.
It never entered my mind.
Once you told me I was mistaken
That I'd awaken with the sun
And order orange juice for one.
It never entered my mind.
You have what I lack myself,
And now I even have to scratch my back myself.
Once you warned me
That if you scorned me
I'd sing the maiden's pray'r again
And wish that you were there again
To get into my hair again.
It never entered my mind.

2nd REFRAIN

Once you said in
Your funny lingo
I'd sit at bingo
Day and night
And never get the number right.
It never entered my mind.

Once you told me
I'd stay up Sunday
To read the Monday
Morning dirt
And find you're merging with some skirt.
It never entered my mind.
Life is not so sweet alone.
The man who came to dinner lets me eat alone.
I confess it,
I didn't guess it
That I would sit and mope again
And all the while I'd hope again
To see my darling dope again.
It never entered my mind.

Disgustingly Rich

{ *Originally sung by Jack Haley, Shirley Ross,*
   Lee Dixon, Hilda Spong, Billie Worth
   and Robert Chisholm }

VERSE

Brenda Frazier sat on a wall.
Brenda Frazier had a big fall.
Brenda Frazier's falling down,
Falling down, falling down,
Brenda Frazier's falling down,
My fair Minnie.
There's money in the movies,
There's money in the ads.
There's money in the old Johns,
There's money in the lads.
Minnie, Minnie, Minnie, Minnie—
Money, Money, Money, Money—
Eenie, Meenie, Money, Mo,
Catch a fortune by the toe.

1st REFRAIN

I'll buy everything I wear at Saks.
I'll cheat plenty on my income tax.
Swear like a trooper,
Live in a stupor—
Just disgustingly rich.
I'll make money and I'll make it quick,
Boosting cigarettes that make me sick.
Smothered in sables
Like Betty Grable's—
Just disgustingly rich.
I will buy land
Down on Long Island
And as a resident
I will pan the President.
I'll aspire
Higher and higher.
I'll get married and adopt a son,
Right from Tony's or from "21."
Swimming in highballs,
Stewed to the eyeballs—
Just disgustingly rich—
Too, too disgustingly rich.

2nd REFRAIN

Break my ankles on the tennis courts.
Get pneumonia doing winter sports.
I won't be civil
Rude as the divil
Just disgustingly rich.
Ev'ry summer I will sail the sea,
On my little yacht, the "Normandie,"
Catch barracuda down in Bermuda—
Just disgustingly rich.
I'll eat salmon,
I'll play backgammon,
Turn breakfast into brunch.
I'll take Errol Flynn to lunch.
I'll aspire
Higher and higher.
I'll buy autos like the autocrats.
I'll drink Pluto like the plutocrats.
Playing the horses,
Getting divorces—
Just disgustingly rich—
Too, too disgustingly rich.

3rd REFRAIN

He'll be photographed with Myrna Loy,
Just to prove he is a glamour boy.
Perfumed and scented,
Slightly demented—
Just disgustingly rich.

I will take a plane to Florida
Where the weather's even horrida.
I'll eat salami
Down in Miami—
Just disgustingly rich.
Get my capers into the papers.
Hoping my folly would
Lead me out to Hollywood.
I'll aspire
Higher and higher.
In the funnies and at Valentine's,
I'll be a picture drinking Ballantine's.
Simple and screwy,
Voting for Dewey—
Just disgustingly rich—
Too, too disgustingly rich.

CODA

We will never even try to swim.
We'll just sit until the sun grows dim.
We'll eat baloney
Down at the Roney—
Just disgustingly rich—
Too, too disgustingly rich.

The pantry in *Higher and Higher*, with Jack Haley (center) and the rest of the "servants" celebrating the fact that a playboy has just offered a million dollars for the hand of a housemaid whom they are passing off as the Deb of the Year. They're all going to be "just disgustingly rich, too, too disgustingly rich."

Gene Kelly

Gene Kelly got his first big break when he was selected to play the incorrigible Joey Evans in Pal Joey. His incomparable dancing and irresistible charm made him an overnight star. During the controversy over whether Joey was just too unsavory a character to be the hero of a musical, Gene, with great accuracy, explained the heel he was playing to the newspapers: "Joey isn't bad; he just doesn't know the difference. He's an ignorant low-class bum with nothing but good looks and a good line."

The Voice of Broadway
By Dorothy Kilgallen

Two Harts in Three-quarter Time

(Our Own Broadway Valentines.)

So far as this column knows they never have met, but our idea of two citizens whose paths the humorous Broadway gods, in their O. Henry wisdom, certainly should cause to cross are the celebrated unrelated Harts—Lorenz and Margie. Lorenz writes songs, and Margie takes here clothes off to them, but the two have in common a fundamental whimsy, an essential gaudiness of legend that would make them compatible characters in Lindy's or the Louvre.

Larry Hart is a quick, dark, darting little man with pointed ears, a gleeful laugh, and the face of a smart faun sitting in on a poker game with the angels. It is no secret that he composes lyrics, for he and Dick Rodgers usually have a hit musical or two kicking around the Broadway boards, but it is a great mystery when he composes his rhymes, for no one has ever caught him working, not even his mother, with whom he lives.

LORENZ HART
Like character from play, but no one minds

Larry calls his mama "The Cop" because she watches him with an eagle eye (an entertaining, if fruitless, pastime), tries to feed him solid food, and shoos his friends out of the house when they stay too late, or past 5 a. m. ...Sometimes at dinner he talks to friends in a secret double-talk language so his mother won't understand what he's saying.

Since last year, when he had pneumonia, Larry's hobby is taking his own temperature. He has thermometers all over the house... He has a penchant for Chinese food, imitating Al Jolson, and dogs. Once he came upon a stray dog in Freeport, L. I., took a fancy to it, and brought it home. Everyone in the house swears he talked to the dog all night...He is one of the more ubiquitous of the cafe crowd, noticeable at the ballet, the first nights, the opera, the more gilded soirees, and at midnight in Sardi's. He loves the music of opera, but thinks that as an art form it is ridiculous, and he and Paul Muni once agreed at a Metropolitan matinee that "Tristan and Isolde" should be performed only for the blind.

Larry terrifies his Negro chauffeur by threatening to grow a beard, explaining that this is a new vogue among intelligent and fashionable people...He never shaves himself, and never writes letters... He adores and bosses his brother Teddy, the comedian, hates Hollywood, and is enchanted with Vivienne Segal because she has a vocabulary as colorful as his own.

He has a habit of confiding a big secret to you, making you swear on your most sacred oath never to reveal it. Then five minutes later you catch him going from table to table in a night club, telling the same sacred secret to everyone in sight...He behaves like a character right out of a Kaufman-Hart play, but no one minds. The other evening he invited Betty Grable and Desi Arnaz to his house for dinner, then forgot to show up himself.

No one was even slightly surprised at his absence—especially Larry.

A while before the opening of *Higher and Higher*, Dorothy Kilgallen wrote this column on Larry in the New York *Journal American*. I think it's the best piece about Larry any reporter ever wrote.

He was a marvelous little fellow—and of course we all admired him for his great talent, so he had a ready audience and in the camaraderie of the theatre, he had ready friends. We all looked up to him because we were all in that lower middle class of actors who hadn't gotten to where our names were over the titles or anything like that, so I had a working acquaintance with Larry. I did do a stupid thing when I auditioned for Rodgers and John O'Hara. I used one of the Rodgers and Hart songs, "I Didn't Know What Time It Was." I was naïve enough not to think about this. I just thought I'd do a ballad for them, an up song. I didn't even know it was a Rodgers and Hart ballad. Years later, when I became a director-producer myself, I learned how songwriters hate this kind of thing because it looks like you're currying favor. A day or two later, they told me I was hired for the part of Joey and I certainly jumped at the chance. I had just closed in *Time of Your Life* where I'd had just a small part.

I was originally a choreographer and did my own choreography for that show. Robert Alton, who did the dances for *Pal Joey*, had known my work for years. I have a hunch that George Abbott saw *Time of Your Life* and might have said, "That's the fellow I want," and he and Larry Hart agreed, but that Richard Rodgers wanted to make sure. I have no way of knowing, but I only auditioned in the theatre that day for John O'Hara and Rodgers. It was during *Time of Your Life* that I'd gotten to know Larry in local saloons around town. I call them saloons because they were not in the Sardi's or Stork Club or "21" class, where Rodgers and George Abbott would go. These were the cheap saloons near Eighth Avenue and Forty-fifth Street where actors hung out. Larry would be there often. He loved actors and he loved to hang around with them. That's how I got to know him, not closely, but in a fun kind of way. We'd stand at the bar, he would tell stories or he'd listen to others tell stories, and he'd laugh while chomping on that big cigar.

We opened *Pal Joey* in Philadelphia and John O'Hara, Larry and I continued drinking after the show, staying up all night. That's how young you can be! But I loved Larry ever since and we had a lifelong friendship. I didn't know then that Rodgers and Hart and O'Hara and George Abbott were creating a musical epic.

Larry particularly, apart from John O'Hara and

Dick, felt that in *Pal Joey* they had created something that was a tour de force, bringing a new kind of seriousness to the musical theatre.

Larry felt certain of a positive reception from the critics. But it didn't happen. After the opening in New York, Larry gave a party for the cast at his home. At a certain point in the evening he listened to a report of the critics' reviews on the phone. They were not that good. Brooks Atkinson of *The New York Times*, the important theatre critic, said, and I quote: "How can you get sweet water from a foul well?" Larry burst into tears and went into his room. We couldn't get him out. He was that hypersensitive a man. And with all his success, he was that easily affected by the diatribe.

The great thing is that Larry was right, though he didn't live to know it. When the show was later revived, Atkinson gave it a good review—as did all the other critics. It is vibrant, progressive, tough, and good theatre, considered a milestone in musical comedy. It was way ahead of its time.

1940

Pal Joey

Opened December 25, 1940, at the Ethel Barrymore Theatre for a run of 374 performances

Music by Richard Rodgers
Book by John O'Hara
Directed by George Abbott
Choreographed by Robert Alton
Designed by Jo Mielziner
Costumes by John Koenig

I Could Write a Book

{ Originally sung by Gene Kelly and Leila Ernst }

1st VERSE

Joey: A B C D E F G—
I never learned to spell,
At least not well.
1 2 3 4 5 6 7—
I never learned to count
A great amount.
But my busy mind is burning
To use what learning I've got.
I won't waste any time,
I'll strike while the iron is hot.

REFRAIN

If they asked me, I could write a book
About the way you walk and whisper and look.
I could write a preface on how we met
So the world would never forget.
And the simple secret of the plot
Is just to tell them that I love you a lot;
Then the world discovers as my book ends
How to make two lovers of friends.

2nd VERSE

Linda: Used to hate to go to school.
I never cracked a book;
I played the hook.
Never answered any mail;
To write I used to think
Was wasting ink.
It was never my endeavor
To be too clever and smart.
Now I suddenly feel
A longing to write in my heart.

Jo Mielziner truly outdid himself with the setting for *Joey*'s pet shop sequence. Peering into the window are Gene Kelly and Leila Ernst. He's snowing her with a story about his boyhood among the gentry.

Gene in Robert Alton's inspired "Joey Looks Into the Future Ballet." The first act of *Pal Joey* ended with Joey dreaming of owning the gaudiest night club Chicago had ever seen.

Zip

{ *Originally sung by Jean Casto* }

VERSE

I've interviewed Leslie Howard.
I've interviewed Noël Coward.
I've interviewed the great Stravinsky.
But my greatest achievement
Is the interview I had
With a star who worked for Minsky.
I met her at the Yankee Clipper
And she didn't unzip one zipper.
I said, "Miss Lee, you are such an artist.
Tell me why you never miss.
What do you think of while you work?"
And she said, "While I work
My thoughts go something like this."

1st REFRAIN

Zip! Walter Lippmann wasn't brilliant today.
Zip! Will Saroyan ever write a great play?
Zip! I was reading Schopenhauer last night.
Zip! And I think that Schopenhauer was right.
I don't want to see Zorina.
I don't want to meet Cobina.
Zip! I'm an intellectual.
I don't like a deep contralto,
Or a man whose voice is alto.
Zip! I'm a heterosexual.
Zip! It took intellect to master my art.
Zip! Who the hell is Margie Hart?

2nd REFRAIN

Zip! I consider Dali's painting passé.
Zip! Can they make the Metropolitan pay?
Zip! English people don't say clerk, they say clark.
Zip! Anybody who says clark is a jark!
I have read the great Kabala
And I simply worship Allah.
Zip! I am just a mystic.
I don't care for Whistler's mother,
Charlie's aunt or Shubert's brother.
Zip! I'm misogynistic.
Zip! My intelligence is guiding my hand.
Zip! Who the hell is Sally Rand?

3rd REFRAIN

Zip! Toscanini leads the greatest of bands.
Zip! Jergen's lotion does the trick for his hands.
Zip! Rip Van Winkle on the screen would be smart.
Zip! Tyrone Power will be cast in the part.
I adore the great Confucius
And the lines of luscious Lucius.
Zip! I am so eclectic.
I don't care for either Mickey—
Mouse and Rooney make me sickey!
Zip! I'm a little hectic.
Zip! My artistic taste is classic and dear.
Zip! Who the hell's Lili St. Cyr?

"He gets the gate." Vera (Vivienne Segal, right) gives Joey his walking papers. His former girlfriend Linda English (Leila Ernst, center) has also decided to drop him, and nobody could say she didn't make the right decision!

Jean Casto singing ''Zip.'' During the show's out-of-town tryout, Gypsy Rose Lee stopped by to give Miss Casto some tips re the art of stripteasing. On the following two pages, Gypsy's sister, June Havoc, can be seen with the *Pal Joey* chorus girls, singing ''That Terrific Rainbow.''

Richard Watts, Jr.

Richard Watts was always a great Rodgers and Hart fan. In the early thirties, when he was the movie critic for the New York Herald Tribune, *he wrote favorable reviews of* Love Me Tonight, The Phantom President, *and* Hallelujah, I'm a Bum. *When he succeeded to the position of the* Tribune's *drama critic, he continued his enthusiasm for Larry and Dick's work, giving raves to* I Married an Angel *and* The Boys from Syracuse. *At the height of the controversy over* Pal Joey, *he wrote this brilliant and persuasive "think piece" for the Sunday* Trib; *he was comparably impressed by the show in his opening night review, in which he wrote "the spiritual kinship between John O'Hara and Lorenz Hart is something to be applauded."*

After a long and embarrassing period of futility, the dramatic season suddenly came to life Christmas week. . . . *Pal Joey* turned out to be an exceptionally brilliant musical comedy by John O'Hara, Richard Rodgers and Lorenz Hart. . . . and so I am going to devote the rest of my first 1941 sermon to a contemplation of this exceptional musical show.

Already *Pal Joey* has become the subject of a fairly heated controversy. It is the contention of squeamish observers that the O'Hara-Rodgers-Hart work, having for its hero an unrelenting heel and for its subject matter a savage study of the insect life of the minor night clubs, cannot—despite its incontestable virtues of vivid writing and enchanting music—be palatable as a musical show. It seems to me that Louis Kronenberger, in *PM*, effectively disposed of this moral objection merely by recalling that a musical comedy called *The Beggar's Opera*, which dealt exclusively with heels and bawds, has managed to be pretty successful over the course of the last few centuries. In strict accuracy, though, it isn't necessary to go back that far. *Louisiana Purchase* treats of some of the shoddiest and most disagreeable political scoundrels in the recent history of American governmental corruption, and, so far as I can see, does it with no particular disapproval. In fact, the fellow who finally gets the desirable heroine is one of the leaders of the Louisiana grafters. Yet *Louisiana Purchase* appears to have been highly satisfactory entertainment for quite a number of paying guests.

As a matter of fact, while the authors of *The Beggar's Opera* and *Louisiana Purchase* gave no signs of distaste for their dubious heroes, Mr. O'Hara has shown every evidence of high contempt for his central character's moral standing. In both the letters of the ineffable Joey, and in the musical comedy based upon them, there is a bitter and savage scorn that is, together with the bite and the contemptuous wit of the writing and the realism of the observation, the chief mark of their distinction. *Pal Joey* is a sardonic and entirely accurate picture of the type of creature reared in the ugly life of the minor cabarets, and I think that, in my limited way, I

have investigated these night clubs carefully enough to attest to the letter-perfect correctness of Mr. O'Hara's reporting. Yet, even though he is a pretty miserable specimen, Joey is by no means unbearable as a musical comedy hero. There is something so naïve about his cheap caddishness, he is so essentially an innocent boob, the simple prey of any smart operator, and, above all, he is so guilefully played by Gene Kelly, that moral judgment becomes suspended and he emerges as an object for Olympian amusement rather than hatred. In particular, it seems to me so pleasant to see believable human beings, even if not admirable ones, in a musical comedy for a change that I think the utterly credible Joey should be accepted with gratitude.

If I am postponing my enthusiastic words for the delightful new Rodgers and Hart score, it is because here for once the book of a musical comedy assumes a power, a forcefulness and a dramatic interest of its own. In truth, it is the only Broadway girl-and-music show I can recall in which the book has enough narrative value to stand by itself. If there is a feeling here and there that the second act of *Pal Joey* falls off a trifle, that, I think, is not due to any lack of merit, but merely to the fact that Mr. O'Hara introduces in the latter half the character of a blackmailing, double-crossing agent, and it is so powerfully drawn a portrait that it tends to shift the focus of the narrative and take the emphasis for the time being off that humorous insect, Joey. It certainly is a novel fault in a musical show when a too strikingly drawn character is to be held against it. It is remarkable, also, to note how completely the quality of Mr. O'Hara's published prose carries over into the theater, and how vivid and pungent is seems. . . .

Bewitched, Bothered and Bewildered

{ Originally sung by Vivienne Segal }

VERSE

After one whole quart of brandy,
Like a daisy I awake.
With no Bromo-Seltzer handy,
I don't even shake.
Men are not a new sensation;
I've done pretty well, I think.
But this half-pint imitation
Puts me on the blink.

1st REFRAIN

I'm wild again,
Beguiled again,
A simpering, whimpering child again—
Bewitched, bothered and bewildered am I.
Couldn't sleep
And wouldn't sleep
Until I could sleep where I shouldn't sleep—
Bewitched, bothered and bewildered am I.
Lost my heart, but what of it?
My mistake, I agree.

He's a laugh, but I love it
Because the laugh's on me.
A pill he is,
But still he is
All mine and I'll keep him until he is
Bewitched, bothered and bewildered
Like me.

2nd REFRAIN

Seen a lot—
I mean a lot—
But now I'm like sweet seventeen a lot—
Bewitched, bothered and bewildered am I.
I'll sing to him,
Each spring to him,
And worship the trousers that cling to him—
Bewitched, bothered and bewildered am I.
When he talks
He is seeking
Words to get off his chest.
Horizontally speaking,
He's at his very best.
Vexed again,
Perplexed again,
Thank God I can be oversexed again—
Bewitched, bothered and bewildered am I.

3rd REFRAIN

Sweet again,
Petite again,
And on my proverbial seat again—
Bewitched, bothered and bewildered am I.
What am I?
Half shot am I.
To think that he loves me
So hot am I—
Bewitched, bothered and bewildered am I.
Though at first we said No, sir,
Now we're two little dears.
You might say we are closer
Than Roebuck is to Sears.
I'm dumb again
And numb again,
A rich, ready, ripe little plum again—
Bewitched, bothered and bewildered am I.

ENCORE

You know,
It is really quite funny
Just how quickly he learns
How to spend all the money
That Mr. Simpson earns.
He's kept enough,
He's slept enough,
And yet where it counts
He's adept enough—
Bewitched, bothered and bewildered am I.

REPRISE

Wise at last,
My eyes at last
Are cutting you down to your size at last—
Bewitched, bothered and bewildered no more.

Burned a lot,
But learned a lot,
And now you are broke, though you earned a lot—
Bewitched, bothered and bewildered no more.
Couldn't eat—
Was dyspeptic,
Life was so hard to bear;
Now my heart's antiseptic,
Since you moved out of there.
Romance—finis;
Your chance—finis;
Those ants that invaded my pants—finis—
Bewitched, bothered and bewildered no more.

PAL JOEY, a "new" musical comedy in two acts taken from John O'Hara's series of letters of the same name. Book by Mr. O'Hara. Music by Richard Rodgers. Lyrics by Lorenz Hart. Dances arranged by Robert Alton; scenery and lighting by Jo Mielziner; costumes designed by John Koenig; staged and produced by George Abbott. At the Ethel Barrymore Theatre.

Joey Evans.....................Gene Kelly
Mike Spears..............Robert J. Mulligan
The Kid.....................Sondra Barrett
Gladys.........................June Havoc
Agnes........................Diane Sinclair
Linda English..................Leila Ernst
Valerie......................Amarilla Morris
Albert Doane..................Stanley Donen
Vera Simpson.................Vivienne Segal
Escort..........................Edison Rice
Terry..........................Jane Fraser
Victor........................Van Johnson
Ernest.........................John Clarke
Stagehand.....................Jerry Whyte
Max..........................Averell Harris
The Tenor.....................Nelson Rae
Melba Snyder...................Jean Casto
Waiter.......................Dummy Spevlin
Ludlow Lowell..................Jack Durant
Commissioner O'Brien..........James Lane
Assistant Hotel Manager.....Cliff Dunstan
    Specialty dancer: Shirley Paige.
    Dancing girls: Claire Anderson, Sondra Barrett, Alice Craig, Louise de Forrest, Enez Early, Tilda Getze, Charlene Harkins, Frances Krell, Janet Lavis, June Leroy, Amarilla Morris, Olive Nicolson, Mildred Patterson, Dorothy Poplar, Diane Sinclair, Mildred Solly, Jeanne C. Trybom, Marie Vanneman.
    Dancing boys: Adrian Anthony, John Benton, Milton Chisholm, Stanley Donen, Henning Irgens, Van Johnson, Howard Ledig. Michael Moore, Albert Ruiz.

By BROOKS ATKINSON

If it is possible to make an entertaining musical comedy out of an odious story, "Pal Joey" is it. The situation is put tentatively here because the ugly topic that is up for discussion stands between this theatregoer and real enjoyment of a well-staged show. Taking as his hero the frowsy night club punk familiar to readers of a series of sketches in The New Yorker, John O'Hara has written a joyless book about a sulky assignation. Under George Abbott's direction some of the best workmen on Broadway have fitted it out with smart embellishments.

Rodgers and Hart have written the score with wit and skill. Robert Alton has directed the dances inventively. Scenery out of Jo Mielziner's sketchbook and costumes off the racks of John Koenig—all very high class. Some talented performers also act a book that is considerably more dramatic than most. "Pal Joey," which was put on at the Ethel Barrymore last evening, offers everything but a good time.

*   *   *

Whether Joey is a punk or a heel is something worth more careful thinking than time permits. Perhaps he is only a rat infested with termites. A night club dancer and singer, promoted to master of ceremonies in a Chicago dive, he lies himself into an affair with a rich married woman and opens a gilt-edged club of his own with her money. Mr. O'Hara has drawn a pitiless portrait of his small-time braggart and also of the company he keeps; and Gene Kelly, who distinguished himself as the melancholy hoofer of "The Time of Your Life," plays the part with remarkable accuracy. His cheap and flamboyant unction, his nervous cunning, his trickiness are qualities that Mr. Kelly catches without forgetting the fright and gaudiness of a petty fakir. Mr. Kelly is also a brilliant tap dancer—"makes with the feet," as it goes in his vernacular—and his performance on both scores is triumphant. If Joey must be acted, Mr. Kelly can do it.

*   *   *

Count among your restricted blessings Vivienne Segal who can act with personal dignity and can sing with breeding. In a singularly sweet voice she sings some scabrous lyrics by Lorenz Hart to one of Richard Rodgers's most haunting tunes—"Bewitched, Bothered and Bewildered." June Havoc applies a broad, rangy style to some funny burlesques of night-club routines and manners. Jean Casto satirizes the strip-tease with humorous condescension. As a particularly rank racketeer Jack Durant, who is a sizable brute, contributes a few amazing and dizzy acrobatics. This department's paternal heart goes out especially to Leila Ernst who is the only uncontaminated baggage in the cast.

*   *   *

Occasionally "Pal Joey" absents itself a little from depravity and pokes fun at the dreariness of night club frolics, and at the close of the first act it presents an admirable dream ballet and pantomime. Joey's hopeful look into a purple future is lyrically danced by Mr. Kelly. There is a kind of wry and wistful beauty to the spinning figures of Mr. Alton's dance design. But the story of "Pal Joey" keeps harking back to the drab and mirthless world of punk's progress. Although "Pal Joey" is expertly done, can you draw sweet water from a foul well?

The famous Brooks Atkinson review of *Pal Joey*. He certainly changed his tune when the revival came along twelve years later. Then he had nothing but praise for everything about the show, and for "the easy perfection of the lyrics."

Take Him

{ Originally sung by Leila Ernst and Vivienne Segal }

1st VERSE

Linda: He was a cutie—
I admit I used to care.
But it's my duty
To myself to take the air.
I won't prevent you from eloping
If you wish.
May I present you
With this tasty dish.

1st REFRAIN

Take him, you don't have to pay for him.
Take him, he's free.
Take him, I won't make a play for him.
He's not for me.
He has no head to think with.
True that his heart is asleep.
But he has eyes to wink with.
You can have him cheap.
Keep him and just for
The lure of it, marry him, too.
Keep him, for you can
Be sure of it, he can't keep you.
So take my old jalopy,
Keep him from falling apart.
Take him, but don't ever
Take him to heart.

2nd VERSE

Vera: Thanks, little mousie,
For the present and all that,
But in this housie
I would rather keep a rat.
Only a wizard could reform
That class of males.
They say a lizard cannot change
His scales.

2nd REFRAIN

Take him, I won't put a price on him.
Take him, he's yours.
Take him, pajamas look nice on him.
But how he snores!
Though he is well adjusted,
Certain things make him a wreck.
Last year his arm was busted
Reaching from a check.
His thoughts
Are seldom consecutive.
He just can't write.
I know a movie executive
Who's twice as bright.
Lots of good luck—
You'll need it—and
You'll need aspirin, too,
Take him, but don't ever
Let him take you.

3rd REFRAIN

Both: I hope that things will go well with him;
I bear no hate.
All I can say is the hell with him;
He gets the gate.
So take my benediction,
Take my old benedict, too.
Take it away, it's too good to be true.

The turning point of *Pal Joey*: Gladys Bumps and Ludlow Lowell (June Havoc and Jack Durant, left) vainly attempting to blackmail Vera Simpson and Joey Evans.

I'm Talking to My Pal*

VERSE

I'm independent.
I'm a descendant
Of quite a family of heels.
I'm never lonely.
I and I only
Know how my pal Joey feels.
Who else would pay for my meals?

REFRAIN

I'm talking to my pal,
Myself, my closest friend.
And that's the only pal
On whom I can depend.
When I come home at night,
A bit too tight to see,
My wallet is all right—
I'd never steal from me.
My friend stands pat
When I am flat.
He only cheats when I do.
I can't be sure of girls,
I'm not at home with men—
I'm ending up with me again.

    * This song, written for Gene Kelly,
was dropped before *Pal Joey* opened.

Larry revising a lyric during *Joey's* Philadelphia
tryout

Larry had been raised in a family and home that bustled with servants, relatives, friends and a constant flow of visitors, and he was unable to adjust to the comparative quiet of his later years. I feel that much of his drinking was due to his inability to be alone. By the 1940s, this had become a serious problem which I think even a long-time associate like Dick Rodgers did not recognize fully, though Dick always claimed he "had to be there always when Larry wrote a lyric."

Teddy and I had dinner almost every night at Larry's apartment. Which is why I never learned to cook! We didn't dare make an outside dinner appointment. But we enjoyed it, and Larry and Frieda were convinced that they hadn't lost a brother and son but had gained a sister and daughter. There were many months when we were in Hollywood; however, when Teddy went off on camp tour with *Room Service*, I began devoting myself to Larry, trying to alleviate Frieda's concern with his drinking. His growing moodiness and changes of personality when he drank were too obvious for her to accept as just show-business boozing. So I took a trip with Larry to Saratoga, where Larry visited Monty Woolley's favorite bars. This was Woolley's home town, Larry reminded me. We stayed at the glamorous Gideon Putnam Hotel, where we ordered all sorts of fabulous food. Larry enjoyed watching me eat, while he nibbled on his food. The weight I gained! He had bellboys betting on the races for him, every horse in each race, of course. That was his "system." I would sit in a corner of a bar reading, while Larry strode up and down buying drinks for all and insisting that John L. Sullivan could lick Joe Louis and Jack Dempsey. "He could lick them all!" To see this bantamweight discuss fisticuffs with the erudition of a college professor was incongruous. The patrons were familiar with Woolley, who actually had been a college professor.

But the Saratoga trip did some good, and when we started for home Larry was a little better nourished and a little less saturated. He told the driver he had hired to continue on to New York instead of dropping us at the station. We played our game of "funny names on store windows," which passed the time on long trips. Tiring of this, Larry got on one of his subjects of late: his grievances against Dick Rodgers. My relationship with Larry had always been wonderful because aside from our strong affection for each other, I did not intrude on his personal life, any more than he intruded on Teddy's and mine. Of late, he had become irritable and tense, and I felt my role was to try to pacify, soothe and calm him. But there were areas in which I felt I had to be honest and frank with him. Not that I offered my advice freely. Larry could be fiercely independent or completely docile. The thing was, you never knew the direction the wind was blowing. But when Larry continued to berate Rodgers for what he believed was a lack of sympathy and understanding or fairness, I spoke up. "Larry, I don't blame Dick for taking this attitude at this time. I'm sure what you say has a lot of truth, but you know that you have been misbehaving and not working and Dick has every reason to be disgusted...."

I had thrown discretion to the winds, because the influences around Larry had precipitated and encouraged a break with Dick, as they had tried to turn Larry against anyone close to him, for their own ends. But I hadn't expected quite this reaction to my words: Larry grabbed me by the shoulders and shook me angrily, roughly and violently. The chauffeur stopped the car in alarm, and a police car passing by got ready to stop also. I wasn't too shook up, but when Larry realized that the impression to onlookers was that I was being strangled, he started to laugh so robustly, and hug me so affectionately, that the chauffeur continued on, reassured. We laughed and laughed, Larry completely relaxed and in good humor again, and we resumed our "funny names on store windows" game. And Larry overlooked what must have seemed to him my treasonous remarks.

Life with Larry was now full of incident. One night as we were about to sit down to dinner, he took Teddy's arm, grinned like a schoolboy and said, "How'd you like to have Vivienne Segal for a sister-in-law?" Teddy, not at all surprised, said, "Great."

But that was the last we heard from Larry on the matter. Several days later we learned that Vivienne had turned him down. Larry wouldn't tell us that. He just seemed more morose than usual. Larry adored Vivienne. No one laughed more heartily at her amusing quips, her salty language and her great sense of humor. Larry would say, "Doesn't she look marvelous? Can you believe she's as old as she is? Didn't she sing great tonight? Isn't she wonderful in the show?"

But for Larry unrequited love was not a bore. In one way or another, it was a disaster.

One day in the summer of 1940, Dick Rodgers wired me, saying he wanted to talk to me. When I went to see him, he said, "Dorothy, you and Teddy have to do something about Larry. You know he's not himself. I don't think in his present state of mind he is responsible." Teddy was on the road with *The Man Who Came to Dinner*. "You know, Dorothy, I've had all sorts of ambitions for us. To have a Rodgers and Hart theatre, to do all kinds of wonderful advanced things in the theatre. But you know how hard it's been to get Larry to do any work at all."

There was a silence between us which we both understood. I didn't quite know what was coming, but I knew it had to be something shattering. He went on. "Larry must be committed. I will help you." I gasped. "You mean by the state?" Dick nodded. "We couldn't do that," I said. Dick continued, "I'd like you to go with me to the office of a psychiatrist I know. Why don't we discuss it with him?"

On leaving, I told Dick I could never consent to Larry being put away against his wishes, and I knew Teddy would feel the same way. The thought of Larry "locked up," as I visualized it then, was abhorrent. He

Teddy, Larry and me in a Miami night club, 1940. Even though Larry's got a drink in his hand, this is one of my favorite pictures of him.

rebelled at any kind of confinement. (Even when he'd had to be at Doctors Hospital, he roamed the halls in a frenzy when his clothes were removed from his room to keep him from leaving before the doctor discharged him.) But I told Dick I would speak to Frieda and Teddy and see what we could do about coaxing Larry to do something voluntarily. Dick shook his head despairingly and repeated, "He'll have to be committed."

He knew as well as the family did Larry's feeling about psychoanalysis. Teddy had often been criticized for not "doing something" about Larry. We knew that he had frequent mental blackouts. We had tried on several occasions to discuss with Larry the help George Gershwin, Josh Logan and so many show people had received. But he had this incredible old-fashioned idea of what psychiatry meant. Or perhaps he was afraid to reveal himself to anyone.

I talked to the psychiatrist quite frankly about Larry's deteriorating condition and explained that several doctors with whom I had conferred emphasized that nothing would help a man in Larry's condition if he himself wasn't ready to ask for help. We discussed the Hartford Rest, which has since changed its name to the Institute for Living (many famous people have been helped there). Also the Menninger Clinic in Kansas City, which was at that time little known. But these were for voluntary patients. Until now it had been all I could do to get Larry to go to Doctors Hospital at different times during the year to dry out. But as I said, after a few days Larry would leave, discharged by his physician or not.

One of us, I don't know whether it was Dick, the psychiatrist or myself, suggested that I should invite the psychiatrist to dinner at Larry's house and pretend he was a friend. The doctor could then observe Larry without the rage that Larry showed when the word "psychiatrist" was mentioned to him.

I remembered that during one of Larry's stays in Doctors Hospital, Dick had called in a Dr. Richard Hoffman, a Park Avenue "shrink" (Larry's doctors felt that a low temperature that had kept him confined for several weeks was psychosomatic). When I visited him that evening Larry was wild. Did they think he was crazy? Who had sent for Dr. Hoffman? I pretended ignorance, while Larry stormed on about those ridiculous questions Hoffman had asked: Why did he like oversized chairs? Why did he like oversized rooms? Did he have a Napoleon complex?

Unfortunately, nothing came of Dick's suggestion that Larry work with this new therapist either.

The beginning of the war years, with many friends and acquaintances in special services scattered throughout the world, brought Larry an uncomfortable and even shocking realization: that times they were a-changing. The frivolous nights of carousing became meaningless where once they had been an end in themselves. If he insisted that he drank for only one purpose, "to have fun," fun wasn't the name of the game anymore. Once he said to Dick, disconsolately, "The world has changed . . . ." Dick's reply was, "It isn't the world that's changed, it's you." They were both right. Larry had changed, and the Second World War did change everybody's thinking. Show people were running to the Stage Door Canteen at every leisure moment. They were involved in political ideologies, mostly to the left, which Larry as a staunch patriot still didn't particularly favor. But he couldn't stir up much enthusiasm for the war. How full of patriotism he had been during World War I when he told his father that he was going to enlist! But he had been turned down, much to Max's secret relief. Larry was underweight, too short.

And Larry was Peter Pan, refusing to grow up. Some of his friends had married and were raising families. And the ones who had been closest since his youth remained in Hollywood in a nine-to-five world rather than the night-into-day routine of Broadway. Many of his aunts and uncles had passed away. Frieda was getting on and so was Mary, who was not responding to Larry's pranks with the high-pitched giggles of her younger days. Doc Bender's brother Charlie had died—he was only in his forties—and the doctor had given Milton himself an ultimatum. The family's inherited blood pressure had taken Charlie, a former opera singer and as close to Doc as Teddy was to Larry. If Bender didn't slow down the same fate awaited him. So

Bender stayed home nights and could no longer be counted on for a night on the town. Most depressing of all, Teddy's marriage gave Larry a room to himself—which he didn't want. Teddy's dry humor, his anecdotes and droll wit had kept Larry amused and in good humor throughout their lives. Now, entering the apartment at the Ardsley, the lights always dimmed (because of Frieda's strong sense of German thrift), the quiet was oppressive. I think that if Larry dragged to his home all sorts of nondescript characters, it was to keep from being alone in the darkened apartment.

He was now a man in his forties who was getting a little breathless from running away from himself—toward oblivion, perhaps.

Once, on the train when we went to Florida during World War II, Larry and I could only get a single compartment. Like Teddy, and everyone else to this day who has to travel with me, Larry complained about the excess baggage I had in the compartment, making quarters even tighter. He got very annoyed when I said coldly to him, "You can't talk to me like that. I'm not married to you!"

The door was open and we found several people, including the porter, staring at us. Here we were sharing the same bedroom and of course we were Mr. Hart and Mrs. Hart! It simply hadn't occurred to us what it would look like! When finally we got the door closed by piling some of the suitcases in the lower berth, we laughed uproariously and Larry clambered up to his top berth agilely. (A good laugh always put Larry in a cheerful mood, often averting a feeling of depression that was never far from the surface.)

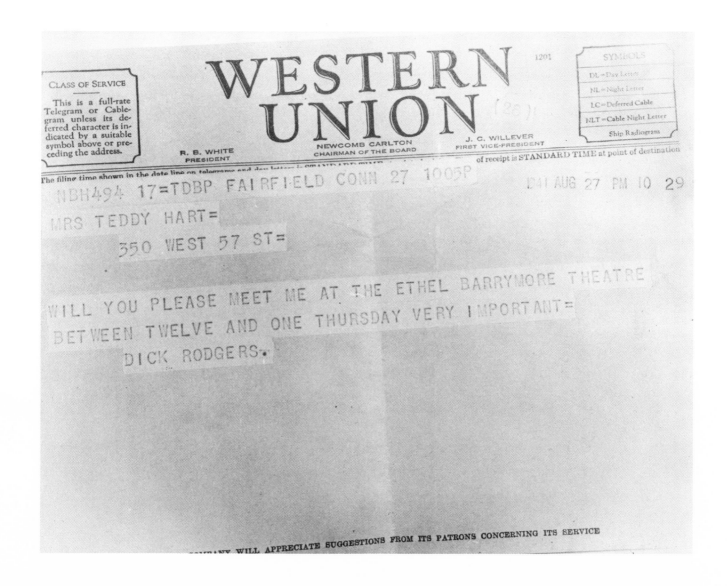

We were in Miami when Teddy, on tour, called from Clarksville, Tennessee, and in a very weak voice advised us that he had been taken off the train with the flu and was in a hospital. The company of the U.S.O. *Room Service* had continued on to its next playing date, a camp some miles away. Just as Larry had accepted the closing of his favorite hotel in Miami, the Roney Plaza, without griping, he now joined me in a slow milk train to Clarksville. We had to change trains several times. Taxis were impossible to get, and we found we would have to take a streetcar at one point since there was no other transportation. And here Larry, in his quixotic way, rebelled. For the first time he complained. Anxious and concerned about Teddy, I persisted. So did Larry. In a stalemate, we walked! Poor Larry in those elevator shoes! But he did walk a long way. Though I had suggested he remain in Miami while I took the trip alone, he had insisted on coming along and I was glad he was with me. (These were sad days for so many young people. They were sprawled in the dirty coaches, the women with tiny babies on the way to join their husbands stationed somewhere, the very young soldiers, catching up on their sleep and looking pathetic and innocent.)

The best accommodation available for Larry and me in Clarksville was a motel with a potbellied stove for heat. I had never visualized Larry in such primitive and uncomfortable surroundings. (I don't think that even in his camp days in his childhood he'd roughed it.) At the hospital we found Teddy a little stronger, and on his way to getting well. One of the nurses, on seeing Larry running in and out of the hospital and not realizing how alike he and his brother looked, said, "Mr. Hart, you're not going to get well running in and out of the hospital like that." Though *I* never saw any real resemblance between them, Larry and Teddy were frequently mistaken for one another. We remained in town until Teddy was well enough to rejoin his show. Larry was surprisingly relaxed and patient during our stay. It was something I was beginning to notice: the frenetic pace he maintained slowed down considerably when he was away from the city. The small Southern town seemed to charm him and there was no sign of the restlessness that everyone considered so much a part of his temperament.

After the tour, late one night, as Larry and I sat before the fire in his room in New York, Larry mentioned what he had discussed with me on several previous evenings: the onset of the middle years. Knowing Larry's bouncy, dynamic, irrepressible personality, one could not visualize a Larry Hart entering a period of decline with any less energy or spirit or vigor.

That night his face had the somber expression very few people, even friends, knew—it was a face completely devoid of humor; morbid and melancholy. He was going to his doctor for treatments, he said with a resigned shrug. He was slowing down, and was beginning to feel his age. I tried to assure him that it was simply a matter of not getting the proper food, the proper rest. . . . Suddenly it occurred to me that I was talking to a man of forty-six as though he were seventy! But Larry's disordered life would have been debilitating to anyone at any age.

Almost with relief he said, "That's the way it should be. Nature sends the message. I'm getting old. . . ." It was about this time that there was a change in the effect of alcohol on his system. It might have been physical, but now it only took a couple of drinks to make him drunk. Psychiatrists claim that alcoholics are childish and dependent, angry people who turn their rage inward on themselves. I think this was true of Larry. Larry had his self-hate, his feelings of being a "freak" in appearance. But there are beautiful people, before the public, adored and admired, who have gone down the same self-destructive path. Where did *their* rage spring from?

Maureen O'Hara in the very last Rodgers and Hart musical written especially for the movies, *They Met in Argentina. Variety*'s critic hit the nail on the head in his review: "It is extremely dubious if *They Met in Argentina* will further the cause of hemispheric solidarity."

Left to right, Larry, Bill Carter, Irving Eisman and Dick Voyno, at a bar in Palisades Park, New Jersey. Dick Voyno was an important producer of musical-comedy recordings. Bill Carter, who married Dwight Wiman's daughter, Trink, is obviously pleading with Larry not to take another drink. I'm afraid Larry does look spiffed in this snapshot.

Larry in 1942

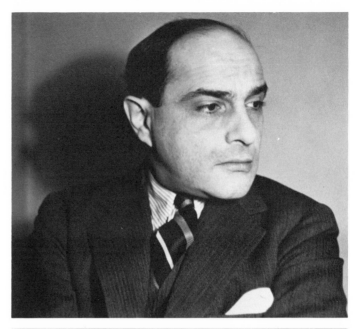

Teddy Hart

By the time of By Jupiter, *Larry's drinking and loneliness were becoming serious problems and were starting to interfere with all phases of his life and work. The many people who loved him became increasingly worried, and none more so than Teddy. No one realizes the heartbreak that Teddy went through in seeing his beloved brother in the condition of his last years. These remarks were made to me by Teddy in 1942.*

If you've known Larry only the last five years or so, you've never known Larry at all. This is not really my brother the way he was. He's a changed person. He was such a great performer. A better comedian than I am. When we lived at the Beresford and slept in the same room, he would read all night. Proust, all the highbrow authors. The light kept me up, but I didn't mind. He seemed to be always on the go, but like I said, many nights he was quiet, reading all the time. He liked to take trips in the car a lot. Once he drove up to New Rochelle to see a cousin. We stopped in at a little store and Larry bought a large rug to take up there. He wouldn't let them deliver it. He dragged it to the car with some help. He got a kick doing things like that. He was like that as a kid—always giving things away. When I was looking for a job in Hollywood, he introduced me to everyone he knew who could help me. Of course, you never really get anywhere that way. But a few days' work here and there helped pay the rent.

When I really got my opportunity it wasn't through Larry. Though I guess it didn't hurt to invite Alex Yokel to swim in Larry's pool. Yokel put me in *Three Men*, but Abbott had to O.K. me. And when I tried to see Jed Harris for *Inspector General*, I sat outside his office all day to see him. When he came out at five o'clock he said, "You're still here. All right, you get the job." But he didn't know I was Larry's brother. During rehearsal he asked me, "Why didn't you tell me you were Larry's brother?" Well, I knew by then you were better off not telling anyone you were related to a celebrity. They figured you didn't need the job.

The thing was, he was always so smart. Even when he was very small I was really in awe of him. But he was always so confident that I would make good—always encouraging and trying to help. You can't believe the kind of guy he was—a dynamo. They called him "The Rehearser" at camp. He never would stop rehearsing. I think he liked that better than anything—directing everybody. He's different now. This is a different Larry that you are seeing—not the man he was. . . .

Ray Bolger as Sapiens in *By Jupiter*. Speaking of this superb role, Ray said "This is the first time in any Broadway show where my assignment has been literally half acting and half dancing, and I'm crazy about it. Not even in *On Your Toes* was I allowed such breadth of pantomime." (Ray collapsed of sheer physical exhaustion several times during the play's run, but he never complained.)

1942

By Jupiter

*Opened June 2, 1942, at the Shubert Theatre
for a run of 427 performances*

Music by Richard Rodgers
Book by Lorenz Hart and Richard Rodgers, from Julian
    Thompson's play *The Warrior's Husband*
Directed by Joshua Logan
Choreographed by Robert Alton
Settings by Jo Mielziner
Costumes by Irene Sharaff

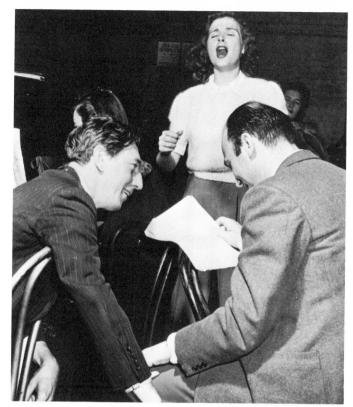

Ray Bolger, Constance Moore and Johnny Green (the show's musical director) at a *By Jupiter* rehearsal. During rehearsals, it was decided that the script wasn't funny enough. So Larry and Josh Logan stayed up half the night at the Ardsley writing new material—and had to walk down twenty-one flights of stairs the next morning, because the elevator had broken.

Nobody's Heart

⊰ *Originally sung by Constance Moore* ⊱

REFRAIN

Nobody's heart belongs to me.
Heigh-ho, who cares?
Nobody writes his songs to me,
No one belongs to me—
That's the least of my cares.
I may be sad at times, and disinclined to play,
But it's not bad at times to go your own sweet way.
Nobody's arms belong to me,
No arms feel strong to me.
I admire the moon
As a moon,
Just a moon.
Nobody's heart belongs to me today.

INTERLUDE

Ride, Amazon, ride.
Hunt your stags and bears.
Take life in its stride.
Heigh-ho, who cares?
Go hunting with pride,
Track bears to their lairs.
Ride, Amazon, ride.
Heigh-ho, who cares?

COMIC REPRISE

⊰ *Originally sung by Ray Bolger* ⊱

Nobody's heart belongs to me.
Heigh-ho, that's bad.
Love's never sung her songs to me.
I have never been had.
I've had no trial in the game of man and maid.
I'm like a violin that no one's ever played.
Words about love are Greek to me.
Nice girls won't speak to me.
I despise the moon
As a moon,
It's a prune.
Nobody's heart belongs to me today.

Wait Till You See Her

⊰ *Originally sung by Ronald Graham* ⊱

VERSE

My friends who knew me
Never would know me,
They'd look right through me,
Above and below me,
And ask, "Who's that man?
Who is that man?
That's not my light-hearted friend!"
Meeting one girl
Was the start of the end.
Love is a simple emotion
A friend should comprehend.

REFRAIN

Wait till you see her,
See how she looks,
Wait till you hear her laugh.
Painters of paintings,
Writers of books,
Never could tell the half.
Wait till you feel
The warmth of her glance,
Pensive and sweet and wise.
All of it lovely,
All of it thrilling,
I'll never be willing to free her.
When you see her.
You won't believe your eyes.

Ev'rything I've Got

{ *Originally sung by Benay Venuta and Ray Bolger* }

1st VERSE

She: Don't stamp your foot at me,
It's impolite.
To stamp your foot at me
Is not quite right.
At man's ingratitude
A woman winks,
But such an attitude just stinks.

1st REFRAIN

I have eyes for you to give you dirty looks.
I have words that do not come from children's books.
There's a trick with a knife I'm learning to do,
And ev'rything I've got belongs to you.
I've a powerful anaesthesia in my fist,
And the perfect wrist to give your neck a twist.
There are hammerlock holds,
I've mastered a few,
And ev'rything I've got belongs to you.
Share for share, share alike,
You get struck each time I strike.
You for me—me for me—
I'll give you plenty of nothing.
I'm not yours for better but for worse,
And I've learned to give the well-known witches' curse.
I've got a terrible tongue, a temper for two,
And ev'rything I've got belongs to you.

2nd VERSE

He: Don't raise your voice at me,
That's very rude.
To raise your voice at me
Is rather crude.
It's wrong essentially when woman yells,
And confidentially, it smells.

2nd REFRAIN

I'll converse with you on politics at length,
I'll protect you with my superhuman strength.
If you're ever attacked I'll scream and say, "Boo!"
And ev'rything I've got belongs to you.
I will never stray from home, I'll just stay put,
'Cause I've got a brand-new thing called athlete's foot.
I'm a victim of colds, anemia, too,
And ev'rything I've got belongs to you.
Off to bed we will creep,
Then we'll sleep and sleep and sleep
Till the birds start to peep.
I'll give you plenty of nothing.
I'll be yours forever and a day
If the first good breeze does not blow me away.
You're enough for one man, that's why I'll be true,
And ev'rything I've got belongs to you.

ENCORE

She: You may have some things that I can't use at all.
When I look at you, your manly gifts are small.
I've a wonderful way of saying adieu,
And ev'rything I've got belongs to you.

He: You won't know how good I am until you try

And you'll let my well of loneliness run dry.
I've a marvelous way of telling you no,
And ev'ryting I've got belongs to yo.
And ev'rything you want belongs to me!
And ev'rything you need belongs to me!

REPRISE

{ *Originally sung by Benay Venuta* }

VERSE

Life has no shape or form
And no design.
It isn't life without that fool of mine.
I used to gad about with any chap
And now I'm sad about my sap.

REFRAIN

He's a living thing that isn't quite alive,
He has brains enough for any child of five.
Oh, he isn't too rich in vigor and vim,
But ev'rything I've got belongs to him.
He's a naughty brat that can't be left alone.
He has eyes for ev'ry skirt except my own.
Even under a tree, he grabs for the limb,
But ev'rything I've got belongs to him.
Something beats in his chest,
But it's just a pump at best.
I'm for him, he's for him.
He gives me plenty of nothing.
When I see that funny face, I know
Something scared his mother twenty years ago.
But I'll never let go, he'll never be free!
Till ev'rything he's got belongs to me!
And ev'rything I've got belongs to him!
And ev'rything we've got belongs to us!

Nanette Fabray had one of her first Broadway breaks when she replaced Connie Moore as Princess Antiope in *By Jupiter.* With her here are Benay Venuta (Queen Hippolyta) and Ray Bolger as Sapiens, the Queen's "suitor."

Despite Rodgers's efforts, Larry went off to Mexico in the summer of 1942 rather than do *Oklahoma!* Larry turned down *Oklahoma!* because he didn't like the original play, *Green Grow the Lilacs.* Oscar Hammerstein II was adapting the libretto and Larry wasn't enthusiastic about Hammerstein as a librettist. He not only didn't feel like working at this point; he didn't want to work with Dick. Yet he must have known the consequences: with Oscar Hammerstein set to write the book, it wasn't too much to figure out that with such a brilliant lyricist available, Dick would ask Oscar to do the lyrics also.

I think Dick had ambivalent feelings about changing partners. As George S. Kaufman has said, "A collaboration is like a marriage without sex." The years together bind the two with invisible cement. There are the wonderful years and memories (and in the case of this partnership, there were also a success and prestige rare in the theatre.) But in a collaborative partnership, there is also a feeling of dependency. "Could I have made it without him?"—each being the half of a whole, each contributing remarkably to the other, as though each song were the result of a single effort. With Dick and Larry, as with all collaborators, there had been irritations and annoyances in their long relationship. But incredibly, there had been none of the serious arguments that so often occur in the heat of production in the theatre. As young men, they had found excitement and fun and pride and satisfaction in their accomplishments. Whatever their apprehensions, they entered middle age with the sentiment and affection of longtime friends.

Dick had no way of knowing how he would be accepted by the critics and the public without Larry. I know Larry had tremendous love and respect for Richard Rodgers. I believe that the love was mutual. After all, it is not remarkable that they split up after twenty odd years, but that they endured and survived during those years.

Two of the last pictures taken of Larry Hart, lyricist, and Richard Rodgers, composer. Note that in the photo on the right, Larry is wearing his shoes with the elevator heels.

It must be remembered that the Rodgers and Hart association was unique. Most composers, most of our top songwriters, have written with a host of collaborators: the Gershwin brothers, Hammerstein, Jule Styne, Sondheim. Only Larry and Dick had such a closely knit, extraordinary association that people never thought of one without the other.

When they first collaborated, Dick was still a teen-ager, and Larry had been the older, the wiser, the sophisticate that Dick looked up to: the theatre-wise, show-wise, worldly-wise self-assured senior partner. As Dick told me, and others, "Larry was incredibly good at knowing where to spot a number, where to stop the story line for the song. *He* knew and did it all in a flash, in a moment, and it was right." Dick learned about the theatre from Larry and he learned it well, and aside from Dick's family, the theatre has remained his whole life. But in 1942, at the time Rodgers suggested *Oklahoma!*, Larry, who had been infatuated with actors and the profession since childhood, had reached an impasse. He didn't know where he wanted to go, but Dick knew. He wanted to climb every mountain professionally. He wanted to be greater than Gershwin, greater than Kern, greater than anybody. Ambition, when you have Rodgers's talent and genius and capacity for hard, relentless work, is admirable and exciting. Dick Rodgers's success is well deserved: he followed his star. Nevertheless, Larry was not a falling meteor, its flame dying in descent to earth. His talents never burned out, and there were several songs written under adverse circumstances in the last months of his life, for the revival of *A Connecticut Yankee*, that were as good as anything he had ever done. His very last song, "To Keep My Love Alive," written for Vivienne Segal in the same show, received the highest praise from the reviewers.

But Larry was in a depressed state long before *Oklahoma!* and long before 1942. Time had caught up with him. Life had lost its savor. Only a few years before, in 1939, his face had lit up when he showed me a financial statement. "Look, Dotsy," he had said, with something like disbelief. "I made a quarter of a million dollars last year." (That was a tremendous sum in that period.) A short year before he had shrugged and said, "I'm sixty thousand dollars in debt. But who cares about money? I'd be just as happy without it."

Being broke to Larry meant borrowing large sums from the bank. His life style remained the same. Larry would never look at the right side of a dinner menu or turn down someone for a loan or ride the subway. His pride in his income was a professional one. He really didn't care about accumulating money. But he would have been helpless without it.

Late in 1942, with Larry at leisure, it seemed time for another trip. Frieda accompanied us to Miami. In Washington, D.C., the train stopped at length at the station. On an adjoining track, a hospital train, with wounded soldiers returned from overseas for hospital care, attracted Larry's attention. It was New Year's Eve. Larry suggested that I go over and wish the boys a happy new year, as it must have been a lonely time for them.

I was shy about entering the train and told Larry I would go if he accompanied me. He shook his head. "They want to see a girl. A female. Go ahead . . . ." That was Larry the sentimentalist, talking like a Tin Pan Alley songwriter! Timidly I edged my way to the window of one of the cars and waved feebly. If only I looked like Marilyn Monroe! That was the kind of girl they really wanted to see, I was sure.

In Miami we stayed at a small hotel, the Roney Plaza having been taken over by the army. Frieda was constantly amused because the ladies sitting on the porch took it for granted that I was Larry's wife. Larry looked glum when she told him this with a sly look at me. For years she had been hoping that Larry would get married. "I wish she *was* my wife," he said quietly. He often spoke now about being a fool for not getting married, and there is no doubt that Teddy's happiness had impressed him. "I love you because you've made Teddy so happy," he said on several occasions. Because he had felt that no woman could really love him, he was encouraged somehow by Teddy's successful marriage.

After a few days, Larry's increasing moodiness and heavy drinking discouraged Frieda. He had made a scene in a restaurant because they didn't have something on the menu he wanted, causing us to leave in embarrassment. He was becoming difficult and almost abusive to his mother, and she decided to return to New York. It was so unlike Larry. He just wasn't himself.

We took an apartment. Fortunately Larry's attitude toward me was always restrained, and his routine in Miami was no different than it was in any other environment. The army was stationed there, but the regular winter visitors were oblivious. I ran into Sailing Baruch, Bernard Baruch's brother, who gave me the name of local psychiatrists who might be of help. Larry's behavior was strange at times, but otherwise remarkably subdued. He flirted with pretty and not-so-pretty waitresses, something I'd never known him to do before. He'd heretofore noticed only elegant women. Though I continued to show him solicitude and tried to hold down his drinking without acting overbearing, Larry accepted my "Brother, dear brother, come home with me now" attentions when he was in the midst of his "John L. Sullivan could lick them all" at his favorite bar. At times when I appeared discouraged, he patted my hand consolingly: "I know, Dotsy, you're trying to keep me from drinking . . . ." and he shook his head as if to say "No use." But I thought he was glad to have someone close by, disapproving perhaps, but not pressuring him.

I knew I was just giving him custodial care, when he needed professional treatment. But if Teddy or I insisted, he would run again, this time away from us.

We had returned to New York, when, early one morning in April 1943, Frieda awoke in unbearable pain. Before the arrival of the ambulance Larry, in panic, ran from the apartment. His mother was seventy-four years old; Larry knew she would not be coming home again. We visited Frieda at the hospital after a hopeless operation. She was being fed intravenously, there was blood plasma being administered and though a second operation had been scheduled, her condition had made it an impossibility. We were going to lose Frieda.

Tears drenched Larry's face as he kissed her hand, pretending in a too loud, too cheerful voice that she would be home soon. His tears never stopped and he never stopped talking, building up to a sort of hysteria. It was frightening because while he thought his laughter was reassuring, his sobbing was agonized, and Frieda wasn't fooled. "Take care of my boys, Dorothy," she whispered. It was too much for me and I ran out of the room. Larry followed, pulling me back. "Don't be a coward. Face it." But *he* couldn't face his mother's funeral. He disappeared just as we left the apartment, and services were held up until he was located at a nearby bar. Then the family drove out to Long Island, to an old Jewish cemetery where Max Hart's lodge long ago had distributed family plots. As we approached the car to return home, Larry nudged Teddy. "There doesn't seem any reason for Uncle Willie to go home."

Uncle Willie, ninety-two, was with us in the car, and he was with us six months later as we drove to the same cemetery. That time we were burying Larry next to Max and Frieda.

After the funeral, we returned to Larry's apartment. Teddy and I rested in Frieda's room on the twin beds, and there were half a dozen people running riot in the kitchen and living room, behaving as though at long last the house were theirs. Mary went about her duties silently, casting mean glances at them and ostentatiously taking the food from the refrigerator to her room, as was her custom when what she called "the riffraff" were about. The bar was busy, and Larry kept running in and out of the bedroom, kissing and hugging me with quick-changing moods, crying and laughing at the same time, as he had at the hospital.

"They're dancing on my mother's grave," Teddy said in disgust. Larry was confused, not too conscious of the impropriety of the actions of these so-called friends. He was drinking and seemed almost incoherent.

A late portrait of Frieda

We finally had to leave Larry in his large apartment in his unhappy state, though at least Mary remained a familiar and sympathetic figure. But how would Larry manage without some family member close by, when so many had their hands out to take advantage of his kindness and generosity?

Then one day Larry turned up and said, "Dotsy, look for two apartments next door to each other. I want to be near you and Teddy." But an actor's salary, good as it was, was not an income. Teddy had been in four shows in six years without a letup, and there had been only one flop, *The More the Merrier* (which failed only because the producer had foolishly allowed Hollywood to buy off William Bendix's contract: Teddy and Bendix had made a hilarious comedy team, but the show didn't work when Bendix was replaced by a straight man instead of another comedian). Still, Larry and I looked at adjoining apartments at the Essex House. It would have been wonderful, but Teddy couldn't afford it. A year before there had been a vacancy in the apartment next door to Larry's at the Ardsley, smaller than Larry's and not so expensive, but still too costly for us. Larry insisted he would pay the difference, but Teddy had struggled too hard for his financial independence. And besides, could we take all the aggravation and confusion in the Larry Hart apartment?

If only Larry could have submitted to a more sensible way of life, we would have enjoyed trying to give him some kind of family home, which he needed. But the sort of hangers-on that had attached themselves to him were people we couldn't tolerate.

"I don't want to work." It wasn't a petulant Larry but an exhausted one. I think the challenge was no longer there; it was all too easy. Perhaps the challenge had gone out of living, too. In 1943, Paul Gallico approached him with the idea of making a musical comedy about the French underground. He had finished the book, called it *Miss Underground*. George Balanchine would do the choreography. With Kron and Bender pressing Larry to do it, he agreed. It progressed fitfully. Emmerich Kálmán, a famous Viennese composer who was set to write the music, and a war refugee who was no longer young, wandered around the large apartment at the Ardsley, looking for a lyricist who did not want to be found.

But as Balanchine says in his interview in this book, because of the war, money could not be raised for the show. It was a difficult time, and even Rodgers and Hammerstein had trouble financing *Oklahoma!*

Then Alex Yokel came along with a book by Richard Shattuck, *The Snark was a Boojum*. This jabberwocky was about six or seven pregnant women in various supposedly hilarious situations. Since Yokel had discovered *Three Men on a Horse*, perhaps he knew something. But when Larry completed half the script, and we didn't find it at all funny, everyone's lack of enthusiasm for what was to be a straight non-musical show got to Larry. He stopped work abruptly. Then Alex came over to the apartment one day, with the intention of spiriting Larry away somewhere to complete the dramatization. He was desperate, not having had a hit since *Three Men*. What followed was just like the scene in *Three Men* where the newlywed Irwin is kidnapped by the three men who want him to continue picking the horses on paper, without being bothered by domestic duties. And if Teddy hadn't been present the scene surely would have been repeated in its entirety. Larry was in no condition to go anywhere. There was actually a tug of war as Larry lay on his bed in a helpless state. We realized then more than ever how dangerous it was to leave Larry in the hands of almost anyone who wanted to use him.

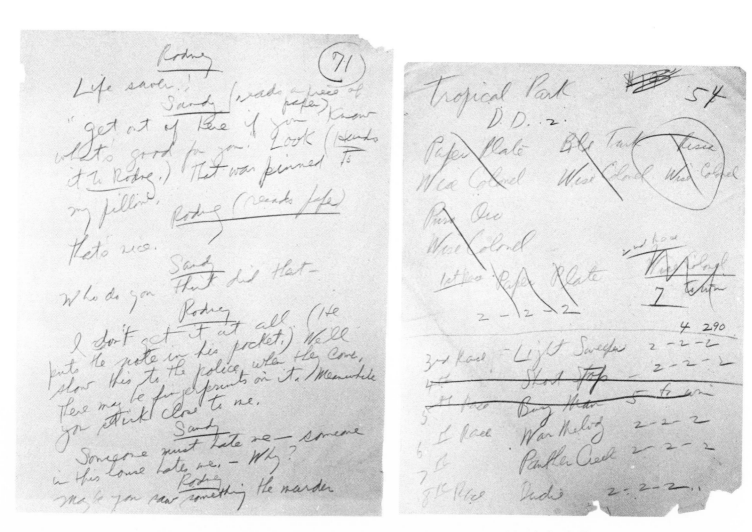

Left, a page of the manuscript of *The Snark Was a Boojum*, which Larry didn't finish. Right, one of Larry's handwritten scratch sheets. He never lost his interest in playing the horses.

Larry once said of Vivienne Segal, "I would rather be caught dead wearing a suit I wouldn't be caught dead wearing than weather one of Viv Segal's storms." It was her fiery temperament, plus her superb soprano delivery, that made Vivienne the perfect singer for "To Keep My Love Alive."

Vivienne Segal

Trained as both a dancer and a singer, Vivienne Segal is one of the brightest star names in the history of American musicals. Larry revitalized her career with the role of Countess Peggy Palaffi in I Married an Angel, *and, after that, she went on to shine as both a singer and a comedienne in* Pal Joey *and in the revival of* A Connecticut Yankee. *When she returned to Broadway in the 1952* Pal Joey, *she was, if anything, a more bewitching Vera Simpson than she had been twelve years before.*

Several months before he died, Larry was helping cast at the auditions for the revival of *A Connecticut Yankee.* I sat with him in the orchestra while girls in turn said their little piece or sang their songs and with the customary "Thank you" were politely ushered off stage. One girl was exceptionally beautiful. I called Larry's attention to her appearance. He shook his head.

"But, Larry, she's *beautiful. . . .*"

Again Larry shook his head. "Talent is beautiful," he said firmly. And this is the way Larry was. If you were his friend and needed money, he'd give you anything. But he wouldn't give you a job in his shows unless he really believed you were the best possible person for the role.

Years before that, I was appearing in Los Angeles in *Music in the Air.* Larry and Dick were out there at MGM and came backstage to say hello. The first thing they said was, "You're a comedienne!" I'd been trying to convince producers of that for years, after having been a musical-comedy star playing idiotic ingenues almost all my life. How long can you try to look eighteen?

Before Larry left, he said, "I'm going to write a part for you soon." We ran into each other in New York several times after that and I kept asking, "Where's that part you're going to write for me?" and he kept repeating, "When the time comes, when I get the right thing, I'll let you know."

One truly marvelous thing about Larry. I could have been his sweetheart, but he didn't feel I was right for something that he was doing; no soap. So I felt he was not just stringing me. I saw him again accidentally at Sardi's one day and he said, oh, so casually, "You're in my next play." He wasn't making a big thing of it. "When you're called for it you'll find out and you'll be good in it."

It was *I Married an Angel.*

Two Rodgers and Hart shows followed: *Pal Joey* and the revival of *A Connecticut Yankee.* I was a comedienne! *Angel* was the first real comedy part I had ever played and the critics were very kind to me. Larry and Dick wrote three new songs for me for *Yankee.* "To Keep My Love Alive" was the last song Larry wrote.

I had a terrible experience with that song. It was the night after he died. The theatre was sold out. Greer Garson was out front, and many other celebrities. I was terribly shaken up because I was fond of Larry. We had

become very good friends. Dick Rodgers has said that I was the only woman Larry ever loved. Larry did ask me to marry him. I loved Larry in a way, but not that way. I told Larry that we would always remain good friends, but that marriage was out of the question.

I thought of this as I went on stage that night. "To Keep My Love Alive" was a difficult number. Each couplet was a different story. I got one of the husbands' names wrong, so I just pulled one of the names out of the second chorus and sang it in the first! By the time I got to the second chorus, I was so confused I simply didn't know how to continue. It had never happened to me before in a long career. Since I was playing a queen, I made a royal bow to the audience, said, "I'm so sorry," and walked offstage. Luckily, I had printed the names of all the husbands I had knocked off in the song on the proscenium. After a quick glance at the names and trying awfully hard to think straight, I walked back on stage, still with queenly dignity, and started the song all over again from the beginning. I received an undeserved ovation. The audience was so understanding and must have realized what I was going through.

1944

A Connecticut Yankee

Opened November 17, 1943, at the Martin Beck Theatre for a run of 135 performances

Music by Richard Rodgers
Directed by John C. Wilson
Choreographed by William Holbrook and Al White, Jr.
Settings and Costumes by Nat Karson

To Keep My Love Alive

{ *Originally sung by Vivienne Segal* }

VERSE

I've been married and married,
And often I've sighed,
I'm never a bridesmaid,
I'm always the bride.
I never divorced them—
I hadn't the heart.
Yet remember these sweet words
"Till death do us part."

1st REFRAIN

I married many men,
A ton of them,
And yet I was untrue to none of them
Because I bumped off ev'ry one of them
To keep my love alive.

Sir Paul was frail;
He looked a wreck to me.
At night he was a horse's neck to me.
So I performed an appendectomy
To keep my love alive.
Sir Thomas had insomnia;
He couldn't sleep at night.
I bought a little arsenic.
He's sleeping now all right.
Sir Philip played the harp;
I cussed the thing.
I crowned him with his harp
To bust the thing.
And now he plays where harps are
Just the thing,
To keep my love alive,
To keep my love alive.

2nd REFRAIN

I thought Sir George had possibilities,
But his flirtations
Made me ill at ease, and
When I'm ill at ease,
I kill at ease
To keep my love alive.
Sir Charles came from a sanatorium
And yelled for drinks
In my emporium.
I mixed one drink—
He's in memoriam
To keep my love alive.
Sir Francis was a singing bird,
A nightingale.
That's why I tossed him
Off my balcony,
To see if he could fly.
Sir Athelstane indulged in fratricide;
He killed his Dad and that was patricide.
One night I stabbed him at my mattress side
To keep my love alive,
To keep my love alive.

ENCORE

I caught Sir James with his protectoress,
The rector's wife, I mean the rectoress.
His heart stood still—angina pectoris
To keep my love alive.
Sir Frank brought ladies to my palaces.
I poured a mickey in their chalices.
While paralyzed they got paralysis
To keep my love alive.
Sir Alfred worshiped falconry;
He used to hunt at will.
I sent him on a hunting trip.
They're hunting for him still.
Sir Peter had an incongruity,
Collecting girls with promiscuity.
Now I'm collecting his annuity
To keep my love alive,
To keep my love alive.

Sir Ethelbert would use profanity;
His language drove me near insanity.
So once again I served humanity
To keep my love alive.
Sir Curtis made me cook each dish he ate,
And ev'rything his heart could wish he ate,
Until I fiddled with the fish he ate
To keep my love alive.
Sir Marmaduke was awf'lly tall;
He didn't fit in bed.
I solved that problem easily—
I just removed his head.
Sir Mark adored me with formality;
He called a kiss an immorality.
And so I gave him immortality
To keep my love alive,
To keep my love alive.

"Thou swell, thou witty," sixteen years later. This time Dick Foran and Julie Warren were the Yankee and Sandy, and the number was still a show-stopper. It was also a hit as sung and danced by June Allyson in *Words and Music*, MGM's not-very-accurate film biography of Rodgers and Hart, made five years later.

After Frieda's death, Larry gave up the apartment at the Ardsley, at William Kron's insistence, and moved to the Hotel Delmonico. (Kron was also involved in the retirement of Mary and the departure of her daughter.) After Larry moved, he gave me his mother's jewelry, while Kron stood by protesting. "Mama wanted Dorothy to have it," he insisted. "It's hers." Kron was not present when he turned over to me the wedding ring Frieda had worn for over fifty years. I wanted Larry to wear the simple gold band. He shook his head: "You should have it." I was tremendously moved. It was then that he told me that he was going to ask his longtime Hollywood friend, Frances Manson, to marry him. He seemed assured of her answer. It was only later that Frances told me he had asked her to marry him many times. Sometime in September of 1943, Larry showed me a copy of Fielding's *Tom Jones*. He seemed excited: "I'm going to speak to Dick about this. It would make a great musical. There are wonderful parts for Teddy and Hope Emerson" (who had recently appeared as husband and wife in a revival of *The New Moon* at Carnegie Hall). I couldn't quite believe what Larry still believed. Did he still consider Dick Rodgers his partner, when Dick had received such acclaim for *Oklahoma!*? I never knew whether he actually approached Dick about *Tom Jones*, because I went to Boston with Teddy for the dog days of *One Touch of Venus*, the Mary Martin show, and the next thing I knew, Larry was calling us from Doctors Hospital where he was writing six new songs for a revival of *Connecticut Yankee*. Laughing all the while, Larry sang the lyrics of "To Keep My Love Alive," and we joined in the fun, feeling things *must* be picking up for Larry.

When the revival of *A Connecticut Yankee* was having its pre-Broadway tryout, Larry called from Philadelphia: "Come. I need you to take care of me." When I arrived at the hotel, Larry was in a puckish mood, a little boy playing hide-and-go-seek with his nanny. He was sharing a suite with Herb Fields, who was back to the early "Herbert Richard Lorenz" association for the revival. All these years he had been working with his sister, Dorothy, writing many hit shows, and he had seen very little of Larry. I had never met him, but now I liked him immediately.

While Larry dressed, Herb told me how dismayed he was at the shocking change in Larry. He told me Larry was drinking constantly and becoming unmanageable. But Larry fussed over me, saw to it that I had the best room, breakfast in bed, and a seat for Oscar Hammerstein's wonderful new show *Carmen Jones*, which was breaking in in Philadelphia also.

Herb was unhappy with *A Connecticut Yankee*, which Richard Rodgers was producing. He didn't like his billing or Larry's billing, but Larry didn't react. He didn't seem to care, even though he had always shown excitement at writing for Vivienne Segal, who was playing Queen Morgan Le Fay. He responded only to the warmth and presence of his old partner and friend. When we ran into Dick Rodgers in the lobby at the hotel, Larry seemed fearful. Larry was in such bad shape, and obviously not up to the half a dozen new songs that were needed. After Larry and I had talked to Oscar Hammerstein, I went to my room in tears. The contrast between the dignified Hammerstein, who had replaced Larry as Rodgers's collaborator, and Larry's pathetic demeanor appeared to penetrate even Larry's befuddled mind. He seemed to cringe. It was wrong for Larry to be seen in public. Had he been back in New York, he would have been in Doctors Hospital. The next day I had to take Larry to Wanamaker's to get him a new overcoat, since he had mislaid three overcoats in the past month. They had been custom-made, and the fact that Larry would accept a store-bought coat—and one from the boy's department at that—showed his indifference to everything going on around him.

It was at William Kron's suggestion that I returned to New York, since he told me he would look after Larry. Why didn't I suspect that Kron, along with others, was trying to keep Larry away from Teddy

Some of Larry's wartime memorabilia. Left, a letter of recommendation he wrote for Irving Eisman, who wanted a job in intelligence rather than a rookie post in the regular army. (Irving, who is pictured on page 163, got the job in intelligence.) Right, the sheet-music cover of a song Larry and Dick wrote at the request of the Air Force.

and me so that they could control him without the family influence? Incredible. That only happened in fiction! The emotional strain of leaving Teddy alone in New York while he was still mourning his mother and was so disturbed about his brother made me question: Where did my duty lie? Could I continue to traipse after Larry watching with heartbreak what was happening to him? Yet what else *could* I do when my presence seemed to give him some comfort?

A few days after I returned to New York and to Teddy, Dick Rodgers called Larry's doctor, who arrived on the scene with a nurse and placed him in Doctors Hospital. Then the day before the opening of *A Connecticut Yankee* Larry called to suggest that I see a friend of his, Jules Glaenzer, vice president of Cartier's. I was to get a gold cigarette case for Herb Fields and something special for Vivienne. These past years Larry had delegated me to buy his Christmas presents or incidentals he might need for himself. But this was different! This would be expensive, and I wasn't sure how much he wanted me to spend. I called William Kron, explaining the problem. "Don't buy anything," he snapped. "Larry can't afford it! And he can't afford to take you out to dinner either!"

Early in the afternoon of the opening of the new show, Larry came by our apartment. He was again on his way to not being sober. Cheerfully, he handed me a dozen pair of theatre tickets to be distributed to certain people he named. We were in for a bad night, because Larry had every intention of being there. Teddy planned to use a little strategy to keep Larry away, since we had been advised by an acquaintance that Dick Rodgers had given orders to the stage manager to have Larry removed from the Alvin Theatre if he became difficult. We understood his position, but did not understand his not asking our help or notifying us about what was likely to happen. Teddy called a cousin, Billy Friedberg, a theatre publicist. He agreed to station himself down the block on West Fifty-second Street, off Broadway. Teddy had to go on to his performance of *One Touch of Venus.*

We anticipated a bad night all around, but Billy was a favorite of Larry's and we figured on his holding action to keep Larry away from the Alvin until after the curtain had gone up. I got to the theatre early, planting myself right under the marquee and keeping an eye on Eighth Avenue. I was counting also on Harry Irving, a writer friend of Larry and Teddy, to be of further assistance if necessary. It was all a terrible mess.

As the audience drifted in, I kept counting off the critics I knew by sight. Once they got in, I could relax a bit. (Opening nights are horrible; I broke out in hives whenever Teddy or Larry opened, and even at an opening that had a casual friend in the cast I fell apart.) I couldn't relax too much though, because I was prepared—almost—for what did happen. A grim-faced, unsmiling Dick arrived. Suddenly I was surrounded by a dozen impatient couples. "But Larry said you had our tickets!" They all said it at once. Since I had already given the tickets I had to those Larry had listed, I was in a quandary. I had even given away my own ticket, to a daughter of Larry's business manager, and she hadn't been on his list! Of course, there were no more tickets available for the opening night.

At this moment I saw Larry headed toward the theatre from the Broadway side. Billy corralled him, putting his arm around him and genially guiding him to a bar a few doors away. Larry almost brushed him

In Philadelphia, Larry posed for this publicity shot with the cast of *A Connecticut Yankee.* On his right are Dick Foran and Robert Chisholm (the show's King Arthur). Larry is supposed to be giving them directions. But, by this time, he was in no shape to direct anybody.

aside, as the entrance was already cleared of patrons, and the curtain bell had sounded. But because he was so fond of Billy and perhaps because he could never resist that one more drink, he disappeared. So had the crowd of disappointed theatre-goers without tickets, victims of Larry's misplaced generosity.

I stood in the foyer as the opening strains of the overture began — that always magical moment for me, for any avid theatre lover. Curtain going up—and then Larry returned. He wasn't sober! I could tell by his walk. In only a few minutes he was right there beside me, checking his coat and hat. It was a chilly, rainy November night. Noisily, Larry tried to drag me into the theatre with him. I was afraid of a scene, so I shook my head, telling him I had given my seat away. I didn't want him to suspect that I was standing guard. A moment later Dick was also in the foyer, ignoring me in his nervousness. He had seen Larry going in. Dick paced, and I stood rigid, staring straight ahead, apprehensive. The first act ended without anything untoward happening. Then Larry was there again, ready to brave the weather for a return to the bar. But he didn't get his hat and coat. I spoke banteringly to him about his not having an overcoat. "I'm fine, fine, Dorothy. Don't worry about me. I'm fine." As he got to the exit, Charlie Abramson, a prominent agent, grabbed him: "Don't go out there, Larry. It's raining." But Larry twisted himself out of Charlie's grasp so that his coat jacket almost remained clutched in Charlie's hand. The second-act curtain had already gone up when Larry was back, staggering. He went into the theatre without a word. I felt that any interference at this point would have created a scene. Ten minutes hadn't elapsed before Larry was in the foyer, his arm held by Eddie, the stage manager, whom I knew. He pantomimed that Larry was not to return to the theatre. I asked Eddie to get a cab and he helped me put Larry into it. I later learned that Larry had disturbed theatre patrons by singing along with Vivienne and laughing at the wrong moments.

The doorman at my apartment house helped me take Larry to my door (he was familiar with Larry's appearance because Larry came to the house almost daily and handed out five-dollar bills to everyone in uniform). Once inside, I put him to bed on the couch. What a sad opening night—and what a sad Larry! How different from the previous openings, with the parties and the waiting for the reviews and all the excitement and Larry rubbing his hands happily. Rumpled though he was, I hadn't removed his clothes. I was waiting for Teddy to get back from his show. This wasn't an opening, it was the end of a man, and that is what I kept seeing and feeling. Could Teddy and I have done something to save Larry from this night? Doctors and psychiatrists we had consulted had said nothing could be done without the patient's "own will and desire to recover." Teddy arrived, troubled after being informed by the doorman of Larry's condition. We exchanged a look of despair. Where to turn now? We sat talking for hours. We should have gotten Larry the psychiatric attention he needed, instead of those futile trips to Doctors Hospital. But the talk of the "crazy house" going on around him by the entourage and even by Frieda held us back. As next of kin, Teddy had the right—no, the duty—to help him recover from this destructive illness. I had tried to tell Dick something of what was going on, about the conspiracy going on around Larry, the manipulation to split him up with his partner, to get Larry away from his family and his friends.

As he had done since Frieda's passing, Larry came by the apartment at all hours, never wishing to be alone at the hotel. He had slept on the sofa so many nights, never too comfortably. When I looked in on him several times during this night, he was perspiring and breathing heavily, but by morning he had left the apartment without telling anyone. (During this sad period I had been going to the doctor for a series of X-rays, with all the symptoms of an ulcer, but happily, the ulcer I thought I had turned out to be an unexpected pregnancy! Larry never knew. As Doc Bender said nine months later, it might have given Larry something to live for, and Teddy and I named our son Lorenz Hart II.)

When I saw Larry next, I tried to show him the reviews of *A Connecticut Yankee*, but he brushed the papers away. Instead, he preferred to talk about Teddy in *One Touch of Venus*. For the first time Herb Fields had liked one of Teddy's performances, and I gathered that it was because Teddy was not the baggy-pants low comic in the show. (He had been dressed by Mainbocher. How odd it had seemed when I accompanied the famous couturier, who was outfitting Mary Martin in the show, to a swank shop for Teddy's clothes! We were so used to buying Teddy his costumes in some second-hand clothes store!)

Teddy was almost a straight man in the show. He would have preferred the Gee clothes and more laughs, but Larry was so proud of him.

Two days after *Yankee* opened, Larry was taken from his hotel apartment to Doctors Hospital at five-thirty on a Friday afternoon, November 19, 1943. A close friend of Teddy's, the actor Seldon Bennett, was with him. Seldon's blood was tested as a possible donor, because Larry had apparently been walking around with pneumonia since the night he was ejected from the Alvin.

Immediately after we were notified, Teddy and I hurried to the hospital. Kron was there, and the doctor advised us not to see Larry as he was delirious and very disturbed — which hampered the necessary treatment. We were lulled by the doctor's words that Larry's condition was "serious but not critical." Hadn't Larry licked pneumonia so easily five years before? Somehow, we didn't consider his changed physical condition in the last few years, for small as he was Larry had a strong constitution, and a fighting spirit,so we were concerned, but not alarmed.

But the next day the news was grim. We were all anxious, including Dorothy Rodgers, who kept reminiscing fondly about the funny and exasperating things Larry had done in the past. Like at a wake. But who could believe that Larry's vital spirit could ever be crushed? We could only visualize the indomitable, indestructible Larry of a few years back, as we kept a continual vigil in the waiting room at the hospital. Friends dropped by. Dorothy Rodgers was there a good deal, also Harry Irving. Sulfa had been administered after a blood transfusion. I knew that Larry had had a bad reaction to sulfa the year before, but it wasn't until later, when I read the hospital records and the complete nurses' chart, that I learned that Larry's heart had stopped twice and only after emergency treatment had started again. At no time was Teddy given a true evaluation or progress report. Again and again we were refused entry to Larry's room, though both Kron and the doctor advised us later that Larry was calling for me. Today, looking back, it seems incredible that Teddy and I could have been so naïve and trusting. But somehow we never for a moment doubted Larry's recovery. And how could we take the chance that a little excitement on seeing us might not change his condition for the worse? When Larry's condition failed to improve, Irene Gallagher, a secretary at Chappell Music Publishers who was a friend of Larry's called up John Golden, the producer, who contacted his close friend Eleanor Roosevelt. A new discovery, penicillin, was being used by the army. It had not yet been released to the public. Mrs. Roosevelt arranged for the new miracle drug to be delivered to Doctors Hospital.

With Larry hallucinating and disoriented, we still sat in the waiting room, not daring to disobey orders and see him. The red tape involved in releasing the medicine meant that Larry couldn't be treated until the twenty-second. Perhaps too late to really help. As it turned out, when the penicillin arrived it was too late.

Nurses'chart: "Patient tossed off his oxygen tent and was difficult to control . . . ."

All this time, Teddy and I lay awake planning for Larry's recovery. He would go to work at MGM, as he had been asked to, and do the *Ziegfeld Follies* for what was then the great sum of $38,000. I would go along, as he had requested, to help settle him, get an apartment and secretary. Then, as he had told me just a few weeks before, he was going to ask Frances Manson, his long-time Hollywood friend, to marry him. Larry knew marriage was his lifeline—a man was a fool to think he could live without a woman.

Why did we have to just wait? Couldn't we go in and hold his hand, as he had held Max's and Frieda's? Why did we have to just wait when he must want to see Teddy, of all people. Couldn't we go in—now? Then suddenly, at exactly nine o'clock on the evening of November 22, the lights went out. The war blackout and darkened the hospital corridor, and at that moment someone exited from Larry's room and shook his head. We could barely see him.

"He's gone."

This is a moment I can't forget, but also can't quite remember; I was in a merciful state of shock that remained for a long time. Harry Irving turned his face to the wall and wept with the heartbreak of a man who had lost a valued friend. Teddy stood too stunned for tears, not yet ready to accept or even believe.

w York Times

U. S. Pat. Off.
News That's Fit to Print.

OCHS, Publisher 1896-1935.

very Day in the Year by
ORK TIMES COMPANY.
a Hays Sulzberger,
ent and Publisher.
us Ochs Adler,
lant and General Manager.
ER N. Nelson, Secretary.
General Adler is on active duty over-

SONG WRITER

The word most frequently used to describe Lorenz Hart was the word that fitted him best, puckish. He never quite grew up. He was the college boy of the Nineteen Twenties to the end. The peculiarly brittle quality of his humor stemmed from Morningside Heights, and two decades of deep immersion in Broadway never quite soaked it off. Especially when blended with the sure suavity of Richard Rodgers' tunes his lyrics were tinpanabulation at its best: sophisticatedly simple, tenderly trite, like "With a Song in My Heart," "Isn't It Romantic," or "My Heart Stood Still"; gaily garrulous, like "To Keep My Love Alive."

From his long and memorable list of lyrics, a score or more gave a pleasure of that tingling sort which a vast public instinctively demands. For twenty years the credit line: "Music by Richard Rodgers; Lyrics by Lorenz Hart" was a signal of almost sure success. They were a remarkable team. Not the lesser of the two was "Larry" Hart, whose facility with simple words added something felicitous to our lives. That his particular genius will be missed along the Broadway where his puckish figure was so familiar goes without saying. And, since Broadway even today contributes greater than its share to the American culture, his death at the age of 48 is more than a local loss.

A POOR TAX BILL

Both the Administration and Congress—and both parties in Congress—share responsibility for the wholly inadequate tax bill which was adopted yesterday by the House of Representatives under a gag rule, without any real debate and apparently without any real awareness of the dangers of inflation The Administration, represent Treasury Department quarter from

K TIMES. TUESDAY, NOVEMBER 23, 1943.

LARRY HART, LED AS A SONG WRITER

Lyricist Who Had Combined His Talents for 20 Years With Richard Rodgers Dies

Lorenz (Larry) Hart, one of America's foremost song writers, died last night in Doctors Hospital after a short illness of pneumonia. He was 47 years old.

Lorenz Hart was Broadway's "Laureate of Lyrics." For more than twenty years he and Richard Rodgers combined their talents to write distinguished musical comedies. Mr. Hart's last contribution to the Broadway musical-comedy scene was the elaborate 1943 revival of the Fields-Hart-Rodgers hit of 1927, "A Connecticut Yankee," which included not only five of the popular numbers from the original version, such as "My Heart Stood Still," but several new tunes.

Born in this city, the son of Max M. and Frieda Hart, he prepared for college at the Columbia Grammar School, and was graduated from Columbia University.

Messrs. Hart and Rodgers met at the university on Morningside. Rodgers, 16 years of age at the time, had just entered as a freshman, and Hart was doing postgraduate work. The student body requested that they join their talents in producing the Columbia Varsity Show of 1920. For Hart, the opportunity was golden. It was a decided change from translating German plays for the Shuberts. The first effort of the two had the audience cheering. So came into being the team of Rodgers and Hart.

From 1920 to 1925 Hart and Rodgers provided such hits as "The Poor Little Ritz Girl," "Garrick Gaieties," "Dearest Enemy," "Peggy-Ann," "Betsy," "The Girl Friend." They wrote "The Greenwich Village Follies," which ran for 211 performances. Then followed such shows as "Chee-Chee," "Spring Is Here," "Ever Green," "America's Sweetheart," "Jumbo," "On Your Toes," "Babes in Arms," "I'd Rather Be Right," "I Married an Angel," "The Boys From Syracuse," "Pal Joey."

Mr. Hart wrote the lyrics for such numbers as "With a Song in My Heart," "Isn't It Romantic?" "Soon," "It's Easy to Remember but So Hard to Forget."

Rodgers and Hart never waited for the muse to strike. When a project was given them, they began work at 11 A. M. and continued with amazing dispatch. For instance, they wrote the entire score of "I'd Rather Be Right" in less than three weeks.

Both wrote lyrics and music for more than a half-dozen motion pictures.

Mr. Hart was not married.

The *Times*'s editorial on Larry, November 25, 1943.

Larry's obituary in *The New York Times*. At his funeral, there was no Rodgers and Hart music, because, as Teddy told the *Times,* Larry "often had said that funerals should be simple affairs, without emotional displays."

Walter Kerr

Larry's reputation rose steadily after his death—and it's still rising today. The 1952 revival of Pal Joey, *with Harold Lang, Vivienne Segal, Elaine Stritch and Helen Gallagher was hailed as masterpiece and ran 542 performances— longer than any of Larry's plays that were produced in his lifetime. Released in 1957, the movie of* Pal Joey, *with Frank Sinatra and Rita Hayworth, was also a great hit, as were several revivals of the show, starring Bob Fosse, at the New York City Center in the early sixties. In the same decade, the* Saturday Review *conducted a poll of the leading living American musical-comedy writers, and the respondents chose more songs with Larry Hart lyrics as their favorite show tunes than by any other lyricist. And in 1963, a new production of* The Boys from Syracuse *was mounted at the Theatre Four, stimulating Walter Kerr to write the following in the October 13 Sunday edition of the* Herald Tribune.

A while ago I was rash enough to write a piece deploring the prevailing custom of basing all musical comedies on old movies or old plays. I now want to modify my position. In fact, I want to admit I was wrong. Wrong. My confession comes not as a result of certain angry letters from composers and librettists who continue to display an exemplary loyalty to the movies they saw when they were in college. . . . I just happened to see *The Boys from Syracuse.* . . . It is like the gentle rain from heaven, that show. All you have to do is sit there and let the lyrics kick their syllables. "I am sinless," sings the condemned old man who is also father to those identical Antipholi, "I am twinless!," and you lean back in your seat in ecstatic relief that someone has remembered —someone *once* remembered—the pleasures to be wrought from compactness, from comic aptness, from the deft and daffy mating of the deadpan and the impertinent mind.

Most lyrics nowadays perform the functions of slave labor. They are always pushing something—the plot, or character, or whatever else the authors have not been able to get into the dialogue. Almost never do we hear a lyric with a leap in its heart, with a slyness in its condescension to the music, or even with an unlikely rhyme.

"This is a terrible city," begins jaunty-voiced Gary Oakes (who should be tapped for further employment

The Broadway revival of *Pal Joey* with Harold Lang and Patricia Northrop as Joey and Linda. Vivienne Segal (far right) as Vera is wondering whether she's still as bewitched, bothered and bewildered as she just sang a couple of minutes ago. When *Pal Joey* was first presented in London, two years later, one entire scene had to be omitted the night Princess Margaret attended the show. But the critic for the London *Daily Herald* wrote, "I never heard such sexy lines sung before on a British stage, but never minded them less."

the minute his contract is up) as he contemplates manfully, and metrically, the unfriendly landscape he has landed in. He isn't being significant, mind you. There is nothing wrong with the city. He isn't doing exposition, either, or recitative, in the manner of imitation Menotti. The tune is not a wail, the phrase is neither broken nor heart-broken. He is really getting ready for an impishly transplanted parody of all those home-town songs that used to keep people steadily moving into the big cities (here, it's called "Dear Old Syracuse") and he is being blunt, brassy, and right on beat about it. If your ear should happen to be particularly pleased by the conversational suddenness of "a girl I'd call pretty," you'll be pleased again, later, even in the ballads, where the mockery is kept —oh, three or four millimeters away.

Theater Four all seem to take a special, most precise delight in making certain that you hear each pleasant, pointedly spaced word. It is no doubt because the lyricist's attitude of mind—cool but secretly confiding, ironic in the presence of poetry but not unaware that the poetry is there—is a comfort to them, too. The women of the house, busy at their sewing because their men give them nothing else to be busy about, seem truly content so long as they can sing.

The lyrics that are so effortless in Ephesus, are, of course, Larry Hart's, and Mr. Hart has been sufficiently praised since he left us. One of the troubles with posthumous praise, though, is that it tends to assume that the kind of thing a man did died with him and can never be recaptured, dare never be tried again. I think somebody *should* try. They might not get the hang of it right off, and people might say that though the lyrics were in Larry Hart's vein they weren't as good as Larry Hart's, but how about if they came out *half* as good? I mean half as crisp, half as perky, half as (deceptively) easy, half as witty in stealing a note from what ought to be the next line. I'd settle.

No need here to dwell on Richard Rodgers, either, the Richard Rodgers who is so adaptable that, after having buttoned his tunes so snugly to Mr. Hart's fit, he was able to unbutton them without thrashing and write just as good music for an altogether different kind of lyricist. When I say "just as good music," I hear a wrinkling of noses. Surely, everyone will say, "better" is the word for what came out of *Oklahoma!* and *Carousel* and *South Pacific.* And perhaps it is. But I'm not going to commit myself. I don't know that *anyone* has written more melodic surprise into what was meant to be a conventional musical comedy than Mr. Rodgers did for *The Boys from Syracuse,* and to hear the still unexpected modulations of "The Shortest Day of the Year" or "You Have Cast Your Shadow on the Sea" is, today as twenty-five years ago, a shocker. Mr. Rodgers never did live along Tin Pan Alley; he was lost at sea as a boy and, when rescued, kept hearing inappropriate sounds. They are still inappropriately perfect. I've decided that I never *will* expect the modulations in "The Shortest Day of the Year," and I'm not going to try.

But what I started out to say was that *The Boys from Syracuse* is, as everyone has always known, based on a play, on two plays, perhaps on three or four plays. Its plot is borrowed, with due credit and a certain pride of race, from Shakespeare's *The Comedy of Errors,* which was borrowed from the *Menaechmi* of Plautus, which in turn may have been borrowed from a couple of oldies by Menander. And it does make hash of my earlier, querulous remarks.

It may not *seem* quite as sober and plodding and sentimental and earnest as so many of the musicals we now borrow from Loew's, Inc., or from The Best Plays of 1947. It may even seem somewhat slapdash, cocky, improvised, and unrestrained. But we must mind our manners and remember our sources with respect. A play is a play is a play, and a play by Shakespeare is a play like anything. . . .

Richard Rodgers

Dick made these remarks on the occasion of the University of Southern California's salute to Larry Hart, in November of 1973. The salute was quite an honor to Larry's memory, former subjects of USC tributes having included Vivien Leigh, Cole Porter and Helen Keller. Among those present to sing the beautiful songs of Rodgers and Hart were Gene Kelly, Benay Venuta, Lisa Kirk, Nanette Fabray, Jack Cassidy, Shirley Jones and, of course, Helen Ford.

In my whole personal life I worked with virtually only two men. And through some quirk of fortune they happened to be the two best lyric writers in the country. I worked with Oscar Hammerstein for many years and with Larry Hart for about twenty-five. It would be awfully hard for me to say which of the two was more accomplished, which of them had more talent. I do know that Larry was more difficult to work with. He was more mercurial, he was harder to find, he was harder to pin down. But when you did, it was awfully well worth it.

He was a sort of genius. He had a way with words that was simply unbelievable. He could write fast when he wanted to write fast. And he could be painstaking when he wanted to be. But he was always good. His words were clever. They were sardonic at times. They were never mean. They were often funny. And more often than most people realize today they were sentimental. As a matter of fact, the big hits of Larry's that still live today were his sentimental songs. Songs like "Where or When", which is not only sentimental but had a philosophy. It was based on the phenomenon called *déjà vu.* And Larry had been there before and made the listener believe that he had been there before.

I'd like to tell you a story that is pretty well known. It is about Larry and me in a taxicab in Paris with two girls. Suddenly a car came out of a side street and just missed us by inches. One girl screamed, "Oh, my heart stood still!" Larry said, "Say, that would make a great title for a song." I called Larry a dirty name for thinking about work.

The next thing I knew we were in London to work on a show. And I found my little black notebook with the words "My Heart Stood Still." I wrote a tune for it. Larry came into the room and I said, "I've got the tune to your lyric." And he said, "What lyric is that?" And I said, " 'My Heart Stood Still.' They're your words and it's my tune and I think we've got a song." And sure enough we did.

With "My Heart Stood Still" he wrote simply. The lyrics were monosyllabic. I don't think there is a two-syllable word in the whole song. The song is still sung today. Larry ran the whole gamut. He ran it well. He was a nice man. A good man. And he was kind. I loved working with him and I loved him. I miss him terribly. But I did have the privilege of working with him and I'm grateful for that.

Irving Berlin

I once asked Larry who his favorite songwriter was. He answered, "Irving Berlin." Then I asked him who he thought the best songwriter was. He repeated, "Irving Berlin." Larry's favorite among the great Berlin's songs was "Lazy." Since "Lazy" was just what so many of Larry's associates in the theatre always accused him of being, I wonder if that particular choice of a favorite song had any special significance. . . .

My generation, you know, are all gone. As someone who has been around for a long time, longer than many, and seen many lyric writers and songwriters come up over the years, my opinion is that Larry Hart was the first of the so-called sophisticated lyric writers. But he also wrote *words*. There is a very important distinction. "Your looks are laughable, unphotographable." That was a clever rhyme, but it tells a story about what he was trying to say about this girl. I'm not splitting hairs, and it's not semantics.

Let's put it this way. Stephen Sondheim is a lyric writer. Stephen Foster was a word writer. Larry Hart was the first of the sophisticated word writers. The important thing in my opinion, and that goes for all songwriters and for all so-called composers, is, How long do they last?

Go back to "Manhattan," which was written over fifty years ago. They still play it. It's better today. It's timeless, because there's still a Manhattan. Larry wrote about Manhattan the way other people are still trying to write about New York. They don't do it as well.

Now he's being criticized. I remember a few years ago Stephen Sondheim, a very successful lyric writer, came out of left field with an unkindly, an unjust interview about Larry Hart as a lyric writer. All I can say is that Larry Hart's lyrics have lasted for so many years. The books that Rodgers and Hart wrote their songs for weren't all successes. Most of them were pretty bad books. But out of those books came very popular songs that lasted.

You can't divorce those lyrics from Rodgers's melodies. They're not just lyrics, they're songs. If Larry had just written those lyrics (which he couldn't have, because he was probably writing to a melody or they were working together) and just printed them, they'd mean nothing. And if you just took the Rodgers melodies, as fine as they are, and just played them as orchestral numbers, they would last four hours. You see, they are *songs*. Larry Hart was a great songwriter, but I repeat, he was not only a lyric writer but a word writer. He had a fine education and could use four- and five- and six- and seven-letter words, and still get down to writing "With a Song in My Heart." I mean, he could be very simple. And very moving, when a lot of others can't be.

Then he could write songs, very sophisticated, like "You Are Too Beautiful." From my point of view, the only way you can tell is, Look at his record. Why has he lasted? In the sixty-five years I've been around as a songwriter, we've had so many great big hits, and you don't hear them anymore. And many of them include my big hits. If there are some songs that last, there must be a reason. There's a quality that has nothing whatever to do with whether you rhyme well or whether you've had any education at all. Whether you can read or write music doesn't make a damn bit of difference.

He floated his words rather than setting them down in books. He was at this point one of those who, in T. S. Eliot's words, "in his own day, made language live." It's still Larry Hart's day, although he died thirty years ago. His language is still new, still capable of telling us surprising things about each other.

—Dr. John C. Hubbard, President,
The University of Southern California,
on the occasion of the USC tribute to
Lorenz Hart, November 1973

The Plays and Films of Lorenz Hart

[Asterisked titles are songs that were dropped before plays or movies opened]

1920

Poor Little Ritz Girl

Cast included Eleanor Griffith, Charles Purcell, Lulu McConnell, Aileen Poe, Florence Webber, Donald Kerr and Elise Bonwit

Mary, Queen of Scots
Love Will Call
You Can't Fool Your Dreams
What Happened Nobody Knows
All You Need to Be a Star
Love's Intense in Tents
The Daisy and the Lark

1924

The Melody Man

Cast included Lew Fields, Fredric March, Betty Weston, Sammy White, Eva Puck and Donald Gallaher

Moonlight Mamma
I'd Like to Poison Ivy

1925

The Garrick Gaieties

Cast included Sterling Holloway, Romney Brent, Betty Starbuck, Libby Holman, Philip Loeb, June Cochrane, Edith Meiser, Lee Strasberg and Sanford Meisner

Gilding the Guild
April Fool
The Joy Spreader
Ladies of the Boxoffice
Manhattan
The Three Musketeers
Do You Love Me?
Black and White
The Guild Gilded
Sentimental Me (And Romantic You)

1925

Dearest Enemy

Cast included Helen Ford, Charles Purcell, Helen Spring, Flavia Arcaro, John Seymour and Harold Crane

Heigh-Ho, Lackaday
War Is War
I Beg Your Pardon
Cheerio
Full Blown Roses

The Hermits
Here in My Arms
I'd Like to Hide It
Where the Hudson River Flows
Bye and Bye
Old Enough to Love
Sweet Peter
Here's a Kiss
*Ale, Ale, Ale
*The Pipes of Pansy
*Dear Me

1926

The Fifth Avenue Follies
(*Night Club Revue*)

Cast included Cecil Cunningham, Doris Canfield, Bert Hanlon, Mignon Laird and Johnne Clare

Do You Notice Anything?
In the Name of Art
Maybe It's Me
A City Flat
Mike
So Does Your Old Mandarin
High Hats
Lillie, Lawrence and Jack
Where's That Little Girl?
Susie

1926

The Girl Friend

Cast included Sammy White, Eva Puck, Frank Doane, June Cochrane, John Hundley, Evelyn Cavanaugh and Dorothy Barber

Hey! Hey!
The Simple Life
The Girl Friend
Goodbye, Lennie!
The Blue Room
Cabarets
Why Do I?
The Damsel Who Done All the Dirt
He's a Winner
Town Hall Tonight
Good Fellow, Mine
Creole Crooning Song
I'd Like to Take You Home
What Is It?
*Sleepyhead
*The Pipes of Pansy

1926

The Garrick Gaieties

Cast included Philip Loeb, Sterling Holloway, Betty Starbuck, Romney Brent, Edith Meiser, Bobbie Perkins, Edward Hogan, William M. Griffith, Blanche Fleming, George Frierson, Dorothy Jordan and Gladys Laird

Six Little Plays
Mountain Greenery
Keys to Heaven
Sleepyhead
Four Little Song Pluggers
What's the Use of Talking?
Gigolo
Queen Elizabeth
A Little Birdie Told Me So
Charming, Charming
Where's That Rainbow?
We Pirates from Weehawken
In His Arms
Chuck It!
I'm So Humble
Havana
Maybe It's Me
Give This Little Girl a Hand
*Come and Tell Me
*Tramping Along
*Paris Is Really Divine
*The Pipes of Pansy
*Little Souvenir

1926

Lido Lady
(*London*)

Cast included Cicely Courtneidge, Jack Hulbert, Phyllis Dare, Johnne Clare, Harold French, Billy Arlington and Bobby Comber

A Cup of Tea
You're on the Lido Now
Lido Lady
A Tiny Flat Near Soho Square
But Not Today
Here in My Arms
The Beauty of Another Day
My Heart Is Sheba Bound
The Dancer
Try Again Tomorrow
What's the Use?
Cheri-Beri
I Must Be Going
*Morning Is Midnight
*I Want a Man
*Chuck It!

1926

Peggy-Ann

Cast included Helen Ford, Lester Cole, Betty Starbuck, Jack Thompson, Edith Meiser, Lulu McConnell and Margaret Breen

Hello
A Tree in the Park
Howdy Broadway

1926

Betsy

Cast included Belle Baker, Allen Kearns, Bobbie Perkins, Al Shean, Pauline Hoffman, Jimmy Hussey, Ralph Whitehead, Dan Healy, Madeleine Cameron, Evelyn Law and Barbara Newberry

My Missus
One of Us Should Be Two
Sing
In Our Parlor on the Third Floor
This Funny World
Follow On
Push Around

Bugle Blow
Cradle of the Deep
If I Were You
Birds on High
Shuffle
*Come and Tell Me
*Show Me How to Make Love
*At the Saskatchewan
*You're the Mother Type
*Six Little Kitzels
*In Variety

1927

One Dam Thing After Another
(*The London Pavilion Revue*)

Cast included Jessie Matthews, Sonnie Hale, Edythe Baker and Melville Cooper

The Election
Shuffle
My Heart Stood Still
Make Hey! Make Hey!
I Need Some Cooling Off
My Lucky Star
One Dam Thing After Another
Paris Is Really Divine
Last Dam Thing of All
*Idles of the King

1927

A Connecticut Yankee

Cast included William Gaxton, Constance Carpenter, Nana Bryant, Jack Thompson, June Cochrane, Paul Everton, Celeste Duth and Gordon Burby

A Ladies' Home Companion
My Heart Stood Still
Thou Swell
At the Round Table
On a Desert Island With Thee
Nothing's Wrong
I Feel at Home With You
The Sandwich Men
Evelyn, What Do You Say?
*I Blush
*Morgan Le Fay
*Someone Should Tell Them
*Britain's Own Ambassadors
*You're What I Need

1928

She's My Baby

Cast included Beatrice Lillie, Clifton Webb, Irene Dunne, Jack Whiting and Ula Sharon

This Goes Up
My Lucky Star
You're What I Need
Here She Comes
The Swallows
When I Go on the Stage
Try Again Tomorrow
Camera Shoot
Where Can the Baby Be?
I Need Some Cooling Off
A Little House in Soho
A Baby's Best Friend
Whoopsie
Wasn't It Great?
Smart People
*How Was I to Know?
*Morning Is Midnight
*The Pipes of Pansy

1928

Present Arms

Cast included Charles King, Flora Le Breton, Busby Berkeley, Joyce Barbour, Franker Woods, Fuller Melish, Jr., Demaris Dore and Gaile Beverley

Tell It to the Marines
You Took Advantage of Me
Do I Hear You Saying "I Love You"?
A Kiss for Cinderella
Is It the Uniform?
Crazy Elbows
Down by the Sea
I'm a Fool, Little One
Blue Ocean Blues
Hawaii
Kohala

The Second Garrick Gaieties: Betty Starbuck and Sterling Holloway singing "Mountain Greenery"

1928

Chee-Chee

Cast included Helen Ford, William Williams, Betty Starbuck, Stark Patterson, George Hassell and Philip Loeb

I Must Love You
Dear, Oh Dear
Moon of My Delight
Better Be Good to Me
The Tartar Song
Singing a Love Song

1929

Spring Is Here

Cast included Charles Ruggles, Glenn Hunter, Lillian Taiz, Inez Courtney, John Hundley, Joyce Barbour and Dick Keene

Spring Is Here
Yours Sincerely
You Never Say Yes
With a Song in My Heart
Baby's Awake Now
Red Hot Trumpet
What a Girl
Rich Man! Poor Man!
Why Can't I?
*A Word in Edgeways
*A Cup of Tea
*The Color of Her Eyes

1929

Heads Up!

Cast included Jack Whiting, Victor Moore, Barbara Newberry, Ray Bolger, Betty Starbuck, John Hundley and Alice Boulden

You've Got to Surrender
Play Boy
Mother Grows Younger
Why Do You Suppose?
Ongsay and Anceday
It Must Be Heaven
My Man Is on the Make
The Lass Who Loved a Sailor
A Ship Without a Sail
Knees
*Sky City
*I Can Do Wonders for You

1930

Simple Simon

Cast included Ed Wynn, Alan Edwards, Doree Leslie, Ruth Etting, Harriet Hoctor, Will Ahearn, Bobbe Arnst, Paul Stanton and Lennox Pawle

Coney Island
Don't Tell Your Folks

Magic Music
I Still Believe in You
Send for Me
Dull and Gay
Sweetenheart
Hunting the Fox
Mocking Bird
I Love the Woods
On With the Dance
I Can Do Wonders With You
Ten Cents a Dance
In Your Chapeau
Roping
The Trojan Horse
Rags and Tatters
Cottage in the Country
*Dancing on the Ceiling
*He Was Too Good to Me

1930

Ever Green
(London)

Cast included Jessie Matthews, Sonnie Hale, Joyce Barbour, Albert Burdon, Jean Cadell and Madeline Gibson

Harlemania
Doing a Little Clog Dance
Dear, Dear
Nobody Looks at the Man
Waiting for the Leaves to Fall
No Place but Home
The Lion King
Quand Notre Vieux Monde Etait Tout Neuf
La Femme A Toujours Vingt Ans!
The Color of Her Eyes
In the Cool of the Evening
Dancing on the Ceiling
Je M'en Fiche du Sex-Appeal!
Hot Blues
If I Give In to You

1931

America's Sweetheart

Cast included Ann Sothern, Jack Whiting, Gus Shy, Inez Courtney, Jeanne Aubert, Virginia Bruce and John Sheehan

Mr. Dolan Is Passing Through
In Califor-n-i-a
My Sweet
I've Got Five Dollars
Sweet Geraldine
There's So Much More
We'll Be the Same
How About It?
Innocent Chorus Girls of Yesteryear
A Lady Must Live
You Ain't Got No Savoir-Faire
Two Unfortunate Orphans
I Want a Man
Tennessee Dan
*God Gave Me Eyes

1931

The Hot Heiress
(Film)

Cast included Ona Munson, Ben Lyon, Walter Pidgeon, Thelma Todd, Inez Courtney and Tom Dugan

Nobody Loves a Riveter
Like Ordinary People Do
You're the Cats
*He Looks So Good to Me

1932

Love Me Tonight
(Film)

Cast included Jeanette MacDonald, Maurice Chevalier, Charles Ruggles, Myrna Loy, C. Aubrey Smith, Charles Butterworth, Elizabeth Patterson and Blanche Frederici

That's the Song of Paree
Isn't It Romantic?
Lover
Mimi
A Woman Needs Something Like That
The Poor Apache
Love Me Tonight
The Son of a Gun Is Nothing but a Tailor
*The Man for Me

1932

The Phantom President
(Film)

Cast included George M. Cohan, Claudette Colbert and Jimmy Durante

The Country Needs a Man
Somebody Ought to Wave a Flag
Give Her a Kiss
The Convention

1933

Hallelujah, I'm a Bum
(Film)

Cast included Al Jolson, Frank Morgan, Madge Evans, Harry Langdon, Chester Conklin and Edgar Connor

I Gotta Get Back to New York
My Pal Bumper
Hallelujah, I'm a Bum
Laying the Cornerstone
Sleeping Beauty
Dear June
Bumper Found a Grand
What Do You Want with Money?
Kangaroo Court
I'd Do It Again
You Are Too Beautiful

1934

Hollywood Party
(Film)

Cast included Jimmy Durante, Stan Laurel, Oliver Hardy, Lupe Velez, Charles Butterworth, Polly Moran, Frances Williams and Mickey Mouse

Hello
Hollywood Party
Reincarnation
*Yes, Me
*Fly Away to Ioway
*The Master's Coming
*You Are
*Black Diamond
*One of the Boys
*The Pots
*You've Got That
*I'm a Queen in My Own Domain
*Keep Away from the Moonlight
*My Friend the Night
*Prayer

1934

The Merry Widow
(Film)

Cast included Jeanette MacDonald, Maurice Chevalier, Edward Everett Horton, Una Merkel, George Barbier, Minna Gombell, Ruth Channing, Sterling Holloway, Donald Meek and Herman Bing

Girls, Girls, Girls
Widows Are Gay
Maxim's
Vilia
Tonight Will Teach Me to Forget

1935

Mississippi
(Film)

Cast included Bing Crosby, W. C. Fields, Joan Bennett, Queenie Smith and Gail Patrick

Roll, Mississippi
Soon
Down by the River
It's Easy to Remember
*Pablo, You Are My Heart
*The Steely Glint in My Eye
*The Notorious Colonel Blake

1935

Jumbo

Cast included Jimmy Durante, Gloria Grafton, Donald Novis, W. J. McCarthy, Arthur Sinclair and Bob Lawrence

Over and Over Again
The Circus Is on Parade
The Most Beautiful Girl in the World
Laugh
My Romance
Little Girl Blue
The Song of the Roustabouts
Women
Diavolo
The Circus Wedding
*There's a Small Hotel

Edgar Connor, Harry Langdon, Al Jolson and Madge Evans in *Hallelujah, I'm a Bum*

1936

On Your Toes

Cast included Ray Bolger, Tamara Geva, Doris Carson, Monty Woolley, Luella Gear, Demetrios Vilan, David Morris and George Church

Two-a-Day for Keith
The Three B's
It's Got to Be Love
Too Good for the Average Man
There's a Small Hotel
The Heart Is Quicker than the Eye
Quiet Night
Glad to Be Unhappy
On Your Toes

1936

Dancing Pirate
(Film)

Cast included Steffi Duna, Frank Morgan and Charles Collins

Are You My Love?
When You're Dancing the Waltz

1937

Babes in Arms

Cast included Mitzi Green, Ray Heatherton, Wynn Murray, Alfred Drake, Rolly Pickert, Grace McDonald, Dana Hardwick, Harold and Fayard Nicholas, and Aljan de Loville

Where or When
Babes in Arms
I Wish I Were in Love Again
All Dark People
Way Out West
My Funny Valentine
Johnny One-Note
Imagine
All at Once
The Lady Is a Tramp
You Are So Fair

1937

I'd Rather Be Right

Cast included George M. Cohan, Joy Hodges, Austin Marshall, Mary Jane Walsh, Florenz Ames, Taylor Holmes and Joseph Macaulay

A Homogeneous Cabinet
Have You Met Miss Jones?
Take and Take and Take
Spring in Vienna
A Little Bit of Constitutional Fun
Sweet Sixty-five

Babes in Arms: Alfred Drake and Wynn Murray

We're Going to Balance the Budget
American Couple
Labor Is the Thing
I'd Rather Be Right
Off the Record
A Baby Bond

1938

Fools for Scandal
(*Film*)

Cast included Carole Lombard, Fernand Gravet, Ralph Bellamy, Allan Jenkins, Isabel Jeans and Jeni LeGon

There's a Boy in Harlem
Food for Scandal
How Can You Forget?

1938

I Married an Angel

Cast included Vera Zorina, Dennis King, Vivienne Segal, Charles Walters, Audrey Christie and Walter Slezak

Did You Ever Get Stung?
I Married an Angel
The Modiste
I'll Tell the Man on the Street
How to Win Friends and Influence People
Spring Is Here

Angels Without Wings
A Twinkle in Your Eye
At the Roxy Music Hall

1938

The Boys from Syracuse

Cast included Jimmy Savo, Teddy Hart, Ronald Graham, Eddie Albert, Muriel Angelus, Wynn Murray, Marcy Westcott, Bob Lawrence, Betty Bruce, John Clarke, John O'Shaughnessy, George Church and Burl Ives

I Had Twins
Dear Old Syracuse
What Can You Do With a Man?
Falling in Love With Love
The Shortest Day of the Year
This Can't Be Love
Let Antipholus In
Ladies of the Evening
He and She
You Have Cast Your Shadow on the Sea
Come With Me
Big Brother
Sing for Your Supper
Oh, Diogenes

1939

Too Many Girls

Cast included Marcy Westcott, Richard Kollmar, Mary Jane Walsh, Eddie Bracken, Desi Arnaz, Diosa Costello, Hal LeRoy and Leila Ernst

Heroes in the Fall
Tempt Me Not
My Prince
Pottawatomie
'Cause We Got Cake
Love Never Went to College
Spic and Spanish
I Like to Recognize the Tune
Look Out
The Sweethearts of the Team
She Could Shake the Maracas
I Didn't Know What Time It Was
Too Many Girls
Give It Back to the Indians

1940

Higher and Higher

Cast included Jack Haley, Marta Eggert, Shirley Ross, Lee Dixon, Leif Ericson, Billie Worth, Robert Chisholm and Hilda Spong

A Barking Baby Never Bites
From Another World
Mornings at Seven

The Dancing Pirate

Nothing but You
Disgustingly Rich
Blue Monday
Ev'ry Sunday Afternoon
Lovely Day for a Murder
How's Your Health?
It Never Entered My Mind
I'm Afraid
*It's Pretty in the City

1940

Pal Joey

Cast included Gene Kelly, Vivienne Segal, June Havoc, Jack Durant, Leila Ernst, Jean Casto, Stanley Donen and Van Johnson

You Mustn't Kick It Around
I Could Write a Book
Chicago
That Terrific Rainbow
What Is a Man?
Happy Hunting Horn
Bewitched, Bothered and Bewildered
Pal Joey
The Flower Garden of My Heart
Zip
Plant You Now, Dig You Later
Den of Iniquity
Do It the Hard Way
Take Him
*I'm Talking to My Pal
*Love Is My Friend
(original lyric of What Is a Man?)

1941

They Met in Argentina
(Film)

Cast included Maureen O'Hara, James Ellison, Buddy Ebsen, Diosa Costello and Alberto Vila

North America Meets South America
You've Got the Best of Me
Amarillo
Lolita
Cutting the Cane
Never Go to Argentina
Simpática

1942

By Jupiter

Cast included Ray Bolger, Benay Venuta, Constance Moore, Ronald Graham, Bertha Belmore, Vera-Ellen and Jayne Manners

For Jupiter and Greece
Jupiter Forbid
Life With Father
Nobody's Heart
The Gateway of the Temple of Minerva
Here's a Hand

No, Mother, No
The Boy I Left Behind Me
Ev'rything I've Got
Bottoms Up
Careless Rhapsody
Wait Till You See Her
Now That I've Got My Strength
*Life Was Monotonous

1943

A Connecticut Yankee

Cast included Vivienne Segal, Dick Foran, Julie Warren, Vera-Ellen, Chester Stratton, Robert Chisholm and Jere McMahon

Six new songs were written for this revival

This Is My Night to Howl
To Keep My Love Alive
Ye Lunchtime Follies
Can't You Do a Friend a Favor?
You Always Love the Same Girl
The Camelot Samba

Occasional Lyrics

1919
Any Old Place with You

1925
Anytime, Anywhere, Anyhow

1929
I Love You More than Yesterday

1930
I'm Hard to Please
Softer than a Kitten
It Never Happened Before

1931
Rest Room Rose

1933
That's the Rhythm of the Day
Rhythm

1934
That's Love
Prayer
The Bad in Ev'ry Man
Blue Moon

1935
What Are You Doing Here?
You Are So Lovely and I'm So Lonely

1940
You're Nearer

1942
Keep 'Em Rolling
The Bombardier Song

1943
The Girl I Love to Leave Behind

Larry and Dick at a rehearsal of *Pal Joey*. Margot Hopkins, their regular rehearsal pianist, is at right.

"This Can't Be Love" from *The Boys from Syracuse:* Eddie Albert and Marcy Westcott

He was always skipping and bouncing. In all the time I knew him, I never saw him walk slowly. I never saw his face in repose. I never heard him chuckle quietly. He laughed loudly and easily at other people's jokes, and at his own, too. His large eyes danced, and his head would wag. He was alert and dynamic. He was fun to be with.

OSCAR HAMMERSTEIN II